THE GO[LDEN]

FLORENCE
and
TUSCANY

*A complete guide to the cities,
the villages and the sites of historical,
artistic and archaeological interest*

BONECHI

Project and editorial conception: Casa Editrice Bonechi
Publication Manager: Monica Bonechi
Editorial Coordination: Giuliano Valdes
Picture research: Franco Filiberto; Alberto Douglas Scotti
Cover: Alberto Douglas Scotti; *Make-up:* Manuela Ranfagni
Editing: Editing Studio, Pisa; Anna Baldini
Drawings: Monica Simoncini
Cartography: Studio Grafico Daniela Mariani, Pistoia; *pages 18, 50, 68:* these plans have
been drawn up by the editorial staff of the publisher.

Text by Various authors

*Photographs from the archives of Casa Editrice Bonechi
taken by* Paolo Bacherini, Renzo Baggiani, Gaetano Barone, Carlo Cantini, Genni
Cappelli, Foto Casadei, Renzo Cecconi, Doriano Ciapetti, Luca del Pia,
Francesco Falaschi, Paolo Giambone, Foto Grassi, Italfotogieffe, Massimo Listri,
Piernello Maroni, Renzo Migliorini, Foto Novi, Nicolò Orsi Battaglini, Andrea Pistolesi,
Valerio Raffo, Andrea Rontini, Jeanette Servidio, Marzio Toninelli, Aldo Umicini

Pages 72 above, 73: Renzo Baggiani; *pages 212, 213d:* Stefano Buonamici;
pages 85, 105, 108, 129 below, 166, 170, 196 left, 229, 232: Editing Studio, Pisa - Foto
Giuliano Valdes; *pages 101, 130, 223 left:* Francesco Giannoni; *pages 90, 91, 206, 213a,b,c,
214:* Sergio Galeotti; *page 72 below:* Italfotogieffe

*Where it has been impossible to verify the origin of photographs, the publisher is
willing to remunerate those who hold the rights and to cite them in all future editions.*

Note
The names of places that have a particular historical, artistic or archaeological interest
have been graphically put into evidence with a larger character.

ISBN 88-8029-724-4

* * *

HISTORICAL INTRODUCTION

ETRUSCAN PERIOD

Historians are still making hypothesis as to where the Etruscans came from, without, however, finding a definite answer; all that can be said, is that towards the end of the 9th century BC, the Etruscans settled in a territory that arrived beyond the frontiers of modern Tuscany. The territories under their influence, soon after their settlement in Tuscany, extended in many parts of the Italian peninsula: from the river Arno to the Tiber, including parts of Campania and the Po Valley. There is very little written evidence on the history of the Etruscans, and the most qualified sources are the Roman and Greek writers, and others that followed: we know that the Etruscans had their own language, religion and customs, and that from a political point of view, they were organised in a confederacy of twelve independent cities (Arezzo, Cerveteri, Chiusi, Cortona, Fiesole, Orvieto, Perugia, Populonia, Roselle, Tarquinia, Vetulonia and Volterra). As above mentioned, from the 6th century BC, the Etruscan territory expanded, and this not for the initiative of the entire population, but as a result of the alliances made and of the will of one or more of these cities. The Etruscan civilisation was at its most during the 7th to 5th centuries BC. New centres

Populonia, necropolis of S.Cerbone: aedicula tomb.

were founded serving principally for their most important activity: trade on land and sea. In fact, Etruscan economy was based on trade, and the Etruscan fleet was so powerful that it achieved hegemony in the Mediterranean, having ports as far as Corsica and Sardinia: the Etruscan fleet was feared by both the Greeks and the Phoenicians. The Etruscans also well exploited the riches of the soil, both through the agriculture and the mining activity: the Piombino coastline and the Island of Elba are still today rich of metals. Etruscan decline began when their economy weakened for the strong competition of the Greeks on the seas. On top of this, there was the heavy defeat at Cumae in 474 BC, the internal rebellions, such as the one in Latium in 510 BC, and the Gallic invasion in the northern part of the territory. From the 4th century BC, the Etruscan territories were conquered by Rome; and its from the Romans that derives the modern name of the region: Tuscia *or* Etruria.

ROMAN AND LOMBARD PERIOD

During the 4th and 3rd centuries BC, the Romans imposed their dominion over a large part of the Italic territories: together with the land, they assimilated the customs, organisation and civilisation of the peoples who lived there. This was also the case for Etruria, later Tuscany, where Latin became the official language of the Etruscans, but at the same time the Romans adopted many of the Etruscan customs. With the fall of the Roman Empire the region was invaded by barbarians: different populations came down in successive waves until the 6th century AD when the Lombards became stable inhabitants of the area; Tuscany served as a

3

defensive barrier against the Byzantine territories in southern Italy. It was divided in duchies, and Lucca became the capital. Other cities, diocese seats, continued to grow in importance and autonomous power, such as Arezzo, Pisa, Florence, Pistoia and Siena.

THE PERIOD OF THE COMMUNES

The Lombard dominion was followed by that of the Franks. Then, at the end of the 9th century, the counts of Lucca acquired the title of Marquises of Tuscia. Thereafter, at the end of the 11th century, for succession

Florence, Palazzo Vecchio: "Judith", Donatello.

Pisa, the facade of the Abbazia di San Zeno, a suggestive example of Romanesque architecture.

reasons, Tuscany became part of the domain of the Lords of Canossa. From the year 1014 (conquest of the Balearic Isles), Pisa took up the role of naval and military force, anti-Saracen, in the Ligurian and Tyrrhenian Seas. In 1080 the first consuls were nominated in Pisa. Then, the influence of the Maritime Republic reached Sardinia (1015), Corsica (1052), and Sicily (1063). After participating in the First Crusade, Pisa expanded its trading with many Mediterranean ports, arriving as far as Constantinople. The decline of the Republic of Pisa, in the 13th century, was consequent to the defeat suffered in the battle of Meloria (1284) against the Genoese, and to the onerous peace treaty imposed by the Florentines at Fucecchio (1293). Siena also nominated its consuls starting from the first half of the 12th century, constituting a pro-Ghibelline Republic that for a long time opposed the Florentine supremacy, until its submission, occurred only during Medici rule. After the death of Matilde of Canossa, in 1115, there was a lack of central authority; at the same time, independent groups of citizens organised themselves into Communes, under the guidance of consuls, and continuously gained strength. Gradually, economic growth favoured the predominance of some cities over others: at the end of the 14th century Florence dominated over all. Slowly, among the citizens that governed the city, the personal interests of some of the families who tended to take over the government, emerged. In Florence, during the 15th century, the power and the rule (signoria) of Lorenzo de' Medici was established, and it endured until, in the century that followed, Florence became a Principality. In fact, in 1480, Lorenzo, approved a political reform, by which the old regulations lost all their value, even if they apparently remained valid, thus succeeding in concentrating the absolute power in his hands. Although the townspeople twice tried to restore the republic (in 1494 and in 1527), the Medici took back the government in 1512 and again in 1531.

THE RULE OF THE MEDICI

The first Medici grand duke, Cosimo, received his title from the pope in 1569, but he had already been trying to conquer and unify Tuscany under a single lord; in 1559, he finally managed to subdue Siena. When he became grand duke, he fortified all the cities under his domain; he also realised the importance of Livorno for trade, and had the port enlarged; he reclaimed the land and started new types of agriculture. Lucca, however, continued to live in full autonomy, without ever becoming part of the Grand Duchy of Tuscany. In 1574, Francesco I succeeded Cosimo, but he was not adeguate for this role, and not alert in the problems of the principate as his predecessor was: his mind was involved in his personal studies and experiments of alchemy and astrology, preferring to leave governing to his ministers. This was not the case, instead, for his brother Ferdinando, who inherited the throne when Francesco died, in 1587. He saw to the economic development of the Tuscan cities and to the well-being of the citizens, to whom he also provided a sort of medical assistance. Ferdinando was particularly able in foreign policy and was esteemed by various foreign princes. The decline of the Grand Duchy began in the 17th century under the rule of Cosimo II, followed by Ferdinando II and Cosimo III: all of them politically neglected the region.

THE HOUSE OF LORRAINE AND THE 19TH CENTURY

In 1723, Gian Gastone, the last of the Medici dynasty, ascended the throne. After him, the succession passed to the Lorraine, and in the second-half of the 18th century, with Pietro Leopoldo, Florence experienced a new period of splendour, and economic and civil progress, thanks to the ideas of the sovereign. In 1808, Tuscany fell under Napoleonic dominion, and the emperor's sister, Elisa Baciocchi, was named Grand Duchess; but after the Congress of Vienna, the region was given back to Pietro Leopoldo's son. In 1860, after having participated partly in the Risorgimento, Tuscany became part of the Italian Kingdom, of which later, Florence would have been capital (1865-1871).

ART HISTORY

ETRUSCAN AND ROMAN ART

Architecture. *The temples and other sacred buildings the Etruscans built, particularly those in wood, have disappeared (except for some foundations), but some of the Tuscan cities still preserve Etruscan walls and city gates in stone, as in Roselle, Populonia, Cortona, Fiesole and Volterra. Historians have learned a lot of the Etruscans from the necropolises, where numerous chamber tombs are still well preserved, at Vetulonia and Populonia; or the vaulted ceiling tomb known as the Tanella di Pitagora at Cortona; and others excavated in the rock at Sovana. The Romans added theatres, which can still be seen in Arezzo, Fiesole and Volterra, and the thermal baths as in Pisa, Volterra and Fiesole.*

Etruscan art (Stele from a necropolis).

Sculpture. *Many examples of Etruscan sculpture are preserved in Tuscany's museums. The most commonly used materials are limestone or sandstone, tufa and terra-cotta. Since the use was for funerary purposes, they consist mainly of stelae decorated with fantastic animals and urns with the lying figure of the deceased on the lid. The Etruscans also worked some bronze pieces, as for example the Arringatore (orator) or Chimera found in Arezzo, now in the Archaeological Museum, in Florence. When the Romans began their colonisation of Italy, they were strongly influenced by these examples and initially copied them, and later assimilated them together with the Greek art.*

Roman art in Tuscany (Fiesole, Roman Theatre).

Example of Romanesque architecture (Empoli, the Collegiate Church).

Painting. *There is a rich heritage of Etruscan tomb painting: the most important centre for this art is Chiusi, but also very interesting are the paintings of the* Amazon Sarcophagus *found in* Tarquinia, *and now in the Archaeological Museum in Florence. In their paintings, Etruscans usually represented* banquets, hunts, games *and* dances, *in bright contrasting colours.*

THE ROMANESQUE STYLE

Architecture. *After the 11th century, the so-called Romanesque style took over throughout Europe. As far as architecture was concerned, it meant a radical transformation of the techniques, as for example the barrel and cross vaults used instead of the timber trusses: this solution allowed more complex architectural structures; the principal innovations in the church, were the transept and the ambulatories around the choir. This new style first appeared in Lombardia and Emilia, from where it spread to other regions, although with some differences: in Tuscany the Romanesque style was taken up in* Florence *and in* Pisa. *Typical of the Florentine Romanesque, is the external facing in polychrome marble in geometric designs, as in the* Baptistery *and in* San Miniato al Monte. *This fashion influenced the area surrounding the city: for example the* Collegiate Church of Empoli *has a façade decorated in the same style.* Pisa, *instead, accentuated some of the Lombard architectural ele-*

ments - open arcaded galleries, corbels, pilaster strips - and used them as external decorations for its churches: examples are the Cathedral, the Baptistery and the Tower, all belonging to this period. Oriental features also influenced the Romanesque style in Pisa, and as a result of this you can see the external facing of edifices in bands of black and white marble with decorative mosaic. Pisan style was widely diffused in Lucca and Pistoia, while Siena remained rather isolated. Little Romanesque architecture is to be found in this city, while the surrounding country is full of parish churches in this style. Forms and elements, characteristic of Lombard Romanesque, prevailed in southern Tuscany, introduced by workers called from the region.

Sculpture. In this period sculpture became independent from the other arts, although it was prevalently used for the decoration of portals and capitals. The human figure, which had been absent from sculpture for such a long time, became again the object of the sculptor, who tried to reproduce its plastic form and separate it from the background, setting it into space, as true to reality as possible. Pisa was the centre for this art: here worked Maestro Guglielmo, who carried out the Pulpit for the Cathedral, now to be seen in the Cathedral of Cagliari; Bonanno Pisano also worked in Pisa, sculptor of the moulds of the Saint Ranieri Doorway (Cathedral), masterpieces which influenced the artists for many years.

Painting. Of all the arts, painting developed more slowly and remained tied to the Byzantine tradition. In Tuscany, none of the frescoes of this period have survived, but there still are a few paintings on wood, above all crosses, carried out with little artistic innovations, with the figures still flat on gold grounds: an example are the painted Crosses of the Pisan School (13th century).

THE GOTHIC STYLE

Architecture. Between 1100 and 1200 a new style of architecture - the Gothic style - was experienced in central-northern France, which then spread throughout Europe, up until the end of the 14th century. The technical solution of this style, was the further development of the structural elements of the Romanesque vault. The arches were lifted and became equilateral: this allowed to put all the weight on the pillars; and, moreover, as the wall between the pillars no longer served as support, it was often replaced by large stained-glass windows. In Italy and Tuscany, this new style of architecture was introduced from France, by the Cistercian monks (Benedictines having their centre in the Abbey of Citeaux in Burgundy). Monastic rule required the architecture to adhere to schemes of great simplicity: an example is still to be found in the romantic ruins of the Abbey of San Galgano near Siena. Other buildings were

Gothic style in Siena (Siena, portal of the "New Cathedral").

then built in Tuscany after these first examples: Santa Maria Novella and Santa Croce in Florence, the Cathedral of Siena, Santa Maria della Spina and the Cemetery in Pisa. These buildings, though, do not have the thrust and lightness of the transalpine Gothic style, consequent to the influence of the Cistercian architecture, that had preserved the solidity, robustness and simplicity of the Romanesque structures.

Sculpture. In the 13th century, with Nicola Pisano, a great artist active in Pisa, Tuscany witnessed a complete renewal in the spirit of sculpture: in the pulpits made for the Baptistery of Pisa and for the Cathedral of Siena, he carried out low reliefs representing profoundly human figures, with faces anatomically detailed, and with a strong character and plasticity. His example was followed by his son Giovanni, who was, however, also open to French influence, as in his pulpit of Sant'Andrea in Pistoia, where his figures have elegance and refinement. Siena also was influence by this new style, mostly in the field of painting, as detailed below.

Painting. In this period, Tuscan painting developed in two quite different directions: the Sienese current of Duccio and Simone Martini, and the Florentine current of Cimabue and Giotto. As mentioned above, the artistic atmosphere of Siena, showed the traces of the influence of French art, and priviledged rhythmical and linear compositions with precious colour effects. Examples of this trend are Duccio's Maestà, now in the Cathedral Museum in Siena, and the same subject frescoed a few years later by Simone Martini, in the Palazzo Pubblico. They are characterised by the lightness of the figures and the richness of their vestment making the atmosphere abstract. In the last thirty years of the 13th century, Florentine painting had turned off in an entirely different direction. Cimabue's Maestà, in the Uffizi, today still testifies the new expressive intensity and the new feeling for space and volume which had then been achieved: it was Giotto, during the 14th century, who spread these innovations throughout Italy, succeeding in representing in his work concrete reality.

THE 15TH CENTURY AND RENAISSANCE

Architecture. In the 15th century Florence became the art centre of Tuscany, and it was here that the new art, based on the complete revaluation of man, of his works, and of reality, developed. Classical art, which best seemed to have interpreted man and nature, became the ideal model. In architecture, the geometric laws of ancient masterpieces were rediscovered, and their beauty was reproduced: on these examples, the first and greatest Florentine architect, Brunelleschi, created in Florence, simple, but at the same time majestic churches, such as Santo Spirito, San Lorenzo, the Pazzi Chapel, the dome of Santa Maria del Fiore. For about a

Della Robbia terra-cotta (Florence, Spedale degli Innocenti).

century, all Tuscan architects followed his teachings: Michelozzo, who left examples of his work in Florence, Pistoia, Montepulciano and Volterra; Giuliano da Maiano, who worked in Siena: Giuliano da Sangallo, in Florence and Prato; Francesco di Giorgio Martini, in Cortona.

Sculpture. Like architecture, sculpture was inspired by the classical rules of harmony, and the study of the single figures was investigated more closely. Donatello *was the artist who had the most followers. His works, commissioned by the Florentine Church, the guilds or private citizens (such as the Medici), are numerous, and they can be found in the Cathedral Museum (Museo dell'Opera del Duomo) and in the Bargello, as well as in the city churches. Many are the sculptors who came close to him:* Desiderio da Settignano, Bernardo *and* Antonio Rossellino, Benedetto da Maiano, Agostino di Duccio, Mino da Fiesole *and* Luca della Robbia, *who, with his glazed terra-cotta figures occupies a unique role.*

Painting. *As far as painting is concerned, Renaissance began with* Masaccio, *who picked up the heritage Giotto had left, about a hundred years earlier, and, at the same time, availed himself of the perspective inventions of Brunelleschi, and of the plastic power expressed by Donatello. The Brancacci Chapel in the Church of Santa Maria del Carmine in Florence is the first example of the results he achieved, on which later painters, such as Paolo Uccello, Andrea del Castagno and Beato Angelico, formed themselves. However, from the second half of the 15th century, painters undertook new studies in their search for a greater freedom of perspective, on the examples of Piero della Francesca (born in Borgo San Sepolcro, and who also worked in Arezzo and Florence). These painters tried to create a more tense illusion of movement, following Verrocchio and Botticelli; and they studied more closely the space-colour effects, which under the influence of Flemish painting, arrived in Florence at the end of the century, and were picked up by Ghirlandaio.*

THE 16TH CENTURY

Architecture. *16th-century art was closely related to the Medici, who promoted many prestigious artistic exploits. Various Florentine buildings were built or transformed at that time, such as the Uffizi, designed by Vasari, or the Palazzo Pitti, which was used by the Medici as their palace. In the country surroundings, the villas, begun in the previous century, continued to be built, and the family used them either as pleasant country houses, or for the supervision of the agriculture activities. Moreover, Cosimo I, took care of the fortifications of various cities:* Livorno, *with its Fortezza by* Antonio da Sangallo il Giovane; Pisa, *where the work was commissioned to* Giuliano *and* Antonio da Sangallo; Borgo San Sepolcro; *and* Florence, *with the so-called Fortezza da Basso and Forte Belvedere, which Buontalenti built to protect the palace. The Church of Santo Stefano dei Cavalieri in Pisa, recalls the Order founded by Cosimo to fight the pirates that endangered the Tuscany coasts: inside, in fact, there are trophies taken from the enemy. Finally, in Florence, there is the so-called* Sagrestia Nuova *(New Sacristy), a Medici tomb in the Church of San Lorenzo, commissioned to* Michelangelo.

Sculpture. *Also in the field of sculpture, the outstanding personality of the century was* Michelangelo, *who worked in Florence in various times. Here, for various clients, he carried out the famous* David, *the figures of* Day, Night, Dawn *and* Dusk *for the Sagrestia Nuova, the statues known as the Prisoners (these works can all be seen in the Florentine museums). His work in-*

16th-century window surrounded by rusticated ashlar (Florence, Palazzo Pitti).

spired, although in different ways, artists, such as, Bartolomeo Ammannati, *sculptor of the* fountain *in* Piazza della Signoria; Cellini, *whose* Perseus, *commissioned by Cosimo I, now stands inside the Uffizi;* Giambologna, *who worked on a series of small bronzes for the gardens of the Medici villas.*

Painting. *At the beginning of the century, three great artistic personalities were simultaneously present in* Florence: Michelangelo, Leonardo *and* Raphael. *The works they left in Florence, can today be admired in the* Uffizi *and in* Palazzo Pitti. *But at the end of the first decade, Florence lost the artistic supremacy that had distinguished the city up to then, in favour of Rome, to which many artists moved. However, in Florence, there are many interesting works from the following period, thanks to* Andrea del Sarto *and* Fra' Bartolomeo. *Around the 1530s, a group of Florentine artists, later called "Mannerists" gave an important contribution to painting and succeeded in bringing, once more, Florence in the limelight. These artists included* Pontormo, Rosso Fiorentino, Bronzino: *they expressed their tormented period in paintings with violent colours and extraordinarily up-to-date.*

THE 17TH AND 18TH CENTURIES

Architecture. *During these centuries Tuscany's art slowed down, it turned back to its own traditions and assimilated very little of what was being experimented in other Italian and European cities. The Medici still commissioned most of the artworks, and, in the 17th century, they began the work on their Chapel to* San Lorenzo, *a sepulchral monument for the Grand Dukes. The architect was* Matteo Nigetti. *In other cities of the region, preference was given to well-known architects from outside Tuscany, such as* Juvarra *and* Bernini, *who built private residences.*

Sculpture. *As far as sculpture is concerned,* Pietro Tacca, *sculptor of the court of the Medici, was the most talented. He was commissioned the statues inside the* Chapel in San Lorenzo *in* Florence *and the* monument to Ferdinand I, *known as the* "Four Moors", *in* Livorno.

Painting. *During these two centuries, painting had some bright spots. Various Tuscan painters, such as* Cigoli, Cristofano Allori, Santi di Tito *and* Matteo Rosselli, *succeeded in renewing Tuscan painting, elaborating again and giving more vital strength to the local traditions. Towards the year 1614, the innovations of Caravaggio's style, were introduced in Florence by the painter* Artemisia Gentileschi, *a follower of the great master, who left various paintings at the Medici court, now in the Uffizi and Palazzo Pitti.*
From the fourth decade of the century, Pietro da Cortona *and* Luca Giordano *were present in Florence.*
The Medici commissioned Pietro da Cortona *the decorations of some of the Palazzo Pitti rooms, while* Luca Giordano *frescoed part of* Palazzo Medici.
Both introduced the great Baroque manner, which did leave its mark, but did not obviously arrive to the greatness one can see in the Rome of the great aristocratic families.

A fountain in maneristic style (Florence, Piazza SS. Annunziata, Pietro Tacca).

The classical shapes of the 19th-century architecture (Florence, Piazza della Repubblica).

THE 19TH CENTURY

Architecture. *In the second half of the century,* Florence *became the capital of the Kingdom of Italy: this brought many changes in the city structure. The centre was transformed with the creation of squares, such as Piazza della Repubblica, built where there once were houses. The old Medieval layout of the streets, was changed in order to line up various blocks of houses according to the 19th-century concepts. The city walls were taken down, to build the ring roads, later extended to Piazzale Michelangelo, a large terrace with view on the city. The unfinished façades of* Santa Maria del Fiore *and* Santa Croce *were completed: the first was commissioned, in 1871, to the architect* De Fabris; *the second, in 1853, to* Matas.

Sculpture. *In this century, the* Academy of Fine Arts, *founded in the 16th century, for those who wanted to study art, played a fundamental role: it was in charge of the official culture, in close relation with the world of politics, and imposed formal rules and iconographic models. All the artist of that time, went through the Academy, although some of them managed to detach themselves from the rigid* conservatism *defended by the school.* Giovanni Dupré, *for example, and* Lorenzo Bartolini, *who also taught in the Academy, recommended their students to combine traditional Tuscan elements with the Neo-classical style, so much in vogue at the time. An example of Bartolini's art can be seen in the Church of Santa Croce. From the year 1855, the group of the "Macchiaioli" painters, who rebelled against the academic teachings claiming the artist's right to search and create, in their paintings, spontaneous and bright effects, also influenced the sculpture of Adriano Cecioni. Examples of his fresh and surprisingly spontaneous works can be seen in the* Gallery of Modern Art *in* Florence.

Painting. *Between the years 1855 and 1867, after decades in which the academic manner of* Ussi, Ciseri *and* Benvenuti *dominated, the "Macchiaioli" painters movement came into being. These painters sought a new way to capture the immediate tones of colour and light, the* instant *emotions and expressions, using "spots" of colour ("a macchia") to create effects closer to reality. They also represented landscapes and life in the fields, subjects up to then ignored. The movement, included the painters* Fattori, Costa, Signorini, Lega, D'Ancona, Abbati, Sernesi *and* Zandomenghi. *A good number of their paintings are exposed in the* Gallery of Modern Art *in* Palazzo Pitti *in* Florence *and the* Museum Giovanni Fattori *in* Livorno.

THE 20TH CENTURY

Architecture. *In* Florence, Livorno *and* Viareggio *the architecture of the beginning of the century was greatly influenced by the* art nouveau, *adopted for many* villas *and* private houses. *Modern works worth mentioning are the* "Artemio Franchi" *stadium in* Florence, *designed by* Nervi *in 1932, and the* Train Station of Santa Maria Novella *built in 1935 by* Michelucci. *Both were modernised on the occasion of the World Soccer Championships* "Italy '90".

Sculpture. *Tuscany did not have any outstanding contemporary sculptors: apart from* Modigliani, *painter and sculptor, who, however, spent most of his life in Paris, painting has been more important than sculpture in this century.*
Worth mentioning are the praiseworthy initiatives of some of the cities of the region, which in the past years have been trying to acquire important sculptures to set in their public squares: in Prato, *for example, there are various works by* Moore; *in* Florence, *in the square of* Porta Romana, *there is* Pistoletto's Dietrofront; *in* Pisa, *beneath the* Tower of the Cittadella, *you will see* Cascella's Wisdom Gate.

Painting. *As already mentioned, in our century, painting has the leading role, thanks to artists from all over Tuscany working in the region and in other European cities, and no longer dependent on the tastes of a patron. These include* Viani, *born in Viareggio;* Rosai *and* Conti, *from Florence;* Severini, *from Cortona;* Soffici, *from Rignano sull'Arno;* Maccari, *from Siena; and,* Modigliani, *from Livorno. The lack of local patrons, however, meant that many of their works were sold to privates and so today are still either in private collections or in museums abroad. Among the ones that can be seen, here in Tuscany, there are the many paintings by* Primo Conti, *which can be found in his house in Fiesole, now seat of an institution that bears his name; and the* Via Crucis, *a mosaic winding along the* Santa Margherita Street *in Cortona, by* Gino Severini.

Art Nouveau decorations adorn Tuscan architecture (Florence, private villa).

THE LANDSCAPE AND THE TRADITIONS

GEOGRAPHICAL OUTLINE

*The landscape in Tuscany is extremely varied, and even short stretches provide surprising changes. The **Apennines** constitute the north-east borderline as far as Arezzo: the highest peaks are **Mount Giovo** (1991 m) and **Falterona** (1654 m). Remarkable are the **Apuan Alps**, rising right on the coast of Massa and Carrara. The highest peak is 1946 m. These mountains always seem covered with snow, instead the white colour is due to the marble they contain. East of Piombino are the **Metalliferous Hills**, while the **Monti dell'Uccellina**, a protected area, lie between Grosseto and the Argentario promontory. East of Grosseto there are a few isolated peaks, such as **Mount Amiata** (1738 m) and **Cetona** (1148 m). Many rivers flow in the valleys lying among these mountains: the largest are the **Valdarno**, the **Valdichiana**, the **valley of the Serchio** (Garfagnana), and the **val di Cecina**. Half-way between the valleys and the mountains there are the many hills, some of which quite unique, as the "crete". The long coastline is sandy from the north to Livorno, where it becomes rocky; rock and sand then alternate all the way to the Lazio border. All that remains of the ancient swamps are the **Orbetello swamp** and the **lake of Burano**.*

PROTECTED AREAS IN TUSCANY

*In Tuscany there are various protected parks: the largest, 54,327 hectares, is the **Apuan Alps Natural Park**, in the provinces of Massa Carrara and Lucca, established in 1985 by the Tuscany Region to preserve the environment endangered by the too many marble quarries. The CAI (Italian Alpinist Club), here has arranged a series of tracks and refuges for the visitors that want to go for outings in the mountains or visit the quarries, some abandoned and others still in use. The **Natural Park of***

Natural Park of Migliarino, San Rossore, Massaciuccoli: the Gombo avenue.

Migliarino, San Rossore and Massaciuccoli, established by the Region in 1979, is the second largest with its 21,000 hectares of beaches, dunes, pine woods and marshy areas along the coast that goes from Viareggio to Livorno; the fauna is particularly interesting: there are dears, boars and many species of birds. San Rossore can be visited on Sundays and public holidays, and with some restrictions, on Tuesdays, Thursdays and Saturdays. Follows in extent the **Maremma Natural Park** on the mountains of the Uccellina. Entrance to this park is at Alberese, where there is a visitor's centre and from which start the interesting walks through the luxuriant vegetation that goes all the way to the sea, still un-contaminated. Visits can be made on Wednesdays, weekends, and public holidays, from 9 a.m. to sunset. The oldest park in Tuscany, institut-ed in 1962 by Mario Incisa della Rocchetta, owner of the land, is the **Fau-nal Refuge of Bolgheri**. In this area the extraordinary variety of wildlife can be easily observed: there are roe dears, boars and acquatic birds. To watch them, without frightening them, there are hidden walks and observation points. Entrance is on a turn off of the Aurelia Road, at 270 km, towards the sea. The other parks are smaller but still very interest-ing. There is the **Tuscan Archipelago National Park**, established in 1989, which includes the Islands of Capraia, Giannutri, Gorgona and Monte-cristo. **Montecristo**, with its wild environment, is probably the most in-teresting island of the Tyrrenian Sea, but it can be visited only with an authorisation for study purposes. **Capraia**, instead, is accessible to all visitors and can be reached by ferry-boat from Livorno. On this island there are various walks that allow the visitor to discover its well-pre-served nature. Near Albinia and Capalbio are the **Faunal Refuges** of **Bura-no** and **Orbetello**, situated on two interesting marshy areas. Here, it is possible to watch from well camouflaged observation points the original fauna of the Maremma: porcupines, otters, and a large variety of birds. To visit the refuges you need a ticket, and the guided tours are on Thursday and Sunday from 10 am to 1 pm, from September to May at Bu-rano, and from October to April at Orbetello.

TRADITIONAL EVENTS

The most exciting event, deeply related to the traditions and culture of local life is, without doubt, the **Palio of Siena**. It is a bare-back horse race between the Contradas of the city (quarters in which the historical cen-tre is divided), held on the 2nd of July and the 16th of August in Piazza del Campo. The prize for the winner is the "palio", a painted cloth, but the glory and the honour that the winner receives from all the people of his Contrada is much more important than the prize itself. In Florence, the people participate just as emotionally in a completely different kind of event, which takes place during the Easter mass, in the Cathedral: the **Scoppio del Carro** (the explosion of the cart). A sort of wooden pyramid on wheels, the cart, is drawn by two oxen up to the Cathedral square. Meanwhile, in the Church of the SS. Apostoli, the ecclesiastic authorities light a large candle rubbing the stones that the Florentine Pazzino de' Pazzi brought back from the first Crusade. It is said that these stones come from the Holy Sepulchre. The candle is then carried in procession to the high altar in the Cathedral, and the bishop, surrounded by the City authorities and trumpet-players dressed in historical costumes, lights a rocket, shaped like a dove, that "flies" towards the cart. As soon as it reaches the cart coloured firecrackers start exploding, and flags and standards pop up. It is also said that the velocity or slowness of the dove flying towards the cart determines the year's harvest. The **Giostra del Saracino**, in Arezzo, also takes the visitor back to Medieval times. The game consists in a contest between various knights with spears fighting against a puppet. This event takes place on the last Sunday of August and the first of September. The nearby city of Sansepolcro, in-stead competes with Gubbio in a cross bow competition, that takes place in September, called the **Palio della Balestra**. Talking about Pisa, mention should be made of the **Luminara di San Ranieri**, an attractive candle illumination of the Lungarni (streets along the river Arno) (16 June), the **Regata storica di San Ranieri** (a regatta), which takes place the 17th of June (the patronal festival) on the Arno river, and the **Gioco del Ponte**, of ancient origins, in which the two "factions" in which the city is divided, "Mezzogiorno" (south of the Arno) and "Tramontana" (north of the Arno) confront each other on the Ponte di Mezzo (the central bridge). In spring, almost everywhere throughout the region, the "bruscelli" are celebrated. These, consist in the representation of historical or religious events, around a tree in flower, symbol of the new season, and at the end, the entire community takes part in a propitiatory dance. The **Carnival of Viareggio** has also become famous, with the parade of allegorical floats attracting crowds of people. Other events that should be mentioned are the **Festa del Volto Santo** in Lucca, the **Balestro del Girifalco** in Massa Marittima, the **Palio dei Micci** in Querceta, the **Palio dei Cerri** in Cerreto Guidi, the **Palio dei Ciuchi** in Incisa Valdarno, the **Festa del Grillo** and the **Rificolona** in Florence.

CUISINE

Tuscan cooking is still today genuine, and it is easy to find good restaurants which serve typical local dishes, especially outside the cities. The basic elements of the dishes are the good olive oil, and the wines. Among the red wines, the most famous is the Chianti, but the Brunello di Montalcino and the Nobile di Montepulciano are also well-known; as far as the white wines are concerned, you should try the Vernaccia di San Gimignano and the Bianco dell'Elba. Traditional first courses, even more than the pasta dishes, are various kinds of soups, such as the zuppa di fagioli (bean soup) and the ribollita, based on vegetables and bread. On the coast, fish dishes are very popular; typical is the caciucco, a highly seasoned stew which is a speciality of Livorno. Game, also, is at the basis of many dishes, especially hare and wild boar, typical of the Maremma. Bistecca alla Fiorentina - a two-inch cut of sirloin broiled rare - and roast arista or loin pork are excellent, too. As far as second courses are concerned, typical Tuscan dishes are the chitterlings pluck: trippa and lampredotto, sweetbread and pork liver. Sausages and salami - salame, finocchiona, soppressata - and ham, salted and very tasty, are excellent; same goes for the pecorino cheese (of ewe milk) made throughout the region. Good pastries can be eaten at the cafés, which often have their own bakeries. Sienese sweets are famous - almonds and honey are at the basis of the panforte, the ricciarelli and the torta di Cecco. Lucca is famous for the buccellato, Florence for the schiacciata and the zuccotto. The speciality of Lamporecchio are the brigidini - large wafers flavoured with anise - which can be bought everywhere. The same is for the almond biscuits made in Prato called cantucci, usually eaten dipped in the Vin Santo.

Montalcino, birthplace of "Brunello" wine, the cellar of the Fattoria dei Barbi (wine producers).

Map of Tuscany
with suggested routes

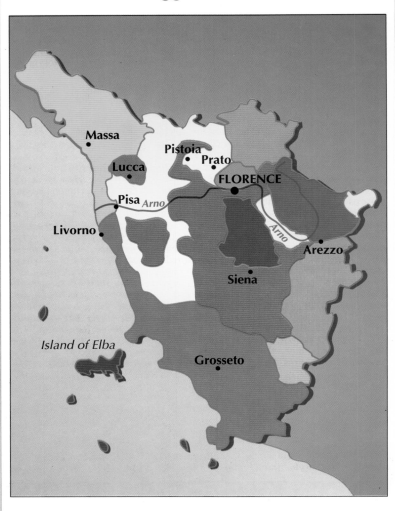

THE VERSILIA, THE APUANE, THE GARFAGNANA AND THE LUNIGIANA

VILLAS OF THE LUCCHESIA

THE MUGELLO

MEDICI VILLAS NEAR FLORENCE

THE CASENTINO AND THE PRATOMAGNO

CHIANTI AND ITS ENVIRONS

THE VALDICHIANA AND THE VAL D'ORCIA

MOUNT AMIATA

THE MAREMMA AND THE ETRUSCANS

THE TUSCAN ARCHIPELAGO

MAIN SUGGESTED ROUTES

Among the many possible routes that can be made in the region, here we want to suggest only the most interesting and peculiar ones. After the brief description of the area concerned, we also suggest a small number of localities which can help the visitor to have a better idea of the landscapes and customs of the area, and a number of other places that may complete each itinerary.

The tourist, however, is free to make his own personal routes and this guide, in alphabetical order, can help him.

MEDICI VILLAS NEAR FLORENCE

In the area surrounding Florence, there are many Villas, that once belonged to the Medici family or to other powerful families, dating from various periods. The most ancient ones were originally castles, that only during Renaissance were transformed into residential villas, but the original structure can often still be seen. The most interesting villas, from an artistic point of view, were built, in fact, during Renaissance, by the most famous architects of the period; the Florentine families spent a great amount of money for their villas, to prove their power, their wealth and rank. The villas were often attached to farms, and especially for the Medici, formed a net-like system from which it was possible to control the region. During the summer, these residences were the meeting points for artists, men of letters and poets, with the powerful members of the families. From their conversations most of the extraordinary art works, that characterised the Medici hegemony, were planned. These villas included extremely elegant buildings and glamorous parks; the gardens were the result of accurate planning and care, to create a surrounding for walks among the fascinating grasslands, boulevards, fountains, stretches of water and artificial caverns, in which grotesque painting could recreate fairy-like corners.

LOCALITIES TO VISIT:
Poggio a Caiano, Pratolino, Artimino, Careggi, Castello

A STOP AT:
- **Villa Corsini**, an imposing building not far from Sesto Fiorentino, in pure Baroque style, now property of the Italian State. It belonged first to the Strozzi family, then to the Rinieri and finally to the Corsini in 1706. The rich façade is divided by tall pilasters and has two stories with framed windows. Also remarkable is the *Garden-park*, with its fine statues and the charming *fountain* by Tribolo.

MUGELLO

This route goes from the plain of Florence to the anti-Apennines, characteristic for the vegetation and the morphology. Between the anti-Apennine range and the Apennine one there is the narrow valley of the Mugello, with its intensive cultivation along the river Sieve, and dotted with small ancient agricultural villages, from where, in old times, the goods were sent to Florence.

The Mugello, already inhabited in prehistory and by the Etruscans and Romans, was also the native land of the Medici family and of many artists, such as Giotto, Beato Angelico and Andrea del Castagno. This area, full of cultivated fields, olive-groves, vineyards, forests and farmhouses, still today preserves its ancient impression, with its castles, villas, Romanesque country churches, hermitages, monasteries, and edifices of the ancient villages (as for example the Palazzo Vicariale in Scarperia). The Mugello is the land where Cimabue, from a bridge, saw the boy, Giotto, drawing a sheep on a slab of stone; the land of the cas-

Environs of Florence, Medici Villa in Poggio a Caiano.

tles of the Ubaldini, proud opponents of Florence; the land of the majolicas of Cafaggiolo; the land of the even more ancient fossilised whale
mandible - called the "fish-bone" - exposed on the façade of a house.
Further into the heart of the Apennines, over the various ancient mountain passes - passo della Futa, giogo di Scarperia, Raticosa, Sant'Agata,
Osteria Bruciata, Muraglione, Colla di Casaglia - the visitor will come upon the most peculiar natural aspects of this area, with its fauna and vegetation still untouched: oaks, chestnuts, beeches, pine-trees, fir-trees,
brooms, junipers, heather and brambles.

LOCALITIES TO VISIT:
Monte Senario Convent, Borgo San Lorenzo, Vicchio, Scarperia

A STOP AT:
- **San Piero a Sieve**, is dominated by the beautiful MEDICEAN FORTRESS OF ST
MARTINO; inside the village, there is the 16th-century PARISH CHURCH - built
again during the 18th century - while not far there is the 15th-century
TREBBIO CASTLE.
- **Barberino di Mugello**, ancient agricultural centre with a 12th-century
CASTLE, with the beautiful 15th-century PALAZZO PRETORIO. Nearby, there is
the VILLA DI CAFAGGIOLO, once a fortress, restructured during the 15th cen-
tury by Michelozzo for the Medici family; a few isolated country churches, the artificial lake of BILANCINO (a dam) still to be finished in connec-

20

tion with which the artistic and environmental surroundings should be emphasised.

- **Passo della Futa**, Apennine pass that takes to the Emilia region, near which there is the GERMAN WAR CEMETERY, that holds the mortal remains of the soldiers of the Second World War.

- **Firenzuola**, village constructed during the 14th century by Florence to oppose the Ubaldini. The latter destroyed it in 1351. Worth seeing are the FLORENTINE AND BOLOGNAN GATES, the FORTRESS and the 14th-15h-century PALAZZO PRETORIO.

VILLAS OF THE LUCCHESIA

The Lucchesia is a gentle territory, full of charm and rich in traces of the past, with delightful corners, a beautiful countryside and, above all, plenty of villas. These villas are remarkable from an architectonic point of view, and, fortunately, they are well preserved. It would not be possible to list them all; the ones described here below are the most prestigious, the most ancient and the easiest to reach.

LOCALITIES TO VISIT:
Segromigno in Monte, Monte San Quirico, Marlia, Massa Pisana

STOP AT:
- **Villa Bigongiari**, formerly Giunigi, is at Farneta; the cube shaped building is enlivened in the façade by a porch with three arcades, breaking up the compact mass.
- **Villa Sanminiati**, 19th-century structure, is at Chiatri, 11 km from Lucca; this interesting building is famous because Puccini here composed his *Tosca*.

Segromigno in Monte, Villa Mansi.

- **Villa Giustiniani**, at Vecoli; according to some historians the construction was carried out by the Civitali circle, most of all for the elegant design, the harmony of the composition and the classical structure.
- **Villa Vanni** (today, Facchinetti) and **Villa de Vera**, at Pozzuolo, are both of the 16th century.
- **Villa Guidi**, at Sant'Alessio (4 km from Lucca), formerly Villa Covani, is enriched by an elegant 18th-century entrance gate and is characterised by a perfect balance of the volumes.
- **Villa Lucchesi**, at San Michele in Escheto (4 km from Lucca), is a 15th-century building partly modified during the 17th century.
- **Villa Totti**, at Mutigliano (6 km from Lucca), is attributed to the circle of Civitali; it has a beautiful fountain decorated with masks.
- **Villa Parensi Mansi**, at San Michele, 7 Km from Lucca; it is a rare 16th-century building with a portico surmounted by a loggia and with a fortified wall.
- **Villa Sardi**, a solid villa, that looks a bit like a fort, and lies 14 km from Lucca, at Sant'Ilario.

The Apuan Alps seen from Bocca di Magra.

THE VERSILIA, THE APUANE, THE GARFAGNANA AND THE LUNIGIANA

The Versilia is a large coastal area dotted with delightful localities traditionally devoted to fishing, agriculture and, from the last century, also a holiday resort. Going north from Livorno you will come across areas of luxuriant vegetation, the typical Mediterranean bush, once full of marshes, and reclaimed during the 18th century. The Tombolo, the San Rossore estate, the Macchia (bush) of Migliarino and the Macchia Lucchese are a series of natural areas, today protected; the stretch of water of Lake Massaciuccoli, often inspired Giacomo Puccini's operas, frequently tinged with that languid feeling the lake can inspire, with its marshy banks arriving under the windows of the musician's house at Torre del Lago. This place was already a holiday resort in Roman age, as you can see by the many finds at Massaciuccoli.

Viareggio was born as a seafaring village. During the belle époque it became a great tourist attraction, and it still is today, having also the Carnival. From here, north, there is a bathing establishment after the other, such as Lido di Camaiore, Forte dei Marmi, Marina di Massa; the hinterland is also interesting, with its small and big villages, with monuments and beautiful panoramas. These in fact are the spurs of the Apuane mountains, which belong to the northern chain of the Apennine mountains, even though, for their particular geological conformation, they are more similar to the Alps. The Apuane, lying between the lower Lunigiana, the Garfagnana and the coast, have a number of high peaks, such as the Pisanino mountain, 1946 m, and, surrounding it, the Cavallo mountain, the Tambura, the Sagro, the Pizzo d'Uccello, all of which are more than 1500 m high. The Apuane have been famous for centuries for the marble quarries, in fact today, they are the world's major centre of marble production. Furthermore, they also attract many mountain-climbers and excursionists that come to admire the beautiful landscapes which can be seen from the paths once used for the transportation of the marble and that cut through the various mountains creating new and fascinating routs.

The Garfagnana is a flourishing green valley bordered on the west by the Apuane Alps, and on the north, by the Apennines. It is of great interest to the tourist, both for the natural beauty, and for the various traces of the past. Already inhabited in prehistoric times, as shown by the tombs dating from the stone age, the area was later under the Ligurians and then passed under the dominion of Rome. During the Middle Ages it was initially subjected to the bishops of Lucca and of Luni and then to various important feudal families, to Pope Gregory XI and Frederick II. In 1248, it was ceded to Lucca; then it was contested by Lucca, Florence and the Malaspina family. In the 15th century, it became the dominion of the Estense and, until 1847, its destiny was that of the Duchy. The Garfagnana is between two mountain chains which, from a geological point of view, differ greatly: the Apuan Alps are bare while the Apennines are much more gentle and full of vegetation.

Although originally the Lunigiana covered a much larger territory, today it is included between the mountain ridge that goes from Mount Gottero to the Magra river, and the chain that from the same mountain goes to La Nuda, and from here, through the mouth of the Carpinelli and Mount Cavallo, arrives to the Apuan Alps. In ancient times, it was inhabited by the Apuan Ligurians who, after a long struggle, were subdued by the Romans. The latter set up a colony of 2000 people and founded the village of Luna, from which the Lunigiana takes its name. During the Middle Ages, the land was divided into various feuds, one of which belonged to the Malaspina, and other parts were divided among neighbouring states (Florence, Genoa and Milan). In 1815, with the Congress of Vienna, the Lunigiana was divided between the Duchy of Parma and that of Modena, which took over the Val di Magra, the Duchy of Massa Carrara, and the Kingdom of Sardinia. Interesting medieval villages, small towns with fascinating traces of an important past, are scattered throughout this area. The many castles of the Malaspina, dotting the landscape, also strike the eye.

LOCALITIES TO VISIT:
- The Natural Park of Migliarino-San Rossore-Massaciuccoli, Torre del Lago Puccini, Massaciuccoli, Viareggio, Camaiore, Forte dei Marmi,

Pietrasanta, Bagni di Lucca, Borgo a Mozzano, Castelnuovo di Garfagnana, Grotta del Vento (Fornovolasco), Carrara, Pontremoli

STOP AT:

- **Lido di Camaiore**, is the continuation, along the coast, of Viareggio, from which it is separated by the Fossa dell'Abate. Bathing establishments and lovely gardens have made Lido di Camaiore a particularly popular holiday resort.

- **Seravezza**, takes its name from the confluence of the Serra and the Vezza, and is traditionally the site of marble quarries since the 16th century, as well as an agricultural centre. Among the city monuments, the tourist should see the PALAZZO MEDICEO by Ammannati (1555), summer residence of the Grand Dukes of Tuscany, the CATHEDRAL, rebuilt in 1503. The Cathedral, bearing 17th-century retouches, houses a *baptismal font* by Stagio Stagi, a 17th-century *pulpit*, a marble *altar-frontal* by Benti and an *astylar cross* by Pollaiolo. The CHURCH OF THE SS. ANNUNZIATA, 15th-century but reconstructed after the war, contains a painting of *Mary's of the Sepulchre* by Pietro da Cortona. Not far from the village (4 km), there is the COUNTRY CHURCH DELLA CAPPELLA, 13th century Romanesque, with its bell tower prior to the 11th century and 15th- and 16th-century decorations.

- **Fosdinovo**, centre of the marquisate of the Malaspina family, who kept it until the 18th century and built a fine CASTLE: this building still dominates the town and the valley below, and from it, you can see a beautiful panorama that reaches the gulf of La Spezia. In the PARISH CHURCH OF ST. REMIGIO there is the 14th-century *tomb of Galeotto Malaspina*, with the figure of the deceased lying on the sarcophagus. The two Oratories are also of interest: one is known as that OF THE SANTISSIMO SACRAMENTO or DEI ROSSI, and the other DEI BIANCHI. The elegant VILLA DI CANIPAROLA lies at the foot of Fosdinovo. This is where the Malaspina sought refuge after losing their feud.

- **Mulazzo**, ancient medieval town with a powerful MALASPINA CASTLE, as well as a beautiful FORTRESS, called TORRE DI DANTE (the great poet sojourned in Mulazzo in 1306). The great navigator, Alessandro Malaspina, was born here.

- **Aulla**, where you can admire the rests of the ancient ABBEY OF ST. CAPRASIO, whose apse is annexed to the PARISH CHURCH. A walk through the charming town, leads to a hill with the fine rectangular fortress with bastions known as LA BRUNELLA, dating back from the early 14th century.

- **Villafranca in Lunigiana**, preserves fascinating rests of the grand MALASPINA CASTLE and the Renaissance CHURCH OF ST. FRANCESCO, with a pretty portico. In the small interior, there are a few important polychrome terra-cotta figures by Della Robbia.

- **Licciana Nardi**, where, facing the town hall, you will admire one of the MALASPINA CASTLES of the area, decorated with a small loggia. Every year, the literature prize "Lunigiana storica", here takes place.

THE TUSCAN ARCHIPELAGO

The Tuscan islands are scattered in the Tyrrhene Sea in front of the coast that goes from Livorno to Orbetello; their size is various, but apart from the Elba Island, they are usually small. These numerous islands and rocks, although invaded by tourists in the summer, still maintain an untouched vegetation and fauna. Where the geological consistence allows it, there are bushes of pine-trees, cork-forests, and forests of ilexes and other plants such as laurel, broom, myrtle, arbutus berry, and heather which are all typical of the Mediterranean bush. Among all these plants there are plenty of animals that live free, as for example martens, wild rabbits and wild goats; birds, also, find here their paradise (sea-gulls, crows, falcons, woodcocks, stilt-birds and mallards). The fauna, though, is even more abundant in the submarine environment, a real paradise for divers.

These islands have been inhabited by the Etruscans, the Greeks, the Ligurians and the Carthaginians, and they always have been exploited for the ore bodies and as strategic watch-outs for the pirates. The Romans built many villas, followed by religious hermitages often attacked by the Saracen pirates, indifferent to the various patronages on the archipelago. Today - apart from some areas that are either penal settlements or

The small port of Marciana Marina is one of the main tourist landings of the island of Elba.

protected areas - the Tuscan islands are frequented, during the summer, by crowds of visitors, that can easily reach them with the many ferry boats.
Given the fact that this route depends on the availability of the air and sea connections, here below you can find the locality of embarkation for the mentioned islands.

For the Island of Giglio: ferry-boats from Porto Santo Stefano.
For the Island of Giannutri: ferry-boats from Porto Santo Stefano.
For the Island of Elba: ferry-boats from Piombino to Cavo, Rio Marina, Porto Azzurro and Portoferraio; from Livorno to Portoferraio. The Marina di Campo airport is connected with Pisa, Milan and other airports.
For Pianosa: this island, the main part of which is closed to tourism since it is a penal settlement, can be reached with the ferry-boat line Piombino-Rio Marina-Porto Azzurro-Pianosa.
For Palmaiola, Isolotto dei Topi and Cerboli: only with private boats.
For the Island of Gorgona: the main part of it is closed to tourists since it is a penal settlement, it is connected with the ferry-boat line Livorno-Gorgona-Capraia-Portoferraio and viceversa.
For the Island of Capraia: ferry-boats from Livorno and Portoferraio.
For the Island of Montecristo and the Scoglio d'Africa: the island is a natural reserve and State property and, excluded from the ferry-boat lines, can only be visited with an authorisation.

25

THE MAREMMA AND THE ETRUSCANS

The Maremma extends from southern Tuscany to north-western Lazio. It is divided in Pisan Maremma (the part north of Piombino) and Grosseto Maremma (the southern part). The hinterland arrives all the way to the Metalliferous Hills, covering an area of about 5000 km square. The coast is interrupted by the promontories of Piombino, Punta Ala and Argentario.

In ancient times, it was a fertile land, on which many powerful Etruscan cities rose. This situation went on until the fall of the Roman Empire, when for the Maremma begun an inexorable decline and a relentless depopulation: the fields were abandoned and this land was forgotten, becoming for centuries infected and malarial.

Only with the great land reclamation operations carried out in 1828 by the Grand Duchy of Tuscany, Leopoldo II, and the following and definitive regenaration interventions done at the beginning of this century, the Maremma, is now almost completely reclaimed, and has returned to being a moderately fertile land with a good agricultural and, above all,

Typical iconography of the Maremma: a "buttero" (cow-boy) on his horse.

26

zoo-technical production. Along its very beautiful coast, there are many famous bathing establishments, such as San Vincenzo, Follonica, Punta Ala, Castiglione della Pescaia, Marina di Grosseto and Porto Santo Stefano.

The presence of raw materials on the land, such as timber and minerals, and the conformation of the area of the cost and also of the hinterland, were the premises for a stable occupation since the Iron Age.

After a progressive development, the small villages of huts united to form cities, well exploiting the local resources, becoming protagonists of the trade fluxes, that during the 7th century BC, interested Etruria. However, it would have been the sea vocation to make the cities of the Maremma become flourishing centres; in fact, at that time the coast had many more inlets than today. In addition to the large gulf of Baratti, that still today is a beautiful protected stretch of water, there used to be a very large internal sea loop: the Lacus Prelius, on which rose Roselle and Vetulonia, and that, after it became marshy, was reclaimed; today it is part of the plain of Grosseto. The presence of the connections between the Island of Elba and the other cities of the coast of the Lazio Etruria, is proved by the findings of objects of exchange, by which it is assumed that these centres went through a period of prosperity until the decline of the Etruscan supremacy on the sea, that is until the year 474 BC, when the Etruscans were defeated at Cuma by the Syracuse navy. Some of the cities, went through a revival between the 4th and 3rd centuries BC, when the Romans conquered this part of land. In 273 BC, with the foundation of Cosa, a Roman colony built to become a port, most of the cities of the coast went through a further decline, pre-announcing the Romanisation of the area.

LOCALITIES TO VISIT:
Orbetello, Castiglione della Pescaia, Massa Marittima, Populonia, Roselle, Vetulonia, Val Fucinaia, Lago dell'Accesa

STOP AT:
- **Talamone**, once an Etruscan city, then simple fisher's village, today is a prosperous summer resort. The town sits on a promontory dominating the sea. Of interest are the 15th-century FORTRESS, probably designed by Vecchietta, and the ruins of the ETRUSCAN TEMPLE OF TALAMONACCIO. The town is mentioned in history books, because in 1860 Garibaldi and the Thousand stopped here to collect arms and ammunition on their way to Marsala.
- **Piombino**, Roman city, today is a rich metal-work centre as well as the port for the Island of Elba. The city offers the visitor the ruins of the WALLS with the SANT'ANTONIO GATE, the fine PALAZZO COMUNALE, built during the 13th century, and only recently brought back to its 15th-century appearance, and the CLOCK TOWER, late 16th-century. What is left of the ancient CITADEL can be seen in the homonymous square with the Renaissance CHAPEL (works by A. Della Robbia). Interesting is also the CHURCH OF ST. ANTIMO, built in 1374, that houses the 14th-century *sepulchre* of Jacopo d'Appiano and two *baptismal fonts*, one of which was made from an Etruscan column, the other is by Guardi (1470).
- **Argentario**, is a large promontory extending 12 kilometres out into the sea. Once it was an island, then it joined the mainland as sand accumulated, forming the isthmus, and creating the ORBETELLO LAGOON. It is a splendid stretch of land: on the west, it falls straight into the sea while on the north, slopes down into a beautiful bay, where PORTO SANTO STEFANO is. There are many tourist resorts, built during the last decades. Along the eastern coast is PORTO ERCOLE, overlooked by a fortress, and embarkation port for Giannutri.
- **Punta Ala**, is a rocky area on the southern tip of the gulf of Follonica. This patch of land is almost untouched, with a beach of fine sand crowned by a dense Mediterranean bush reaching down to the sea. In the last twenty-five years, Punta Ala has become an exclusive residential area.
- **Follonica**, industrial town, as well as famous seaside resort; it has a large beach, bordered by a flourishing pine-wood. The PARISH CHURCH OF ST. LEOPOLDO, dating back from the years 1836-1838, is of interest for the original combination of materials used for the construction - cast iron, stone and wood. An interesting visit can also be made to the recently established MUSEUM OF IRON AND CAST IRON

MOUNT AMIATA

Mount Amiata (1738 m) is the highest peak of southern Tuscany and its natural characteristics are very beautiful. It is a volcanic mountain of the Quaternary period. The mountain is crossed by short streams of water and springs; in recent years, it has become a popular winter holiday site: there are, in fact, quite a number of sophisticated lifts, refuges and ski slopers. The Amiata is also a fairly populated mountain, and the villages, such as Abbadia San Salvatore, Piancastagnaio, Santa Fiora, Arcidosso, Castel del Piano, preserve precious traces of the past.

LOCALITIES TO VISIT:
Abbadia San Salvatore, Piancastagnaio, Santa Fiora, Arcidosso

A STOP AT:
- **Castel del Piano**, is an ancient medieval village, having its oldest part in a higher position, surrounded by the 16th-century built-up area and the modern part on the outside. Among the most ancient monuments, is the CHURCH OF ST. LEONARDO, built in the 15th century, the CLOCK TOWER and the CONFRATERNITY ORATORY .
- **Bagni San Filippo**, spa near the Formone river, with hot springs of sulphurous water with calcium carbonate - the legend says that they come out from where Saint Filippo Benizzi laid his stick - that can give relief for rheumatic, arthritic, cutaneous and inflammatory diseases.

THE CASENTINO AND THE PRATOMAGNO

The Casentino and the Pratomagno are two areas situated close by the Apennines between Florence and Arezzo, among the highest peaks and the valley of the Arno. Here, in fact, there is Falterona, with the springs of the most important Tuscan river, and many other mountains featuring an untouched nature.
These mountains, among which there are a number of small Etruscan villages, have an extremely rich vegetation, with plants such as chestnuts, maples, yews, elms, bay oaks, ash-trees, birches and silver firs, all typical of the Apennine chain, to which man has added the alder and the pine-tree.
The Foreste Demaniali Casentinesi have been instituted to protect these beautiful forests, and the access is forbidden. Among these high valleys, the streams, the olive groves and the cultivated fields, there are ancient villages, with churches, castles, palaces and squares that still retain their 14th-century appearance. Religious communities, instead, have chosen the most isolated areas to build, in the last centuries, hermitages, still today destination for pilgrims and for meditative retiring.

LOCALITIES TO VISIT:
Vallombrosa, Hermitage of Camaldoli, Poppi, Bibbiena, Sanctuary of Verna, Sansepolcro, Anghiari

STOP AT:
- **Caprese Michelangelo**, is the birthplace of the famous artist, from which this hamlet takes its name. Built before the year 1000, it was the dominion of various families before becoming part of the Florentine territory in 1384. Of the same period, is the CASTLE, restored and now museum of moulds of Michelangelo's works and sculptures of contemporary artists. The house, where the 6 March 1475 Michelangelo was born, is the PALAZZO DEL PODESTÀ - the father of the artist, in fact, was a podestà - which is, also, today a museum that houses documents relative to the great works of the artist.
- **Romena**, where you will find the beautiful COUNTRY CHURCH OF ST. PIETRO, 12th-century, in part restored. Both the inside and the outside, are Romanesque: the inside, has pillars with fine capitals that divide the two naves from the aisle; along the naves, there are paintings of the 13th and 14th centuries.
Nearby, there is the CASTLE OF ROMENA, built around the year 1000 and scene of many fights, as well as of the episode involving Mastro Adamo, of which Dante writes in his *Divine Comedy*. In ruins for many centuries, the fortress has been recently restored and integrated.

- **Subbiano**, probably was built during the 11th century to control a strategically important bridge. In the centuries that followed, it passed from the Guidi counts to the Tarlati of Pietramala, and then became a vicariate of the Florentine Republic. As well as the ruins of the CASTLE, there is the ancient PALAZZO PRETORIO with, on the façade, numerous stone armorial bearings of the vicars sent here from Florence.

- **Terranuova Bracciolini**, has a quite unusual layout: it is similar to the nearby San Giovanni Valdarno, which also develops around two parallel streets with a square plan in between; the town blocks are all proportional in area to each other, and once they all had their own parish church. As for San Giovanni, it is said that the town plan is a design of Arnolfo di Cambio, but this has not been proven yet. Most of the original city WALLS are still standing, but the gates were destroyed under the bombings of the 2nd World War. Before this war, there were also many palaces, as for example the one where the Florentine representative lived: unfortunately, only a few remain today, of which the most important, is the PALAZZO CONCINI, of the Renaissance.

- **Loro Ciuffenna**, still retains its medieval aspect, and is one of the most enchanting in the Pratomagno. Etruscan in origin, it developed especially during the 13th and 14th centuries, becoming an important market centre. The CHURCH OF SANTA MARIA ASSUNTA is in the oldest part of the town and is interesting especially for the panel painting of the *Madonna and Saints* by Lorenzo Bicci and the *Annunciation* by Carlo Portelli, a 16th-century painter born in Loro Ciuffenna.

CHIANTI AND ITS ENVIRONS

Chianti is the land where the famous wine is produced, and today it extends far beyond its original historical boundaries – Classical Chianti – comprising the countryside of Pisa, Siena, Pistoia, Arezzo and to the north-east of Florence. The original area of the Chianti region, with its gentle hilly countryside, is bordered by the basin of the Arno to the south of Florence, and that of the Ombrone, north of Siena. The area was already inhabited by the Etruscans and then passed under the Roman rule. In the 8th century, it became a large feud of the noble Firidolfi family. Later, this land was disputed between Siena and Arezzo, and then between Siena and Florence. The landscape that the Chianti offers to the visitors is rich in many ways: it is rich in roads, often unpaved and still retaining their ancient charm, and steep paths winding up to villas and castles, churches and farmhouses. The Chianti is a "holy" land (there are small churches everywhere, all having an ancient history) and a land of towers, rich in castles (they can be counted by the dozen) where the atmosphere is still medieval. To name just a few, at Montefiridolfi there is the one called "del Gabbiano", another at Poggio Petroio, others at Monte Campolese, Tignano, Uzzano, Verrazzano, Vicchiomaggio; the imposing and scenic Castle of Brolio of the Ricasoli barons, the one at Vertine, Tornano, Cacchiano, San Polo in Rosso, and the keep of Montegrossoli, the tower of Barbischio, the Castle of Meleto, the Fortress-castle of Volpaia, the ones at Fonterutoli, Orgiale, Monterinaldi; and many others to be found everywhere, increasing the charm of this land. It is hardly necessary to say, that the principal activity in this region is agriculture: an agriculture which produces a wine famous in every corner of the world, the "Chianti Classico Gallo Nero", and an olive oil that is just as prized.

The Chianti territory is formed by marl limestone (alberese), by sandstone (macigno) and clayey schist (galestro). Over half of the land is covered by tall trees: oaks, chestnuts, ilexes, firs, and in part by the Mediterranean bush including shrubs, brambles, bushes, hedges and aromatic plants. The other half is cultivated: large vineyards covering the hillsides in geometric patterns, and large olive groves stretching to the horizon. The wine of this land, known for centuries for its delicious aroma, is the result of a perfect blend of four types of grapes: the Sangioveto and the Canaiolo (black grapes), the Malvasia and the Trebbiano (white grapes).

The result is the Chianti Classico, a ruby-red wine with a full dry flavour, the just right amount of tannic acid and the typical perfume of violets: it is the masterpiece of this generous land which has managed to keep its flavour untouched.

Beyond the Brolio Castle there are the noble Chianti vineyards.

LOCALITIES TO VISIT:
San Casciano in Val di Pesa, Tavarnelle Val di Pesa, Castellina in Chianti, Gaiole in Chianti, Radda in Chianti, Greve in Chianti, San Gimignano, San Miniato, Montalcino, Buonconvento, Volterra, Colle Val d'Elsa, Monteriggioni

STOP AT:
- Badia a Passignano, is a medieval monastic centre with the CHURCH OF ST. MICHELE, originally Romanesque then transformed in the 16th century, and the annexed ex-monastery containing the *Last supper* by Ghirlandaio. As well as the 13th-century TOWER, also see the CHURCH OF ST. BIAGIO (Gothic-Romanesque) and the CAPPELLINA DEI PESCI, built in 1798.
- Semifonte, was an important medieval town before it was destroyed by the Florentines in 1202. You will see its ruins around the fine CHAPEL OF ST. MICHELE, 16th-century, designed by Santi di Tito, surmounted by an accurate copy, reduced to 1/8, of Brunelleschi's dome on the Cathedral in Florence. Nearby, rests of residences and furnaces have been found; also the TOWER DEL BORGO and the annexed building - maybe an ex-convent - and the TOWER DEL MORELLO.
- San Donato in Poggio, castle already existing before the year 1000, was chief town of one of the "Terzi" of the Barberino League. In the village, with buildings having 13th-century elements, there are the Renaissance

PALAZZO MALASPINA and the CHURCH OF SANTA MARIA DELLA NEVE, late 14th-century featuring Gothic details. Not far is the country CHURCH OF SAN DONATO, of Romanesque structure already present in the 10th century, with a beautiful bell tower; nearby, you will find the ORATORY OF THE MADONNA DELLE GRAZIE DI PIETRACUPA: the church was built at the end of the 16th century, while the outside loggias in the 17th century.

- **Certosa di Pontignano**, built in 1343, but still retaining the Sienese Romanesque atmosphere, often damaged, it was restructured in the 17th century, receiving frescoes by Poccetti, the picturesque cloister and the monk's cells.

- **Brolio**, early medieval, was one of the castles harshly disputed between the Florentine and the Sienese from the 13th to 15th century. It contains the KEEP and the PENTAGONAL WALLS, late 15th century; about 450 metres long. Inside the castle, in which Bettino Ricasoli lived, there is the PALAZZO PADRONALE, neo-Gothic, and the CHAPEL OF ST. JACOPO.

- **Badia a Coltibuono**, fine example of the Chianti Romanesque style, was built in the middle of the 11th century and for a long time the Vallombrosan monks lived there. The CHURCH OF ST. LORENZO has a Latin cross plan covered with trusses and a barrel vault, as well as a dome on the transept, to which corresponds, on the outside, an unusual pagoda roof. The MONASTERY, to the right of the church, holds a beautiful cloister and a refectory.

THE VALDICHIANA AND THE VAL D'ORCIA

The Valdichiana is among the most representative historical regions of Tuscany. This territory was once lacustrine and marshy, the relicts of which are the lakes of Chiusi and Montepulciano. The Chiana region, today rendered pleasant, fertile and productive by the reclamation operations culminating in the construction of the Maestro della Chiana Canal, is a typical area of transition from characteristic Tuscany to nearby Umbria, lying between the basins of the Arno and the Tevere. Its delightful hills, green with cypresses, olive groves and forests, are intensively cultivated and full of fine vineyards.

The area has always attracted tourists for its great variety of archaeological sites, Roman and Etruscan settlements, Romanesque monuments and picturesque medieval hamlets, as well as for the many fine spas; moreover, in recent years, the increase of farm holidays has made this land even more inviting. The natural landscape of the Valdichiana encloses the typical and ideal Tuscan landscape: the farm-house at the top of the hill, enlivened by the patterns of the specialised cultivation, accessible from an unsurfaced road framed by towering cypresses. On the slopes of the Cetona mountain you can visit ancient pre-historic sites, and beyond it lies the natural and scenic landscape of the Val d'Orcia, with its 'crete' (hills with no vegetation), 'calanchi' (eroded clay slopes with small sharp ridges), 'biancane' (countryside not cultivated), scattered rural sites, parched fields, ploughed turf and cypress groves. The pleasantness of the environment and the great number of cultural sites justifies the institution of the Artistic Natural and Cultural Park of the Val d'Orcia.

LOCALITIES TO VISIT:
Chianciano Terme, Chiusi, Sarteano, Cetona, San Casciano dei Bagni, Pienza, Montepulciano, Torrita di Siena, Sinalunga, Trequanda, San Quirico d'Orcia, Bagno Vignoni, Castiglione d'Orcia.

STOP AT:
- **Monticchiello,** hamlet still retaining its medieval harmony. KEEP, WALLS and TOWERS are 13th-century. In the PARISH CHURCH, dating from the same period, there are frescoes of Sienese setting and a painting by P. Lorenzetti.

- **Montefollonico,** pretty medieval village with ancient GATES. Romanesque Church OF ST. LORENZO, Churches OF THE TRAIANO, OF THE COMPAGNIA and OF ST. BARTOLOMEO.

- **Petroio,** like the near Castelmuzio still preservs its medieval schemes. Ruins of the WALLS and of a TOWER, once part of the 13th-century layout. Fine paintings in the PARISH CHURCH.

FLORENCE

HISTORICAL SURVEY - *Florence lies at the foot of the Tusco-Emilian Appennines, in the large plain cut by the Arno river and surrounded by hills. After being inhabited in prehistoric times, during the 8th century BC, an Italic people, with a Villanovan culture settled in the area between the Arno and the Mugnone rivers, but little is known of these remote times. In 59 BC, the Roman city was founded, with the square ground plan of the* castrum. *The* decumanus *was laid out along what are now the Via del Corso, the Via degli Speziali and the Via Strozzi, while the ancient* cardus *corresponds to the line between Piazza San Giovanni, the Via Roma and the Via Calimala. Marcus Aurelius (or Diocletian) chose it as the seat of the* Corrector Italiae, *the governor responsible for Tuscany and Umbria. With the arrival of the Barbarians, Florence was first besieged by the Ostrogoths of Radagaisus (405), who plundered the surrounding countryside, although Florence managed to resist protected by Stilicho's troops inflicting an overwhelming defeat on the enemy. Next came the Byzantines, who occupied Florence in 539, and the Goths who took over the city in 541. Under Lombard domination (570), the city managed to safeguard its autonomy, while under the Franks, the number of inhabitants diminished, and the city lost most of its territory. Around the year 1000, the ascent of Florence began and continued through various centuries in spite of numerous controversies, wars and internal struggles. New walls were built around the city, new civic and religious buildings went up, and at the same time the arts, literature, and trade continued to prosper. In 1183, the city became a free Commune, although it had already actually availed itself of this freedom for many years. The first clashes between two factions, the Guelphs and the Ghibellines, date to those years. The first were followers of the Pope, the second of the Emperor. These clashes were to lacerate the civil fabric of the city up to 1268. The Ghibellines were the first to gain advantage and expelled the Guelph families from the city in 1249. But Florence's roots were Guelph, and the followings years these won. The Ghibellines sought refuge in Siena, where they were overtaken by the Guelph*

Florence, the beautiful panorama of the city from Piazzale Michelangelo.

troops, who were, however, badly beaten in the battle of Montaperti. As a result, Florence was once more Ghibelline for various years until the battle of Benevento (1226), when the Guelphs once more defeated their bitter rivals, once and for all. Despite the unstable social and political situation, this period witnessed an upsurge in the arts and in literature. This was the time of Dante and the "Dolce Stil Novo", of Giotto and Arnolfo di Cambio. In the 15th century, the city's rise continued. Florence was a trading city, but also the new cradle for Italian and eventually European culture. Many powerful families (Pitti, Frescobaldi, Strozzi, Albizi) contended the supremacy of the city. Finally, a powerful family of bankers – the Medici – distinguished themselves. The first to govern would have been the founder Cosimo I, later known as the Elder. His successors were to govern up to the first half of the 18th century, making Florence the leading city during the period of Humanism and the Renaissance. Great personalities, such as Leonardo da Vinci and Michelangelo, worked here during this period, when Florence was at its highest prestige. In 1737, to the Medici succeeded the house of Lorraine, and the government continued along the lines of a moderate liberalism, although by that point the great period of Florentine culture was fading away. In 1860, during the Risorgimento, Tuscany was annexed to the kingdom of Italy with a plebiscite. For a brief period, Florence became the capital of the new nation. During World War II, serious damage was inflicted on the historical centre and various important buildings were lost. Despite this and the flood, which invaded the city in 1966, Florence has retained its charm.

BAPTISTERY OF ST. GIOVANNI - The Florentine Baptistery seems to have been built originally around the 4th-5th century, in an area occupied by a large Roman *domus*, and the peripheral parts extended as far as the area later occupied by Santa Reparata. The site was near the northern gate of Roman Florence (located between the Baptistery and the *Via Cerretani*), and the religious building was always octagonal in plan, with a semi-circular apse and set on a podium with steps. In the 11th century, the Baptistery became the city cathedral, since Santa Reparata was being rebuilt. San Giovanni (the Baptistery) too was refaced both inside and out, while in 1128, the smooth pyramidal roof was finished and topped by a lantern with columns (1150).

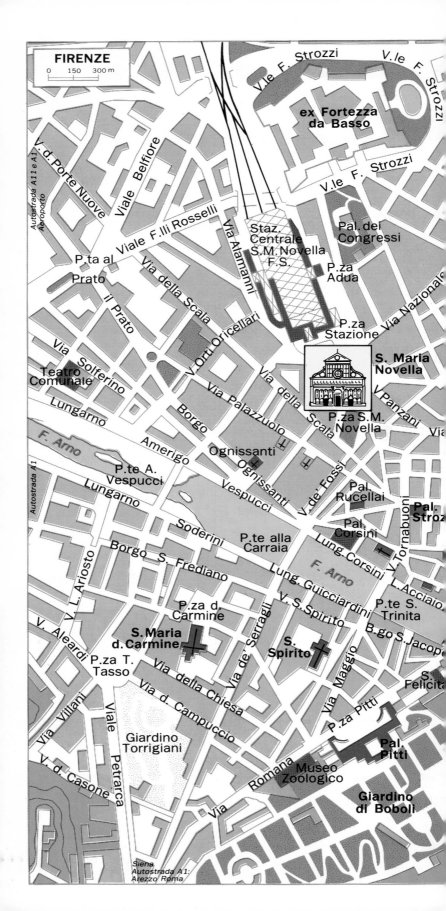

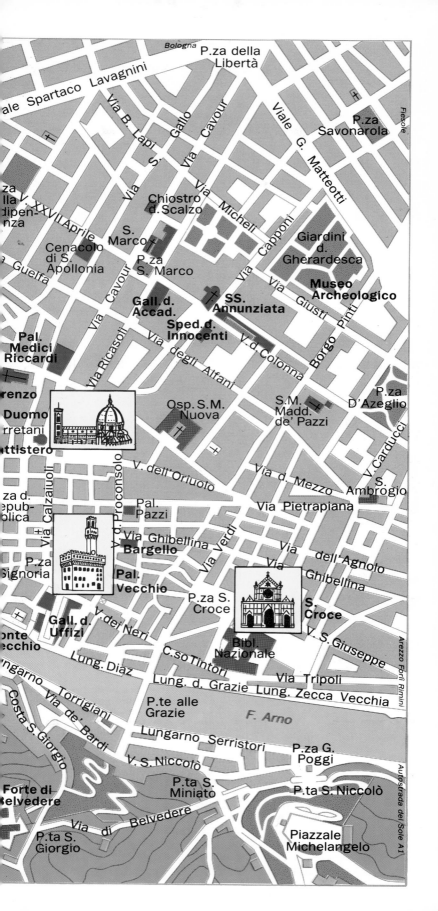

Florence, panorama with the Baptistery, the Cathedral and Giotto's Bell tower.

The **apse** – also called *Scarsella* – was rebuilt in a square shape in 1292, and in 1293, when the work carried out by the corporation of the *Arte di Calimala* (wool merchants' guild) was finished, the Baptistery looked as it does today. The building, where the Florentine Republic invested its knights, is still today faced on the **exterior** by green and white marble. Each side is divided into three areas by pilaster strips supporting an entablature below and round arches with windows above. The higher entablature has an attic divided into blind compartments.

The three bronze **doors** are particularly important. The *South door*, which is the oldest and is decorated with scenes from the *Life of St. John the Baptist* and the *Allegories of the Theologian and Cardinal Virtues*, is by Andrea Pisano (1330-1336). The *North door,* with *Stories from the New Testament, Evangelists and Doctors of the Church* is by Lorenzo Ghiberti (1403-1424), with the help of Donatello, Bernardo Ciuffagni, Paolo Uccello and Bernardo Cennini. And lastly, the *Eastern door,* known as the *Gates of Paradise* with ten panels (now replaced by copies) representing *Stories from the Old Testament* is by Lorenzo Ghiberti, and is considered one of the greatest masterpieces of 15th-century sculpture.

The **interior** has an inlaid pavement with decorative motives of eastern style. On the walls from left to right you may admire a Roman *sarcophagus*, the *sarcophagus of Bishop Ranieri* and the *tomb of the antipope John XXIII* (1427), designed by Michelozzo and Donatello, who also executed the lying statue. The Baptistery also houses a marble baptismal font dating 1371, attributed to the school of Pisa.

The tribune in the apse has Byzantine style mosaics on the vault, dating 1225 by Fra' Jacopo. Other mosaics cover the entire **cupola**, at which Florentine artists, probably helped by Venetian craftsmen, worked between the 13th and the 14th century. These artists include Cimabue, Coppo di Marcovaldo and Gaddo Gaddi. The tondo above the apse represents *Christ* surrounded by scenes of the *Last Judgement*. The opposite side contains *Stories of the Baptist,* scenes from the *Life of Christ,* and from the *Life of Joseph and Mary,* as well as *Stories from Genesis.* The *Angelic Hierarchies* are represented around the lantern.

CATHEDRAL - The Cathedral of Florence, dedicated to *Santa Maria del Fiore*, is the fruit of the commitment of a large number of artists who worked on it over a period of centuries. At the end of the 13th century, Florence, then a Commune, was already flourishing and the build-up area had spread considerably. The extant cathedral of Santa Reparata was by then too small to house the citizens, and no longer sufficiently prestigious for the city. In his *Cronache*, Giovanni Villani writes that "the citizens came to an agreement on the renewal of the principal church of Florence, which was of a simple form and small in comparison to a city of this kind; and they gave orders to make it larger and set the façade further back, and to make it all in marble and with sculptured figures". In 1294, the Art Guilds, that supported the government, decided that Arnolfo di Cambio should construct a new cathedral, and when the building was completed, the preexisting church should be torn down. At the time **Santa Reparata** was situated where the front part of the cathedral now stands. The Church had been built in the 4th-5th centuries on the ruins of a Roman *domus,* and it had a nave and two aisles with a single apse. During the Byzantine wars, the church was destroyed, and then rebuilt between the 8th and 9th centuries. Although the perimeter was basically the same, two side chapels were added to the structure and the columns were replaced by pilasters with strips. Between the years 1000 and 1100, a crypt with a raised choir was created in the area of the apse, which was flanked by two bell towers outside. The new cathedral building yard grew around and inside this church and although work continued for decades, Santa Reparata continued being the cathedral until 1375. Work on the new cathedral, begun on September 8, 1296, was interrupted in 1302 when Arnolfo di Cambio died. His place as masterbuilder was taken by Giotto, in 1334. However, the social situation and various natural calamities (the economic crisis due to the bankrupt of the Bardi and Pe-

Florence, the Southern Portal of the Baptistery.

ruzzi banks, the flood of 1333, the popular uprisings and the plague of 1348) slowed down the construction. After Giotto's death in, 1337, Andrea Pisano, Francesco Talenti and Giovanni di Lapo Ghini worked on the Duomo. In 1375, Santa Reparata was demolished to the height of two and a half metres and the plans for the cathedral were changed, so that part of Arnolfo's structure was torn down. The building was finally finished with the exception of the dome, which had been included in the original project but turned out to be more difficult to build than planned. The competition for the dome was won in 1420 by Brunelleschi, who proposed to build the enormous aerial structure without the use of fixed centring, thanks to the adoption of interconnected ribbing and herring-bone bricks. The dome was finished in 1434, and the cathedral was consecrated in 1436, 140 years after it had been begun. The lantern at the top of the dome was also designed by Brunelleschi, but as Vasari notes, "because he was now old and would not live to see the lantern finished he stipulated in his will that it should be built with the model and the written instructions that he left; otherwise, he insisted, the fabric would collapse as it was vaulted in an ogive and needed the weight pressing down on top in order to strengthen it. He failed to see this edifice completed before he died, but he raised it to a height of several feet...". Arnolfo's **façade** was torn down in 1587, and designs for a new one abounded. Not until 1871 were the plans by De Fabris approved, and they were then carried out in 1887. This façade, which is the one we now see, employed the same types of marble as those used in the revestment of the sides: Carrara white, Prato green and Maremma rose. Above the three portals, with *Stories from the Life of the Virgin*, there are three lunettes with, left to right, *Charity,* the *Madonna with the Patrons of the City,* and *Faith.* The gable of the main entrance has a *Madonna in Glory.* Statues of the *Apostles* and of the *Virgin* are on the frieze running between the side rose windows and the central one. The tympanum, with a bas-relief of *God the Father,* is set above a row of busts of artists. Four doors open in the sides of the cathedral articulated by pilasters and tall mullioned windows with two lights. On the bell tower side, there are the *Bell tower Door* and the *Canons Door,* while on the other side are the *Balla Door* and the *Mandorla Door.* The latter is 15th-century, and is decorated in the lunette with a mosaic of the *Annunciation* by Ghirlandaio, a tympanum by Nanni di Banco, and *statues of the Prophets* by the young Donatello. The **interior** is very spacious, both in height and width, following the dictates of Italian Gothic architecture. The three broad aisles are divided by composite pillars from which spring large moderately pointed arches. The spaciousness of the bays unifies the area of the cathedral, enhacing its width. At the bottom of the naves there is a large area occupied by the high altar, around which there are the three apses, each divided in five parts. Under the stained glass windows designed by Ghiberti, and the clock with Paolo Uccello's *Prophets* (1443), the **interior façade** bears the 14th-century lunette with the *Coronation of the Virgin* by Gaddo Gaddi, and the *tomb of Antonio d'Orso,* by Tino di Camaino, 1321 circa. The **left aisle**, apparently very simple, contains various masterpieces: at the beginning is the aedicule with a statue of *Joshua,* by Ciuffagni, Donatello and Nanni di Bartolo, and the neighbouring *Aedicule of St. Zanobius* painted at the end of the 14th century by Vanni del Biondo. Between Benedetto da Maiano's *bust of A. Squarcialupi* and Ciuffagni's *Aedicule with David* (1434) there are the two *equestrian monuments,* once frescoed, of *Giovanni Acuto* (John Hawkwood) and *Niccolò da Tolentino.* The former was painted by Paolo Uccello in 1436, representing the soldier of fortune in such a severe pose that it communicates immobility, while in the latter (1456), Andrea del Castagno has a livelier plasticity giving a sense of vitality to the knight. In front of the arch of the fouth bay, under the stained-glass window designed by Agnolo Gaddi, are the panels with *SS. Cosmas and Damian* (by Bicci di Lorenzo, 15th century), and *Dante Alighieri* (by Domenico di Michelino, 1465). In the left tribune, is Lorenzo di Credi's *St. Joseph* in the first room on the left, and once it contained Michelangelo's marble *Pietà,* now in the nearby Cathedral Museum. Two marble aedicules flank the door of the **New Sacristy** surmounted by a lunette in glazed terra-cotta by Luca della Robbia. This *Resurrection,* which Luca made in 1444, is exalted by an ascending movement that is both linear and sculptural, and is enriched by colour. On the opposite side, beyond the high altar – a 16th-century work by Baccio Bandinelli – there is the door to the **Old**

Florence, the Cathedral of Santa Maria del Fiore.

Sacristy with Luca della Robbia's other lunette of the *Ascension*. The right tribune contains a Giottesque fresco with the *Madonna* and a *St. Philip* by Bandini. Beyond this, in the south aisle, is a painting of *St. Bartholomew Enthroned* by Franchi (15th cent.) and the aedicule with a *Prophet* by Nanni di Banco (1408), set between the medallions with *Giotto* (by Benedetto da Maiano, 1490) and with *Brunelleschi* (by Buggiano, 1446). Here, a modern staircase descends to the pre-existant church of Santa Reparata. The great **dome**, which Brunelleschi had conceived as bare, was however painted by Giorgio Vasari and Zuccari between 1572 and 1579. Scenes from the *Last Judgement* are set in three concentric bands with the *Prophets* at the top of the vault in a trompe l'oeil lantern with a railing. A passageway set in the dome, leads to the frescoes – recently restored – and, from the terrace above the high altar, continues up to the lantern at the top of the cathedral.

GIOTTO'S BELL TOWER -The cathedral bell tower was begun in 1334 by Giotto, masterbuilder for the construction of the Cathedral. Actually he soon became more interested in the bell tower than in the church, and

39

even made a model of the tower which is now in Siena in the Metropolitan Artwork Museum. Until his death, in 1337, he built the bottom part of the bell tower composed of two closed stories decorated with hexagonal and rhomboid reliefs, by Andrea Pisano, Luca della Robbia, Alberto Arnoldi and workshop. The relief panels on the lower band, now replaced by casts, represent the *Life of Man in the Creation and in the Human Arts* executed by Andrea Pisano and Luca della Robbia on Giotto's designs. His influence is clear in the relief given to the figures and the simplified masses. The theme was influenced by the fact that Giotto had been named master builder by the Corporation of the Arts, which at the time controlled the government in Florence. It was therefore to compliment his patrons that he included the following subjects in this order: *Tilling of the Land, Sheepraising, Music, Medicine, Hunting, Weaving, Legislation, Mechanics, Navigation, Justice, Agriculture* and *Theater.* The upper row, which dates from the second half of the 14th century, represents the *Planets,* the *Virtues,* the *Liberal Arts* and the *Sacraments.* The two upper stages were finished by Andrea Pisano, who took Giotto's place. He created a series of sixteen niches between the pilaster strips which contained *statues of the Prophets, Sibylls* and the *Baptist,* surmounted by an equal number of false niches. Between 1350 and 1359, Francesco Talenti finished the bell tower, adding two levels with the two gabled mullioned windows with two lights with their lovely twisted columns and the story with the single mullioned window with three lights. On the top, more than 81 metres high, he created the large terrace supported by small arches and with an openwork balustrade.
The sense for solidity is typical of Italian Gothic and the steeple Giotto had included in his original plan was not carried out.

CATHEDRAL MUSEUM - The Cathedral Museum is installed behind the apse of the cathedral. The entrance is surmounted by a fine *Bust of Cosimo I* by Giovanni Bandini.
Inside there are numerous examples of Romanesque sculpture, statues and architectural pieces from the ancient façade of the Duomo and the Baptistery. Among the finest statues on the ground floor, there is *Boniface VIII in the Act of Blessing,* the *Madonna and Child* and the *Madonna of the Nativity* by Arnolfo di Cambio, and the famous *St. Luke* by Nanni di Banco. Nearby you will find the room that houses illuminated manuscripts and chorales and precious reliquaries.
The museum also contains the *Magdalen,* an intense and vibrant wooden statue by Donatello. On the first floor are the two choir stalls, one by Donatello and the other by Luca della Robbia, and various statues once set on Giotto's campanile. They are of the prophets *Habacuc, Jeremiah* and another *Prophet,* all by Donatello, *Abraham* and *Isaac* by Nanni di Bartolo.
In the room to the right is the fine *Altarpiece of St. John the Baptist,* a large monument on which Michelozzo, Verrocchio, Antonio del Pollaiolo and Bernardo Cennini collaborated. On either side are the statues of *Our Lady of the Annunciation* and the *Archangel Gabriel* by Jacopo della Quercia. In the room to the left are the original relief panels from Giotto's bell tower, made for the two tiers: they are by Andrea Pisano, Alberto Arnoldi and Luca della Robbia.
Other examples of painting and sculpture include a noteworthy diptych with scenes from the *Lives of Christ and the Madonna,* it is of Byzantine school and dates from the late 13th century; Michelangelo's *Deposition,* formerly in the Cathedral (the central figure is supposed to be a self-portrait), and the Baptistery altar, in silver, with gilding and enamel.

LOGGIA DEL BIGALLO - This pretty Gothic structure is on the corner of *Piazza del Duomo* and *Via Calzaioli.* Attributed to Alberto Arnoldi (1352-58), it consists of two arcades richly decorated with reliefs and statues. Once seat of the Mercy Company it is now a **Museum** with works by important 15th- and 16th-century artists.

PIAZZA DELLA SIGNORIA - It is among the most beautiful Italian squares, and it occupies a large area. The piazza was enlarged later, between the 13th and 14th centuries, thanks to the demolition of the houses of various Florentine Ghibelline families, including the Uberti and the Foraboschi. The imposing complex of **Palazzo Vecchio** towers over the piazza on the north side. To the right of the façade of Palazzo Vecchio is the

Florence, a beautiful view of Palazzo Vecchio dominated by the Tower of Arnolfo.

lovely **Loggia dei Lanzi**, a late Gothic structure by Benci di Cione and Simone Talenti (1376-91). To the left of the palace, is the beautiful *Fountain of Neptune,* or *Fontana di Piazza,* by Bartolomeo Ammannati (1563-75) and, to one side, the *Equestrian Monument of Cosimo I* (1594) by Giambologna.

FONTANA DEL BIANCONE (THE NEPTUNE FOUNTAIN) - This very scenic sculptural group was carried out between 1563 and 1575; the powerful figure of *Neptune* standing out in the centre of the Fountain, is not one of Ammannati's best works (the artist may have been inspired by a drawing of Leonardo). Best are the bronze statues representing *River Allegories* of satyrs and nymphs by Ammannati and some of his young collaborators, including Giambologna.

EQUESTRIAN STATUE OF COSIMO I DE' MEDICI - The monument is on the left of Palazzo Vecchio. It has a very dignified and noble air in the proud pose of the *condottiere* and in the powerful muscles of the horse, which Giambologna, as a mature artist, was capable of creating (1594). The bas-reliefs of the pedestal show the *Entry of Cosimo into Siena, Pio V Giving Cosimo the Insignia of the Grand Duke, The Tuscan Senate Giving Cosimo the Title of Grand Duke.*

LOGGIA DEI LANZI - Built by Benci di Cione and Simone Talenti between 1376 and 1391, it consists of large round arches on compound pillars, although there is also emphasis on horizontal rhythms. Of late Gothic style, the Loggia is very elegant. The fine reliefs above the pillars are allegories of the *Virtues,* designs by Agnolo Gaddi. On either side of the stairs two *lions* flank the access: one is an example of classic art, the other is by Flaminio Vacca (1600).

Various outstanding examples of sculpture are preserved **inside** the Loggia: in front to the left, is Cellini's famous *Perseus* (1553), replaced by a copy (the original is now in the Uffizi Gallery). On the right is a copy of the *Rape of the Sabine women* by Giambologna (1583) (the original is now in the Galleria dell'Accademia); at the centre are *Hercules and the Centaur,* also by Giambologna (1599), *Ajax with the Body of Patrocles,* a restored piece of Hellenistic sculpture, and the *Rape of Polyxena* by Pio Fedi (1866). Six antique Roman statues of women are set against the back wall.

PALAZZO VECCHIO - Begun in 1294, as a palace-fortress for the residence of the Priors, Arnolfo di Cambio conceived the building as a large block crowned by merlons.

The characteristic feature is the powerful thrust of the **Tower** rising up above the palace and similar in style to the upper part of the mansion. The building is in rusticated ashlars of "pietra forte" giving the large three-storied building with its fine mullioned windows with two lights within round arches an air of severity.

A row of statues is set in front of the building. On the left, at the foot of the palace is the *Marzocco,* the lion, the heraldic symbol of the city (a copy of Donatello's original of 1438, now in the Museum of the Bargello); to the right of the Marzocco is the copy of Donatello's *Judith* (1460), followed by a copy of Michelangelo's *David* and *Hercules and Cacus* (1534) by Baccio Bandinelli. On the left of the observer is the large *Fountain of Neptune.*

Immediately **inside** is the first **courtyard** rebuilt by Michelozzo. The columns were stuccoed and gilded and the walls were frescoed with *Views of the Austrian Cities* by Vasari on the occasion of the wedding of Francesco de' Medici with Joan of Austria, in 1565. At the centre there is a *Fountain* by Battista del Tadda with a *Winged putto holding a spouting fish* (1467) by Andrea del Verrocchio. Under the portico there is a fine

Florence, the Loggia dei Lanzi in Piazza della Signoria.

Florence, the Sala dei Gigli in Palazzo Vecchio.

sculpture of *Samson and the Philistine* by Pierino da Vinci. After the courtyard, two spacious flights of stairs (by Vasari) lead on each side to the large **Hall of the Fivehundred** built by Cronaca and decorated by a team of painters chosen by Vasari. The ceiling is decorated with allegorical panels of the *Triumph of the Grand Duke Cosimo I*; the four *Quarters of the City* (in the medallions in the ceiling); the sixteen *Cities of the Duchy* (in the compartments at the four corners), the six *Stories of Medici Tuscany* (in the rectangular and square compartments of the central part), the seven *Stories of the Wars for the Conquest of Pisa* (in the rectangular, octagonal and square compartments on the left side), and the seven *Stories of the Wars against Siena* (in the panels on the right side). On the entrance walls are the large allegories of *Cosimo I founding the Order of the Knights of St. Stephen,* by Passignano, and further down, the three great *Stories of the Conquest of Pisa*. These are followed by three marble sculptures: the *Three Labours of Hercules* by Vincenzo De Rossi, and the *Statue of Cosimo I* by Baccio Bandinelli. The back wall has *Leo X* by Baccio Bandinelli in the central niche; in the side niches are *Giovanni delle Bande Nere* and *Alessandro de' Medici* by Bandinelli, a niche on the right contains *Charles V Crowned* (Bandinelli and Caccini). On the wall facing the entrance, above left, *Cosimo receiving the Insignia of the Grand Duchy from Pope Pius V,* by Cigoli; above right, *Cosimo acclaimed Duke of Florence,* also by Cigoli; further down, three large *Stories of the Conquest of Siena* by Vasari. Michelangelo's sculpture of *Victory* is on the wall to the right.

A door at the far right of the entrance leads to the **Study of Francesco I,** a small chamber created by Vasari. The walls are lined with panels painted by Bronzino, Naldini, Santi di Tito, Stradano and with bronze

43

statues by Giambologna, Ammannati, Vincenzo De Rossi. The small study is also decorated with stuccoes, and frescoed in the lunettes with the portraits of the *Grand Duke Cosimo* and *Eleonora of Toledo,* by Bronzino. A small staircase leads to another chamber known as **Tesoretto of Cosimo I** (by Vasari) with the Grand Duke's magnificent desk.

From the Hall of the Fivehundred, a decorated corridor leads to the **Hall of the Twohundred** (1441) by Giuliano and Benedetto da Maiano, with a fine carved coffered ceiling by Michelozzo; on the walls there are tapestries woven in the Medici tapestry workshops on designs by Bronzino.

Entrance to **Leo X Apartments** is from the Hall of the Fivehundred. These include many rooms rich in paintings and frescoes: the *Hall of Leo X,*

Florence, the elegant prospect of the Church of Orsanmichele.

frescoed in 1560 with scenes from the *Life of the Pope*; the *Hall of Clement VII*, the *Hall of Giovanni delle Bande Nere*, the *Hall of Cosimo the Elder*, the *Hall of Lorenzo the Magnificent*, the *Hall of Cosimo I*. A staircase to the second floor leads to the **Elements Apartments**, by Battista del Tasso. The name derives from the *Allegories of Earth, Air, Water and Fire* painted in the first room, by Vasari. Mention should also be made of other charming rooms: the *Room of Hercules*, the *Terrace of Saturn*, the *Terrace of Calliope*.

A gallery overlooking the Hall of the Fivehundred, leads to the **Apartment of Eleonora of Toledo** by Vasari, which begins with a beautiful *Chapel* frescoed by Bronzino. Then comes the *Room of the Sabines* (once reserved to the ladies of the court), the *Room of Esther* (dining room), the *Room of Penelope,* the *Room of Gualdrada* (the bedroom of the Grand Duchess). A *Chapel* known as the *Cappellina della Signoria,* frescoed by Ridolfo del Ghirlandaio (1514) and with a tender *Holy Family* by Mariano da Pescia on the altar, leads to the *Audience Hall*, with its fine carved ceiling by Giuliano da Maiano (1478). The *Hall of the Gigli*, so-called because of its decoration of golden fleur de lis on a blue field, leads to the *Sacristy*, with the *Portrait of Niccolò Machiavelli*, by Santi di Tito. The bronze original of Donatello's *Judith,* restored and presented to the public in 1988, is on exhibition in the Hall of the Gigli. In the adjacent *Cloak-room,* embellished with 53 painted panels in the doors of the wardrobes, is the large *Map of the World* by Danti. A staircase leads to the **Quarter of the Mezzanino** (Apartments), and to the old *Gallery* from where one can go to the **Tower** of the palace, where Cosimo the Elder and Savonarola were imprisoned, and from which it is now possible to see a magnificent view of the city.

MUSEUM ALBERTO DELLA RAGIONE

MUSEUM ALBERTO DELLA RAGIONE - The museum is in a small old palace in *Piazza della Signoria*, and houses a rich collection of contemporary Italian painting: from Rosai to De Pisis, from De Chirico to Morandi, from Carrà to Guttuso, and sculpture, from Fontana to Manzù and Marino Marini. The museum was given to the city in 1970, by Alberto della Ragione, a well-known collector.

CHURCH OF ORSANMICHELE

CHURCH OF ORSANMICHELE - The structure was once a loggia used as a communal granary which later became an oratory. Built by Arnolfo di Cambio in 1290, it was transformed between 1337 and 1404.

The **exterior** appears as a large cube with the arcades of the loggia at the base, closed by a delicate late Gothic marble decoration of elegant form; the upper part is more uniform with walls in "pietra forte" and two tiers of large mullioned windows with two lights.

A series of tabernacles and statues runs along the walls of the church. On the *via Calzaiuoli* are *St. John the Baptist* by Ghiberti (1414-16), the tabernacle by Donatello and Michelozzo with the group of the *Doubting Thomas* (1464-83) by Andrea del Verrocchio, and Giambologna's *St. Luke* (1601). On the *via Orsanmichele* are *St. Peter* (1408-13) by Donatello, *St. Philip* (1405-10) by Nanni di Banco, the *Four crowned Saints* (1408) also by Nanni di Banco, and the *St. George* (1416) by Donatello (bronze copy of the marble original now in the Bargello Museum). On the *via dell'Arte della Lana* are the *St. Matthew* (1420) by Ghiberti, the *St. Stephen* (1426-28) also by Ghiberti, and *St. Eligius* (1415) by Nanni di Banco. In the *via dei Lamberti* are *St. Mark* (1411-13) by Donatello, *St. James* by a pupil of Ghiberti, *Madonna and Child* (1399) attributed to Simone Talenti, and *St. John the Evangelist* by Baccio da Montelupo. The terra-cotta medallions are by the Della Robbia brothers.

Inside there are a series of frescoes and panels dedicated to the *Patron Saints* (14th-16th century). Over the altar is a marble group of *St. Anne, Virgin and Child* by Francesco da Sangallo. But the masterpiece, is the magnificent tabernacle by Orcagna (1355-59) in International Gothic style, and finely decorated with remarkable sculptures and mosaics. The panel framed by the tabernacle is by Bernardo Daddi.

LOGGE DEL MERCATO NUOVO AND FOUNTAIN OF THE PORCELLINO

LOGGE DEL MERCATO NUOVO AND FOUNTAIN OF THE PORCELLINO - The Loggia del Mercato Nuovo is a basic structure on a square ground plan built by G. B. del Tasso (1547-51). A characteristic market of typically Florentine craft objects (straw, leather) is held here. On the south side of the loggia is Pietro Tacca's famous *Fountain of the Boar* (1639) later called *Porcellino* or Piglet by the Florentines.

PALAGIO DI PARTE GUELFA - The fine 14th-century **façade** was restored in the 19th century, while the back, on the *via di Capaccio*, is by Brunelleschi. The building is a mixture of various styles (14th, 15th, 16th century). **Inside** is a large hall, by Brunelleschi, with a wooden ceiling by Vasari, and a fine terra-cotta lunette by Luca della Robbia.

MUSEUM OF HISTORY OF SCIENCE - This interesting collection of objects comes from the rich collections of the Medici and the House of Lorraine. Among these are some of Galileo's instruments, such as a telescope and compasses, thermometers and aerometers from the Accademia del Cimento, and a collection of antique surgeon instruments.

PALAZZO DEL BARGELLO - The Bargello palace looks like a fortress and has a powerful **crenellated tower** (the *Volognana*) above the severe façade. It was built in 1255, as the headquarters of the *Capitano del Popolo*; it then became the residence of the *podestà* and afterwards was used by the Council of Justice. From 1574, the Bargello (or Captain of Justice) resided here and it was then called with today's name. The **exterior**, divided by frames, has architraved windows below and mullioned windows with one and two lights above; the building is topped by a crenellation which projects on arches and corbels.
The **interior** opens around the courtyard with pillars supporting arcades on three sides. A picturesque open staircase of the 14th century by Neri di Fioravante leads to the upper loggia, designed by Tone di Giovanni (1319). Since 1859, the palace has been the seat of the **National Museum** which contains Renaissance sculpture and masterpieces of the minor arts from various periods.

NATIONAL MUSEUM OF THE BARGELLO - The enormous **Entrance hall** is on pillars with solid vaulting, and has heraldic decorations on the walls with the coats of arms of the *podestà* (13th-14th century). From here you enter the scenic **Courtyard**, irregular and original. The coats of arms of many *podestà* are here, as well as the picturesque insignia of the quarters and the districts into which the city was once divided, under the portico. The 16th-century statues, set against the walls, are by Bandinelli, Ammannati, Giambologna and Danti. On the same wall, there also are some pieces of the Medici armoury. The courtyard leads to a **Hall**, with a collection of 14th-century sculpture, including Tino da Camaino's *Madonna and Child with Angel,* a meditating *Madonna and Child* of Venetian school, and the base of a holy water font by Nicola Pisano. In the Room close to the open staircase there are important works by Michelangelo: the *Bacchus* (1496), an early work of great power and softness, the *Pitti Tondo,* with the *Madonna teaching Jesus and St. John to read* (1504), the *David* or *Apollo* (1530), and the *Brutus* (1540). There are also works by Ammannati, Giambologna (including his famous *Mercury-* 1564), Tribolo, Danti, Francavilla and Sansovino, who made a *Bacchus* of his own to compete with Michelangelo's. The bronze *bust of Cosimo I* by Cellini, made for Portoferraio in Elba and brought back in 1781, is also in the same room.
The **Open staircase** leads to the **Loggia**, embellished by works by various 16th- century artists.
The first room to the right, once the Hall of the General Council, is now the **Donatello Room**, and contains many of his works such as the *St. George* (1416) with its composed energy, made for the niche in Orsanmichele; the young *St. John,* slender and mystical; the marble *David* (1408); and the bronze *David,* the first delicate Renaissance nude made around 1430. Also by Donatello, are the *Marzocco,* the symbol of the city, and the lively bronze *Amor-Attis,* revealing a classic influence.
In addition to works by Luca della Robbia, Ghiberti, Vecchietta and Agostino di Duccio, the room also contains the trial panels which Ghiberti and Brunelleschi made, in 1402, for the competition for the second door of the Florentine Baptistery (there were six participants). Ghiberti's relief succeeds in giving us a complete view of the story of the *Sacrifice of Isaac*, while Brunelleschi's panel, well articulated, gives the impression of a juxtaposition of parts.
Access to the **Collection of Decorative Arts**, mostly based on the donation of the Carrand Collections, is from the hall. Goldwork and enamels from the Middle Ages to the 16th century, seals and various metal objects are in the **Hall of the Podestà**. In the adjacent **Chapel of the**

Florence, Palazzo del Bargello on Piazza S. Firenze.

Podestà, where those condemned to death passed their last hours, there are Giottesque frescoes of *Paradise, Hell* and *Stories of the Saints*. This floor is completed by the **Hall of the Ivories**, with rare carvings dating from antiquity to the 15th century; the **Hall of the Goldwork**, with numerous works of sacred art, and the **Hall of the Majolicas**. The second floor of the Bargello contains other rooms dedicated to great artists: the first, known as the **Giovanni della Robbia Room**, contains a number of the master's sculptures, including the predella with *Christ and Saints,* the *St. Dominic,* the *Pietà* and the *Annunciation*. The following **Andrea della Robbia Room** houses the *Madonna of the Architects* and other works in glazed terra-cotta.

In the **Verrocchio Room** are the *Resurrection,* the *bust of a young woman,* the *Madonna and Child,* the bronze *David,* and other works by the master, as well as various busts and sculptures by Mino da Fiesole, and the group of *Hercules and Antaeus* by Pollaiolo, a vibrating force of the two struggling figures. Other bronze sculptures are in the **Hall of the Bronzes** with the fireplace of Casa Borgherini by Benedetto da Rovezzano; the **Hall of the Arms** houses military vestments from the Middle Ages to the 17th century. The museum is completed by the **Hall of the Tower** with tapestries and the **Medici Medal show-case**, with works by artists such as Pisanello, Cellini, Michelozzo and others.

CHURCH OF BADIA - The church of Badia, Benedictine, was founded before the 11th century but was completely reconstructed in the 17th century.
The **façade** has a fine portal by Benedetto da Rovezzano (1495). The lovely slender **Bell tower** still has some of its Romanesque structure at the base (1310), but the top is Gothic. The **interior**, Greek-cross plan, contains a number of masterpieces of Renaissance sculpture: to the right of the entrance is the *tomb of Giannotto Pandolfini*, by Rossellino's workshop; the fine bas-relief of the *Madonna and Child with SS. Leonardo and Lorenzo* (1464-69) is by Mino da Fiesole, to whom the *tomb of Bernardo Giugni* (1469-81) is also attributed. The left chapel leads to a room of the original construction, frescoed by a follower of Giotto, probably Buffalmacco (1340); on the wall to the left of the entrance, the fine panel of the *Apparition of the Virgin to St. Bernard* (1480), is one of Filippino Lippi's finest works. Near the apse is the entrance to the **Small Cloister of the Aranci**, with a 14th-century fresco cycle of *Scenes from the life of St. Bernard* by an unknown painter.

ALIGHIERI HOUSES - The complex of the Alighieri houses, mostly restored, lies in the centre, in a widening between the lanes. At present the small piazza, squeezed between two tower-houses, has a low building on one side, with a long shed roof on brackets that covers the entrance; inside: exhibitions and the well.

UFFIZI GALLERY - The gallery of the Uffizi is the most famous picture gallery in Italy, and one of the best known in the world. It offers a complete outline of the various schools of Florentine painting, represented by important works and real masterpieces. It also includes numerous collections of other Italian schools (particularly the Venetian), and a good number of Flemish paintings, as well as the famous collection of self-portraits. Another interesting collection is the one of the antique statues and tapestries.
The Uffizi was commissioned to Giorgio Vasari by the Medici and should have become the seat of the administrative and judicial offices (Uffizi means offices). Begun in 1560 and finished twenty years later, it consists of two wings with a portico at the bottom, connected by a third construction with an arcade facing the river Arno. On either side of the central courtyard powerful pillars contain niches with 19th-century statues of *famous Tuscans*, while the upper floors of the building have windows (1st floor) and a running loggia (2nd floor). On the ground floor there are the interesting remains of the Romanesque church of **St. Piero Scheraggio** (brought to light and restored in 1971), with fine frescoes by Andrea del Castagno. On the first floor, there is the **Drawings and Prints Cabinet**, a vast collection begun in the 17th century by order of Cardinal Leopoldo de' Medici. The visit to the Gallery begins on the second floor. This great museum became a public patrimony in 1737, when Anna Maria Ludovica de' Medici, the last of this prestigious family donated it. During the night between 26 and 27 May 1993, the Uffizi and the nearby Academy of the Georgofili, were the object of a terrorist attack: the explosion of a car bomb caused severe damage to the artistic and historical surround, and, what is more, five people died.
The gallery consists of 45 rooms divided into sections.

Room 1 (The Archaeological Room). The room contains a *torso* in green basalt, Roman copy of a *Doryphoros* by Polykleitos.
Room 2 (Tuscan painting of the 13th century and Giotto). This room contains some of the greatest works of this period, such as the *Madonna in Maestà* by Cimabue (1285), a fundamental work which testifies to the passage from the Byzantine and Romanesque tradition to a major awareness of the development of forms. The figures are rigorously symmetrical, in relation to the fine architecture of the throne. The room also contains the *Rucellai Madonna (Madonna Enthroned with Six Angels)* (1285) by the Sienese painter Duccio di Buoninsegna, a work laid out along the lines of Cimabue's pictorial schemes, but original in its composition,

Florence, the upper gallery of the Uffizi.

with grace and softness of forms; and Giotto's *Ognissanti Madonna (Madonna and Child Enthroned with Angels and Saints)* (1310), which marks the beginning of a new direction in Italian figurative art. Note the layout of the picture, with the superposition and retreating of the figures hinting perspective.

Room 3 (Sienese painting of the 14th century). Here, you can see works by Pietro and Ambrogio Lorenzetti, as well as the splendid *Annunciation with Saints* (1333) by Simone Martini: a large triptych centred on the intimate and touching dialogue between Gabriel and the Virgin; the figures at the sides, *Saints Ansano and Giulitta,* are by Lippo Memmi, Simone Martini's brother-in-law.

Room 4 (Florentine painting of the 14th century). Many works by the most prestigious Florentine masters are collected here: Taddeo Gaddi, Bernardo Daddi, Giottino, Giovanni da Milano.

Room 5-6 (International Gothic). Among the art works in this room, note the brightly coloured *Adoration of the Magi* (1425) by Gentile da Fabriano, a panel populated by many figures in rich costumes, and also, Lorenzo Monaco's lively triptych of the *Coronation of the Virgin* (1413).

Room 7 (Early Renaissance Florentine painting). The outstanding paintings in this room include the *Madonna and Child with St. Anne* (1420-24) by Masaccio, finished by Masolino da Panicale (the group of the Virgin and Child, touching in its realism, is by Masaccio); the *Battle of San Romano* (1456) by Paolo Uccello, a large work in three panels, of which only one, with the knights in a battle, is in the Uffizi. In this painting, the daring search for perspective of the artist creates a fascinating, almost abstract ensemble. Then there are the *Portraits of Federico da Montefel-*

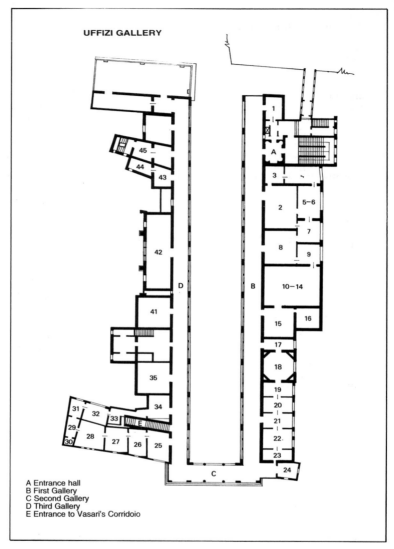

UFFIZI GALLERY

45
44
43
42
41
35
34
31 32 33
29 28
30
27 26 25
E

1
A
3
2 5-6
7
8 9
10-14
16
15
17
18
19
20
21
22
23
24

D
B
C

A Entrance hall
B First Gallery
C Second Gallery
D Third Gallery
E Entrance to Vasari's Corridoio

tro and his wife Battista Sforza (1465), two splendid profiles by Piero della Francesca, who here reaches a remarkable purity of line and a profound introspection.

Room 8 (Florentine painting of the 15th century). Also known as the Filippo Lippi room because of the many works of this great master here on exhibit, including the *Virgin adoring the Son,* the *Coronation of the Virgin,* the *Madonna and Child with an Angel,* as well as interesting works by Alessio Baldovinetti, such as the *Madonna and Child with Saints* and the *Annunciation.* The room also contains early works by Botticelli, such as the *Madonna of the Rose Garden,* and the *Madonna Enthroned and Saints* by Lorenzo di Pietro, called Vecchietta.

Room 9 (Florentine painting of the 15th century, known also as the Pollaiolo room). This room contains numerous works by the brothers Antonio and Piero del Pollaiolo. Among the paintings of the first artist, there is the famous *Portrait of a Lady, Hercules and Hydra* and *Hercules and Antaeus;* and by the second, the *Virtues* and the *Portrait of Galeazzo Maria Sforza.*

Room 10-14 (The Botticelli rooms). Some of the greatest masterpieces of the artist and of the entire 15th century are hung here, including the famous *Primavera* (1477-78), a magnificent allegory set in a classic atmosphere. The soft airy figures and the extreme number of details, have made the painting one of the most famous paintings in art history. Just

50

as famous is the *Birth of Venus* (1486), in which the softly modeled figure of the goddess, standing on a shell, or rather floating in air with great lightness, dominates the picture. Botticelli also painted the realistic *Adoration of the Magi,* the touching *Annunciation* and the sophisticated *Madonna of the Magnificat* and the *Madonna of the Pomegranate.* Mention should also be made of the bright *Adoration of the Magi* by Filippino Lippi, and the panel paintings by Lorenzo di Credi and Ghirlandaio.

Room 15 (Dedicated to artists active between the 15th and 16th centuries, known also as the Leonardo room). Among the works of this room, mention must be made of Verrocchio's *Baptism of Christ,* where Leonardo's unmistakable touch can be seen in the face of the angel in profile and in the landscape in the background; Leonardo's *Adoration of the Magi,* although not finished is considered the great artist's first masterpiece; also, in this room, his *Annunciation,* a work with a 15th-century layout, but already bearing the unmistakable touch of his hand.

Room 16 (Room of the Maps). Works exhibited here include important paintings by Hans Memling, such as the *Madonna and Child Enthroned with two Angels, Saint Benedict,* the two stupendous *Portraits of an unknown Man* and *Portrait of Benedetto Portinari.*

Room 17 (Room of the Hermaphrodite). This small room contains the sculpture of the *Hermaphrodite* and the group of *Cupid and Psyche.*

Room 18 (Known also as the Tribune). Its name derives from the magnificent tribune by Buontalenti (1585-89), octagonal in plan, with fine decorations in the cupola where the sections have mother-of-pearl applications. As well as examples of antique sculpture, the room contains a vast collection of 16th- century portraits, including Andrea del Sarto's enigmatic *Portrait of an unknown Lady,* and outstanding portraits by Bronzino, Pontormo, Rosso Fiorentino and many other Mannerist artists. The centre of the room is dominated by the *Medici Venus,* a 1st-century BC copy of a Greek original of the 5th century BC. It is one of the most famous examples of classical sculpture in Florence – a marble with gentle forms and luminous effects of light and dark.

Florence, Botticelli's "Primavera", one of the most celebrated masterpieces in the Uffizi.

Room 19 (The Signorelli and Perugino Room). Noteworthy is the *Holy Family*, a tondo by Luca Signorelli with an intimate and supernatural atmosphere; also in this room, the famous *Madonna and Child* by Signorelli, and some intense portraits by Perugino, including those of *Don Biagio Milanesi* and *Baldassare Vallombrosano,* and that of *Francesco delle Opere,* paintings of a very introspective nature.

Room 20 (Dürer and German painting). The room contains fine portraits by Lukas Cranach the Elder, including the famous *Portrait of Luther* and of his wife *Caterina Bore,* that of *Friedrich III* and *Johann I of Saxony.* But the most important artist represented here is Albrecht Dürer, with his *Adoration of the Magi,* a far-reaching and monumental painting, the *Apostle Philip,* the *Calvary* and the deeply touching *Portrait of his Father.*

Room 21 (The Bellini and Giorgione Room, including Venetian 15th-century painting). Outstanding are Giovanni Bellini's fanciful *Sacred Allegory,* a painting with a fantastic and contemplative atmosphere, illuminated by beams of mystical light, and Giorgione's two masterpieces, *Moses undergoes Trial by Fire* and the *Judgement of Solomon.*

Room 22 (Flemish and German Masters). Notice here the *Adoration of the Magi* by Gerard David and the *Portrait of Sir Richard Southwell* by Hans Holbein.

Room 23 (The Correggio Room). Among the art pieces in this room, the most beautiful are the *Madonna and Child in Glory,* the popular and tender *Rest on the Flight into Egypt,* and the moving *Adoration of the Child,* all by the founder of the Emilian school, Antonio Allegri called Correg-

Florence, Uffizi Gallery, Michelangelo's famous "Tondo Doni".

gio. Also of interest are two rather naive portraits attributed to Raphael's early years, the portrait of *Elisabetta Gonzaga* and that of *Guidobaldo da Montefeltro*. Also in this room, paintings by Andrea Mantegna: the *Triptych* depicting the *Epiphany*, the *Circumcision* and the *Ascension*, and the small and touching *Madonna of the Caves.*

Room 24 (The Room of Miniatures). This room contains a number of Italian, French, German and English miniatures, dating from the 15th to the 18th century.

Room 25 (The Michelangelo Room). As well as important paintings, such as Mariotto Albertinelli's *Visitation, Annunciation* and *Nativity,* and Rosso Fiorentino's *Moses Defends the Daughters of Jethro,* attention centres on the *Holy Family* or *Doni Tondo* by Michelangelo, the artist's only finished panel painting. The group of three holy figures fills up the small space, and the monumentality and sculptural quality, that were to characterise the artist are already here evident.

Room 26 (The Raphael and Andrea del Sarto Room). The room contains many masterpieces, including Andrea del Sarto's *St James* and his statuary *Madonna of the Harpies,* but the most remarkable is Raphael's *Pope Leo X with Cardinals Giulio de' Medici and Luigi de' Rossi,* one of the artist's finest works, revealing his ability in catching the psychology of his posers, evident in the search for expression in the faces of the three figures, and a great attention to detail. Raphael's transparent *Madonna of the Goldfinch* is also particularly lovely. Although it is an early work, it does not follow any longer Perugino's schemes, but is clearly influenced, in its pyramidal composition, by Leonardo.

Room 27 (The Pontormo and Rosso Fiorentino Room) The room is almost entirely dedicated to the great Florentine Mannerist painters. Most interesting are Pontormo's disquieting *Supper at Emmaus* and Rosso Fiorentino's intimate *Madonna and Child.*

Room 28 (The Titian Room) The room contains many masterpieces by the great Venetian painter: the penetrating *Portrait of Bishop Ludovico Beccadelli,* the famous *Venus and Cupid* and the *Portraits of Eleonora Gonzaga della Rovere* and *Francesco Maria della Rovere.* But the finest of all is the *Venus of Urbino,* one of the greatest works of Titian's maturity: a magnificent nude in warm tones and frank sensuality.

Room 29 (The Parmigianino Room). In addition to various important works by painters such as Luca Cambiaso, Girolamo da Carpi, Beccafumi and Perin del Vaga, the room contains various masterpieces by Parmigianino, such as the *Portrait of a Man, Madonna and Child with Saints* and the elegant and sophisticated *Madonna of the Long Neck.*

Room 30 (Emilian Painting). This room houses works by Emilian artists of the 16th century, such as Niccolò Pisano, Niccolò dell'Abate, Dosso Dossi.

Room 31 (Room of Dosso Dossi). As well as the *Sorcery* by Dossi, the room contains various works by Sebastiano del Piombo and Lorenzo Lotto.

Room 32 (Room of Sebastiano del Piombo). Here you will find the fine *Holy Family* by Lorenzo Lotto, and two *Male Portraits* by Paris Bordone, as well as Sebastiano del Piombo's famous *Death of Adonis,* influenced by Raphael, in the softness of colour and by Michelangelo, in the powerful forms.

Room 33 (16th-century Painting and Foreign Artists). Particular attention should be given to the powerful portrait of *François I of France on Horseback* by François Clouet; *Christ Carrying the Cross* by Luis de Morales, a painting full of realism and human suffering; as well as a good number of paintings by Florentine artists of the late 16th century.

Room 34 (The Veronese Room). In this room, the most beautiful paintings are the *Holy Family with Saint Barbara* (being restored), with its warmth and intense vibrant colours, the small *Saint Agatha Crowned by Angels,* and above all the *Annunciation,* a painting with an original perspective, all by Veronese. Also see Moroni's famous *Portrait of a Man with a Book* and the mystical *Transfiguration* by Savoldo.

Room 35 (The Tintoretto and Barocci Room). This room contains some of the masterpieces by late Mannerist painters: a penetrating *Portrait of a Man* by Tintoretto, his *Portrait of Jacopo Sansovino* and his delicate *Leda and the Swan,* a canvas with intense colours and an almost dazzled luminosity. Next to these, there are various paintings by Federico Barocci, the greatest Mannerist painter of central Italy, represented here by his large canvas of the *Madonna of the People,* his most famous painting, a lively surprising image, full of figures who point to the Virgin in astonishment, his *Noli Me Tangere,* a delicate painting, and then his *Portrait of a Girl* and the *Stigmata of St. Francis,* simple and immediate in the composition.

Room 41 (The Rubens Room) Imposing canvases of *Henry IV at the Battle of Ivry* and the *Triumphal Entry of Henry IV into Paris,* two of the best works of Rubens' maturity, are hung here. Also see the fine series of *Portraits* by Van Dyck, Sustermans and Rubens.

Room 42 (The Niobe Room). The room was commissioned to Gaspare Maria Paoletti in 1779, by the Grand Duke Pietro Leopoldo. The statues of the group of the *Niobe* discovered in Rome in 1583 and transferred to Florence in 1775 are shown here. The statues are Roman copies of Hellenistic originals of the 3rd and 2nd centuries BC.

Room 43 (The Caravaggio Room). Three fundamental works by Caravaggio attract the attention: the *Medusa,* an impressive image intensified by the violent beams of light which fall on her face; the *Adolescent Bacchus,* an early work representing a youth, somewhat effeminate, and the dramatic *Sacrifice of Isaac* where, in true Caravaggesque style, a beam of light illuminates the face of the boy who is about to be sacrificed.

Room 44 (The Rembrandt Room). The room contains various masterpieces by Rembrandt: the two lovely *Self-Portraits* – the study of himself as an old man characterised by his personal ability for introspection, and that of the artist as a young man, with its self-assured, almost arrogant expression. Note also Rembrandt's famous *Portrait of an Old Man,* also called *The Rabbi,* which reveals the artist's acute eye and gift for psychological analysis.

Room 45 (Painting of the 18th Century). This is the last room in the Gallery. A number of 18th-century works, particularly by Italian and French painters, are on exhibit here. There are canvases by great *vedutisti* (panorama painters), such as Canaletto, Bellotto and Francesco Guardi, and expert artists from north of the Alps, such as Jean Baptiste Simeon Chardin and Jean Etienne Liotard, as well as a series of portraits by Rosalba Carriera.

Between the door leading to Room 25 and the one leading to Room 34 is the entrance staircase to **Vasari's Corridor**, built by Vasari in 1565, and joining the Gallery to Palazzo Pitti. Along the Corridor are hung important paintings by Italian and foreign artists, and the entire painting collection of *Self-Portraits* (Raphael, Titian, Bernini, Rubens, Rembrandt, Velazquez, Canova, David, Ingres, Corot, Delacroix, and many others) of famous artists up to the 20th century.

PONTE VECCHIO - It is the city's oldest bridge, built, as it appears today, in 1345 by Neri di Fioravante, with its elegant structure on three arches. A characteristic feature of the bridge is the row of small houses on either side; in the 14th century, the features were much more regular, and as time passed they have aquired the picturesque variety, you can admire today. At the centre of the bridge, the buildings are interrupted, and an opening allows a fine view of the Arno and the other bridges. A bronze bust of *Benvenuto Cellini* by Raffaello Romanelli (1900) has here been placed. Above the houses, on the upstream side of the bridge, is *Vasari's Corridor,* built by Vasari for Cosimo I to go from Palazzo Pitti to Palazzo Vecchio. The shops on either side of the bridge are still working and are the workshops of artisan goldsmiths.

CHURCH OF ST. FELICE - The church of St. Felice has a Renaissance façade by Michelozzo. Remarkable are the carved wooden 15th-century doors. The building dates from the Middle Ages, but it was frequently remodeled between the 14th and 16th centuries.

The **interior** is small with a nave and two aisles on columns, and a large 16th-century gallery over the first half. Noteworthy on the first altar to the right is the fresco of the *Pietà* by Nicola Gerini; a *Madonna and Saints* by Ridolfo del Ghirlandaio, and a fresco in the lunette of the *Assumption* by an unknown 14th-century painter, at the sixth altar. On the seventh altar to the left, the fresco with *St. Felix resuscitating St. Maximus of Nola* (1635) is by Giovanni da San Giovanni (the *Angels* are by Volterrano). Above the choir, is a painted *Cross* in the style of Giotto, while the triptych on the first altar to the left with *SS. Rocco, Anthony Abbot and Catherine of Siena* (1480) is attributed to Filippino Lippi or a follower of Botticelli.

Florence, a view of Ponte Vecchio.

BARDINI MUSEUM - This collection contains many important paintings, antique furniture, precious tapestries, archaeological objects from Roman times, weapons and wooden sculpture. Among the most remarkable are a bust of *St. John* by Andrea Sansovino; a marble *Charity* by Tino di Camaino; some terra-cotta figures by the Della Robbia; a panel with *St. Michael Archangel* by Antonio del Pollaiolo.

PONTE SANTA TRINITA - After Ponte Vecchio, this is considered the most beautiful bridge in the city. It was built by Bartolomeo Ammannati, with Michelangelo's suggestions. Fine statues are set at the entrances to the bridge: on the side towards the city, *Spring* by Pietro Francavilla is on the left, and *Summer* by Cacini is one the right. On the opposite side are *Autumn,* also by Cacini, and *Winter* by Taddeo Landini.

CORSINI GALLERY - Installed in Palazzo Corsini, the Gallery includes a rich selection of paintings from the 16th and 17th centuries, by great artists such as Signorelli, Filippino Lippi, Raphael, Andrea del Sarto and Pontormo.

CHURCH OF SANTA TRINITA - The church already existed in the 11th century and was rebuilt and enlarged in the 13th and 14th centuries.
The **façade** is linear and decorated with a lovely stone medallion by Buontalenti (1593).
The **interior** is simple and severe, with a nave and two aisles separated by pillars. In the first chapel of the right aisle, stands out a fine 14th-century *Crucifix;* in the third, a *Madonna with Saints* by Neri di Bicci (1491); in the fourth, the *Annunciation* by Lorenzo Monaco (1425), and in the fifth, a lovely altar by Benedetto da Maiano. At the end of the crossing, there is the **Sacristy** and then the **Sassetti Chapel**. The fresco over the entrance arch depicts the *Tiburtine Sibyl announcing the Birth of Christ to Augustus;* inside, *Scenes from the Life of St. Francis;* behind the altar, the *Miracle of the Resuscitated Child;* above the altar, *St. Francis Receiving the Rule from Pope Honorius,* all by Ghirlandaio (1483-86). On the

55

walls are the *tombs of the Sassetti family,* by Giuliano da Sangallo and, on the altar, the *Adoration of the Shepherds,* also by Ghirlandaio.

Next comes the **Major Chapel**, with a triptych of the *Trinity and Saints* by Mariotti di Nardo (1416) on a 15th-century altar, while parts of frescoes by Alessio Baldovinetti are in the vault. In the second chapel, is the *tomb of the bishop of Fiesole Benozzo Federici,* a marveluous work by Luca della Robbia (1454-56), decorated with a charming frieze of painted and glazed terra-cotta tiles. In the fifth chapel of the left aisle, is a wooden statue of the *Magdalen* begun by Desiderio da Settignano (1464) and finished by Benedetto da Maiano (1468). Also see in the third chapel, the *Annunciation* by Neri di Bicci (1491) and in the fouth chapel, the *Coronation of the Virgin,* probably by a pupil of Neri (1491).

CHURCH OF THE SS. APOSTOLI - Begun in 1075, the church of the SS. Apostoli was a prototype for many other Florentine churches, with its archaic Roman forms. Although it is not big, the building is very solemn. The **interior** is full of atmosphere, with a fine painted timber shed roof on compound pillars dividing the church into a nave and two aisles. On the third altar of the **right aisle** there is a panel of the *Immaculate Conception* by Giorgio Vasari (one of his best works). The apse contains the *tomb of the archbishop Antonio Altoviti* carried out from a design by G. B. Dosio (1574). In the **left aisle** see the tabernacle by Andrea della Robbia, the *tomb of Donato Acciaioli* (1339) of Pisan school, and the *tomb of Oddo Altoviti* by Bernardo da Rovezzano (1507).

PALAZZO DAVANZATI - Built around 1330, the base is in rusticated *pietra forte*; in the upper floors the external facing is smoother, and broken by a series of windows, built with the typical Florentine arch with its round arched intrados. Above is the 15th-century terrace covered by a gabled watershed. The palace is one of the most remarkable examples of 14th-century private houses and is today the seat of the **Museum of the Antique Florentine House**, an interesting collection of furniture and objects from the 15th and 16th centuries.

MUSEUM OF THE ANTIQUE FLORENTINE HOUSE - The museum contains a perfect reconstruction of households, particularly from the 15th and 16th centuries. Dining rooms, wedding chambers, and meeting halls, are all furnished with magnificent tapestries, small-scale sculpture and various household objects.

The **staircase** from the delightful **internal courtyard** leads to the exhibition rooms. Note on the various walls the ancient writings (dating from the time when the building was used as public offices) which have today been collected into an amusing *corpus*, which gives us an insight into the Florence of the past.

PALAZZO STROZZI - This typical example of a Renaissance palace was designed by Benedetto da Maiano, in 1489. Its construction continued, under various supervisors (among which Cronaca), until 1538, when the work was suspended, although incomplete on the south side.

The lower part in rusticated *pietra forte* ashlar, is by Benedetto da Maiano and is characterised by the wide portal with the arches in rusticated ashlar, and the row of rectangular windows; the upper part is attributed to Cronaca, as well as the two dentellated cornices in between the floors, in a classical style, and the big cornice at the top of the building. On the front, as on the sides, the upper floors have rows of mullioned windows with two lights with the external arch in rusticated ashlars.

The palace has a courtyard on several floors, supported on the lower part by columns, in the intermediate floor by engaged pilasters, and at the top by columns forming a fine loggia. The **many rooms**, some of which still maintain their Renaissance appearance, are currently used for cultural happenings and art exhibitions.

CHURCH OF ST. MARIA MAGGIORE - Begun in the 10th century in Romanesque style, St. Maria Maggiore was almost completely rebuilt in Gothic style, at the end of the 13th century.

The linear severe **façade** has a lovely 14th-century *Madonna* of Pisan school on the pointed arch portal. The **interior**, in Cistercian style, is extremely simple: a nave and two aisles set in pointed arches on square pillars with cornices with dentils and square chapels. Traces of 14th-century frescoes by Agnolo Daddi, Spinello Aretino, Paolo Uccello and Masaccio can still be found on some of the walls. The two episodes from the *Story of King Herod,* painted in the style of Spinello Aretino in the **Sanctuary**, are particularly fine. In the left chapel is a relief in gilded wood of a *Madonna and Child,* while, in the right aisle, is a noteworthy altar on which is a painting of *Saint Rita* by the modern artist Primo Conti.

PALAZZO RUCELLAI - The design for the palace was created for the Rucellai family by Leon Battista Alberti, and the project was carried out by Rossellino, between 1446 and 1451. The classical **façade** is divided into three stories by horizontal string-courses with decorations supported by pilasters. These divide the flattened rustication into sections that have simple windows set into the lower story and mullioned windows with two lights into the upper stories.

RUCELLAI CHAPEL - Not far from their palace the Rucellai had their chapel, and commissioned to Alberti the **Shrine of the Holy Sepulcher**. The rectangular structure in the shape of an apse, has Corinthian pilasters and a crenellated entablature along the top of the black and white marble walls. It is topped by a canopy with a dome. Inside are frescoes by Baldovinetti and a terra-cotta *Christ*.

CHURCH OF SANTA MARIA NOVELLA - Begun in 1279, by Sisto da Firenze and Ristoro da Campi, it was finished in 1348, by Jacopo Talenti, with the bell tower in Romanesque Gothic style (1330).
The marvelous **façade** was remade between 1456 and 1470 by Leon Battista Alberti, who designed the portal and the wall above, divided into compartments by inlaid marble and framed by the coats of arms (heraldicsails) of the Rucellai, who commissioned the great work. Two

Florence, the geometric façade of Santa Maria Novella.

large upside-down volutes join the sides with the centre divided by four engaged pilasters and closed by a triangular tympanum.

The **interior** is divided into a nave and two aisles by pillars carrying pointed vaults. A fine mosaic *Nativity* based on a cartoon by Filippo Lippi, is set over the central door. In the second bay of the **right aisle** is the *tomb of the Beata Villana,* by Rossellino (1451), and the **Chapel of the Pura**, a Renaissance structure built in honour of a miraculous *Madonna,* a 14th-century fresco, in the left-hand corner. In the right arm of the crossing is the terra-cotta *bust of St. Antonine* and, above, the *tomb of Tedice Aliotti, Bishop of Fiesole,* by Tino di Camaino. A flight of steps leads to the **Rucellai Chapel**, with remains of frescoes of the *Martyrdom of St. Catherine* by Giuliano Bugiardini; at the centre of the pavement is the fine *tombslab for Leonardo Dati* by Ghiberti (1423). From the crossing, there is the entrance to: the **Bardi Chapel**, with the *Madonna of the Rosary* by Vasari (1568), and remains of 14th-century frescoes; and the **Chapel of Filippo Strozzi the Elder**, with important frescoes, including scenes from the *Lives of St. Philip and St. John Evangelist* by Filippino Lippi (1503). On the back wall there is the *tomb of Filippo Strozzi* by Benedetto da Maiano (1491). The **Sanctuary of the Tornabuoni**, houses a fine bronze *Crucifix* by Giambologna on the altar, and frescoes on the vault and on the walls with scenes from the *Lives of St. John the Baptist* (on the right) and *of the Virgin* (on the left) by Domenico Ghirlandaio (late 15th century). The **Gondi Chapel**, by Giuliano da Sangallo, has fragments of frescoes by 13th-century Greek painters, and on the back wall, the famous *Crucifix* by Brunelleschi; next come the **Gaddi Chapel** with the *Miracle of Jesus* by Bronzino on the altar; the **Chapel of the Strozzi family of Mantua**, displays frescoes of the *Last Judgement* on the back wall, *Hell* on the right, and *Paradise* on the left, by Nardo di Cione or by Orcagna. A large panel of the *Triumphant Christ* by Orcagna (1357), is on the altar. Next comes the **Sacristy**, built by Jacopo Talenti (1350); on the left, a marble lavabo in a glazed terra-cotta niche by Giovanni della Robbia (1498).

Masaccio's *Trinity,* an extremely important fresco, is in the **left aisle**; on the second pillar there is a *pulpit*, designed by Brunelleschi, with classical decorative elements, and bas-reliefs by Buggiano (1462). The gate to the left of the façade leads to the Cloisters of the **Large Convent** (now used for civil and military purposes): the **First Cloister** is the oldest, it is in Romanesque style (1350), and the various frescoes with *scenes from the Old Testament* by Paolo Uccello, have been detached, and are now exposed in the refectory.

Nearby, is the famous **Spanish Chapel**, built by Jacopo Talenti (1359) in honour of St. Thomas of Aquinas: on the entrance wall are the scenes from the *Life of St. Peter Martyr* and above, in the vault, the *Ascension.* The side walls are decorated with allegories of the *Triumph of Wisdom and the Church Militant and Triumphant* by Andrea di Buonaiuto (1366-68). The so-called **Small Cloister of the Dead**, in Romanesque style, and containing a number of *tomb slabs,* leads to the **Great Cloister**, the largest in the city, with over fifty arches, and completely frescoed by the greatest Florentine painters of the 15th and 16th centuries. At present it is not open to the public for it is now part of a school for *Carabinieri*.

CHURCH OF OGNISSANTI - The church of Ognissanti, built in 1256, has often been reconstructed, particularly in the 17th century, and little of the original features remain.

The **façade** is by Matteo Nigetti (1638), and is one of the first examples of Baroque architecture in the city. The spacious and well-balanced **interior** has large Renaissance altars. On the second altar to the right, there is a fresco of the *Madonna of Mercy* by Domenico Ghirlandaio; under this is a *Deposition*, also by Ghirlandaio. Towards the centre of the right aisle, you will see a fresco with *St. Augustine* (1480) by Botticelli, and across, on the left wall, Ghirlandaio's *St. Jerome* (1480). On the right, on the pavement of the chapel in the crossing, there is the *tomb of Mariano Filipepi* and his children, including the great Botticelli. The fine dome has frescoes by Giovanni da San Giovanni; in the **Sacristy** see the painted wooden *Crucifix* of the school of Giotto, and a fine fresco, the *Crucifixion,* attributed to Taddeo Gaddi.Next to the church there is the **Cloister**, of the school of Michelozzo, with scenes from the *Life of St. Francis* by Jacopo Ligozzi (1625). A door leads to the **Refectory**, which contains a fine *Last Supper* by Ghirlandaio.

THE LAST SUPPER OF FOLIGNO - Inside the ex-Convent of St. Onofrio, of the so-called Franciscans from Foligno, the refectory contains the fresco of the *Last Supper* by Perugino and assistants (1490). In the painting, beyond Christ and the Apostles, the architecture opens out on a country scene with *Christ on the Mount of Olives*.

QUARTER OF ST. LORENZO - One of the most picturesque and typical quarters of Florence, St. Lorenzo covers the piazza, dominated by the large Church of St. Lorenzo, and a multitude of small narrow streets leading to the "Mercato Centrale", the largest food market. Long rows of stalls surround the large structures of the Market, turning the area into one of the most busy shopping areas in Florence.

STATUE OF GIOVANNI DELLE BANDE NERE - This imposing marble work portrays the famous commander seated, and with a scepter in his hand. It is considered one of Baccio Bandinelli's best works. The sculptor also made the finely carved base (1540).

CHURCH OF ST. LORENZO - Consecrated by St. Ambrose in 393, it is the oldest church of the city. It was rebuilt along Romanesque lines in 1060. The present building dates from 1423 and was designed and carried out

Florence, the bare façade of the Church of St. Lorenzo.

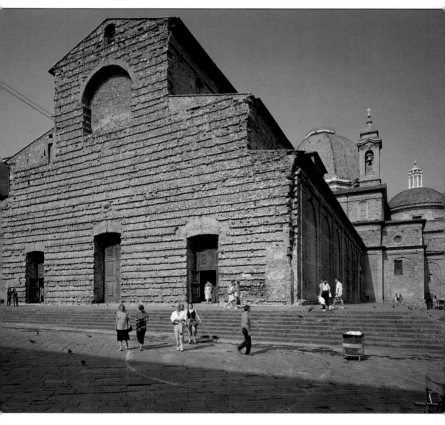

by Brunelleschi. The simple bare **façade** lacks the marble covering; Michelangelo's design was never carried out. The **internal façade**, which Michelangelo also designed, is comprised of three doors between two pilasters with garlands of oak and laurel, and a balcony on two Corinthian columns.

The **interior** has a nave separated from the side aisles by Corinthian columns. The ceiling, in white-ground coffering has beautiful rose windows. The second chapel of the **right aisle**, contains the *Wedding of the Virgin* by Rosso Fiorentino (1523) with the bright colours, typical of the Mannerist painters; next to it is the Gothic *tomb slab of F. Landini*, organist, carved in 1398. After the two paintings of *St. Lawrence* and the *Adoration of the Magi*, comes the ciborium, dating 1461, by Desiderio da Settignano.

In the right-hand chapel of the transept, there is a Roman *sarcophagus*, used to bury Niccolò Stenone; in the main chapel, is a marble *Crucifix* by Baccio da Montelupo, while the central **dome** is frescoed with *Florentine Saints in Glory* by Vincenzo Meucci (1742). The left transept contains the wooden statue of the *Madonna and Child*, a polychrome late 14th-century work; the painting of *Saints* by the school of Ghirlandaio, and Filippo Lippi's *Annunciation* diptych. The Annunciation dates from 1440, and has a remarkable feeling for space, due to the figures in third dimension and the perspective sudy of the building in the background. The **left aisle** contains the large fresco of the *Martyrdom of St. Lawrence* by Bronzino (1565-1569), and the marble choir, which may have been designed by Donatello. Under the arches of the last two bays of the nave, there are Donatello's two bronze *pulpits*, similar to two large classic arches on columns. The Dionysiac scenes which fill in the empty spaces recall ancient monuments. The panels painted by Donatello's pupils – Bellano and Bertoldo – include the *Crucifixion*, the *Deposition*, part of the *Passion of Christ, St. John the Evangelist*, and the *Flagellation* on the left pulpit, and the *Martyrdom of St. Lawrence*, the *Resurrection*, and the other part of the *Passion* on the right pulpit.

The **Old Sacristy**, at the back of the left transept, was built by Brunelleschi, between 1419 and 1428. Built before the church, the sacristy is the first example of Renaissance architecture, and of the work of Brunelleschi, in Florence. A dome covers the square room, and a square apse opens off one wall. The structural lines are stressed by stone molding. Eight tondos by Donatello (1435-1443) with the *Four Evangelists* and *Scenes from the Life of St. John* are set into the corner pendentives and on the walls. The bronze doors and the stucco reliefs over the doors are also by Donatello, while the *funeral monument to Piero and Giovanni de' Medici* (1472) is by Andrea del Verrocchio. Andrea Cavalcanti made the balustrade of the apse, on a design by Donatello, as well as the *sarcophagus of Giovanni Bicci de' Medici and his wife*. On the opposite side, near the right transept of the church, there is the New Sacristy with the entrance from outside.

MEDICI CHAPELS - This big complex containing the Medici family tombs, is attached to the back of the Church of St. Lorenzo and it includes the underground quarters and various other rooms of the church.

The entrance is on the *Piazza Madonna degli Aldobrandini* and it leads to a vast and low hall, designed by Bountalenti, in which the visitor can admire the *tomb of Cosimo the Elder*, the one of *Donatello*, and of the various members of the *House of Lorraine*, as well as other grand-ducal sepulchers. From here one moves up to the **Princes Chapel** in part by Nigetti (Buontalenti also worked on the design), dating from 1602, and finished in the 18th century. From the outside, the building is Baroque, with a high drum, and big windows, supporting a large dome faced in brick, similar to the dome on the cathedral.

The **interior** is octagonal in plan, entirely lined with semi-precious stones and marble in Baroque style. The base is decorated with the *16 coats of arms* of the Tuscan grand-ducal cities. Above are the six *coffers or tombs* of the Grand Dukes *Cosimo III, Francesco I, Cosimo I, Ferdinando I, Cosimo II, Ferdinando II*, over two of which stand *statues of the Grand Dukes* by Tacca. Narrow rooms open off from either side of the altar. Once sacristies, they now contain a collection of relics and the *treasure* which includes glass vases, church furniture and reliquaries dating from the 17th and 18th centuries.

A corridor leads from the Princes Chapel to the **New Sacristy**. This room, designed by Michelangelo around 1520, reverses the restrained balance of Brunelleschi's room in St. Lorenzo (Old Sacristy) in a dynamic concise series of wall decorations. Under the dome, with its perspective coffering, the walls of the square space have niches, pilasters and molding. Facing the tomb with the altar designed by Michelangelo, there is the *sarcophagus of Lorenzo the Magnificent and Giuliano de' Medici,* surmounted by statues of *St. Damian* (by Raffaello di Montelupo), the *Madonna and Child* (by Michelangelo) and *St. Cosmas* (by Giovannangelo Montorsoli). The *tombs of Giuliano, duke of Nemours,* and of *Lorenzo, duke of Urbino,* face each other at the centre of the other two walls. Michelangelo placed the sarcophaguses with the *Allegories of Time* under the statues of the dukes set in niches: Giuliano's tomb is watched over by *Day* and *Night,* while *Dusk* and *Dawn* watch over Lorenzo's. The accurate anatomical depiction of the figures, which are in part unfinished, expresses the intrinsic meaning through exterior form, and here Michelangelo created one of his greatest masterpieces.

PALAZZO MEDICI-RICCARDI - The palace that Cosimo the Elder had built as his official family residence – the first Renaissance example – is by Michelozzo. The building, as it was originally built between 1444 and 1464, was shorter than what we see now; only in 1517 the open arched loggia on the ground floor was filled in, and the gabled windows, attributed to Michelangelo, were added. When the palace was bought by the Riccardi, the **façade** was made longer (between 1600 and 1700), and the inner building was enlarged, changing the aspect of the original project.
On the exterior the building is a powerful construction with rusticated ashlars on the ground floor and arcades in smooth ashlars; above the dentellated cornice moldings of classic inspiration, Michelozzo raised

Florence, Palazzo Medici Riccardi: on the corner the Medici coat of arms.

the upper floors with each stage smoother than the preceding one; so the first floor is in smooth ashlars and the second in flat finely fitted blocks of stone. On the upper floor there are mullioned windows with two lights with a medallion surmounting the column, inscribed in round arches; the palace is crowned by a bracketed cornice obviously inspired from antiquity.

Inside is the **First Courtyard**, with arcades and a series of mullioned windows with two lights, and a loggia, decorated with 15th-centurys graffiti by Maso di Bartolomeo and medallions by Bertoldo. Various antique works of art are to be found in the courtyard and, in front of the entrance, there is an *Orpheus* by Baccio Bandinelli. Entrance to the **Chapel**, by Michelozzo, is through the courtyard. The ceiling is coffered and there is an inlaid floor (1465). The *Arrival of the Magi in Bethlehem* is on the walls. In this fresco, Benozzo Gozzoli (1459-60) painted portraits of the famous persons present at the Council of Florence, in 1439 (John VII, Lorenzo, Piero the Gouty with his daughters, Galeazzo Maria Sforza, Sigismondo Malatesta, as well as Benozzo himself and Fra' Angelico).

The palazzo also contains the **Gallery**, a 17th-century hall with stuccoes, the vault of which was frescoed by Luca Giordano with the *Apotheosis of the Medici Dynasty* (1682) surrounded by various mythological allegories. This gallery communicates with the **Riccardi Library**, housing many volumes, manuscripts and incunabulae; the vault of the Exhibition Hall is decorated with the fresco of *Intellect Released from the Bonds of Ignorance,* by Luca Giordano (1683).

ACADEMY GALLERY (GALLERIA DELL'ACCADEMIA) - The Gallery houses an extremely important sculpture collection by Michelangelo. The **room** that leads to the Tribune, with tapestries on the walls, contains the *Palestrina Pietà,* whose attribution to Michelangelo is controversial; the unfinished *St. Matthew,* made for the Florentine Cathedral; and the four *Prisoners* (or slaves) which were created for the tomb of Julius II in St. Pietro in Vincoli in Rome, never finished, like these male figures who seem to be trying to free themselves from the marble grip.

At the centre of the spacious **Tribune** there is the original of the *David* (1501-04) commissioned to the great sculptor to replace Donatello's *Judith* on the balustrade of the Palazzo dei Priori. The room also contains an important collection of paintings of the Tuscan school, from the 13th and 14th centuries.

Three small rooms are to the right of the Tribune and contain various shrines attributed to Bernardo Daddi, and a fine *Pietà* by Giovanni da Milano. To the left, another series of three small rooms contain works by famous masters of the 14th century: most remarkable are a fine *Polyptych* by Andrea Orcagna, and two series of panels representing scenes from the *Life of Christ* and *Scenes from the Life of St. Francis,* by Taddeo Gaddi. To the left of the Tribune, there is another large hall, containing Florentine works of the 15th century, including Lorenzo Monaco's *Annunciation,* Filippino Lippi's *St. John the Baptist and the Magdalen,* the *Madonna of the Sea,* attributed either to Botticelli or Filippino Lippi, and a fine panel from a wedding chest, known as the *Adimari wedding chest,* by an unknown Florentine painter of the 15th century. Inside the Gallery there is the group of the *Rape of the Sabine women*, a 16th-century work by Giambologna, once in the Loggia dei Lanzi.

Florence, Michelangelo's "David", famous sculpture of the Academy Gallery.

CHURCH AND CONVENT OF ST. MARCO - The Convent has been known since the 12th century. In 1437, Cosimo the Elder commissioned Michelozzo to restructure it, therefore it is the first convent built in the elegant simple forms of the Renaissance.

The fine **Cloister** has a simple stone structure with brick cornices. Light arcades delimit the space on the ground floor. On the first floor are fine lunettes frescoed by Poccetti, Rosselli, Coccapani, Vanni, Cerrini, Dandini and other famous artists. But most of the frescoes in the cloister are by Fra' Angelico, who passed the greater part of his life within these walls; his works include: *Crucifixion with St. Dominic* at the entrance to the cloister and the lunette over the door with *St. Peter Martyr*; in the lunette of the **Chapter Room**, a *St. Dominic*, and inside a magnificent *Crucifixion*; over the door of the refectory a *Pietà*; on the door of the Hospice, *Jesus as a Pilgrim* and, inside, the *Madonna dell'Arte dei Lanaioli* (1433), the *Last Judgement, Scenes from the Life of Christ*, the *Deposition*. In the Refectory, a fine *Supper of St. Dominic*, a fresco by Sogliani, and on the walls the *Last Judgement* by Fra' Bartolomeo.

A staircase leads to the next floor, with Fra' Angelico's famous *Annunciation* at the top; off the corridor is the splendid **Library**, by Michelozzo, and at the end of the corridor, **Cosimo's Cell** with a *Crucifix* in the antechamber and an *Adoration of the Magi* in the cell, both by Fra' Angelico. In the left corridor, you can admire an *Enthroned Madonna between Saints*, and in the cells that open off the corridor, other lovely works, all by Fra' Angelico: the *Annunciation*, the *Transfiguration*, *Christ in the Praetorium*, the *Marys at the Tomb*, the *Coronation*, the *Presentation in the Temple*. At the end of the corridor is **Savonarola's Cell**, with a portrait of the martyr painted by Fra' Bartolomeo.

A flight of stairs on the right leads down to the **Small Refectory**, with a large fresco of the *Last Supper* by Ghirlandaio.

The **Hall of the Hospice** contains a number of panel paintings: the most remarkable are Fra' Angelico's *Last Judgement* and *Deposition*.

The **Church** was restored in 1437 by Michelozzo himself; it was later remodeled by Giambologna (1580) and then by Silvani; the simple façade was redone between 1777 and 1780.

The **interior** is linear and the carved and gilded ceiling is remarkable. On the door is a *Crucifix* of the school of Giotto, while works on the altars include, on the right, *St. Thomas Aquinas* by Santi di Tito and a *Praying Madonna* of Byzantine school. Nearby is Michelozzo's **Sacristy**, which contains a *sarcophagus* with a bronze statue of *St. Antoninus* by Fra' Domenico Portigiani (1602). Nearby is the **Chapel of St. Antoninus**, with marble and bronze decorations by Giambologna and Francavilla, and other works by Alessandro Allori and Battista Naldini; the frescoes in the dome are by Poccetti. To the left of the presbytery see the lovely **Chapel of the Sacrament**, decorated with frescoes by Poccetti and canvases by Santi di Tito, Passignano and Empoli.

MUSEUM OF GEOLOGY AND PALAEONTOLOGY - The current arrangement dates from the beginning of this century. Extremely interesting is the large collection of vertebrates and fossil finds from the Valdarno. On the second floor there are thousands of examples of invertebrates.

BOTANIC MUSEUM - It is the largest in Italy and one of the best-known museums of its kind in the world. The various sections include: the **Central herbarium** (1842), with about four million specimens; the interesting **Tropical herbarium**; and a **Xylotheque**. Adjacent to the museum there are the **Botanical Gardens**, founded in 1545, by order of Cosimo I de' Medici, which contain extremely rare tall trees.

MINERALOGY MUSEUM - It is an enormous collection of over 25,000 samples of minerals from all over the world, begun by Cosimo I de' Medici. The *Elbana Collection* (5000 pieces) is particularly interesting. Exceptional pieces include, a Brazilian topaz weighing 151 kilos, the Elba tourmalines and the Sardinian azurites.

CHURCH OF SS. ANNUNZIATA - When it was originally built (1250), outside the second circle of walls, it was an oratory. As time passed, the church was enlarged to the present size. Entrance to the church is through the so-called **Small Chapel of the Vows**, built by Antonio Manetti from designs by Michelozzo (1447). The space is remarkably scenic with

Florence, the portico in front of the Church of SS. Annunziata.

lunettes frescoed with scenes from the *Life of the Virgin* (right wall), and outstanding works such as the *Assumption* (1513) by Rosso Fiorentino, the *Visitation* (1513) by Pontormo, the *Marriage of the Virgin* (1513), the *Birth of the Virgin* and the *Voyage of the Magi* (1511) by Andrea del Sarto. The small cloister is also decorated with *Scenes from the Life of St. Filippo Benizzi* by Cosimo Rosselli; and the *Punishment of the Blasphemers,* the *Healing of a Woman Possessed,* the *Resurrection of a Child,* the *Healing of a Child,* by Andrea del Sarto. The **interior**, restructured in the middle of the 17th century, consists of a single great nave with arches, set between pilaster stips, that lead to the chapels on either sides; the church is enriched by the magnificent coffered ceiling by Volterrano (1664). The large tribune of the choir, with a hemispherical cupola designed by Leon Battista Alberti (1444), is also particularly fine. To the left of the entrance, is the **Tabernacle of the Annunciata** by Michelozzo, built around a 14th-century fresco of the *Annunciation* traditionally considered miraculous. The tabernacle consists of four Corinthian columns surmounted by rich entablature; the dome is by Volterrano, the gate, in bronze ropes, is by Maso di Bartolomeo (1447), the silver altar is by Egidio Leggi (1600).

Rossellino's *funerary monument to Orlando de' Medici* is in the fifth chapel on the right; the chapel to the left of the right transept contains the *tomb of Baccio Bandinelli* with his *Pietà*. Near the presbytery, in the centre, there is the **Giambologna Chapel** transformed by the sculptor for his own burial (1598). Michelozzo's terra-cotta statue of *John the Baptist* is at the back of the left transept; the fourth chapel of the left side, is decorated with an *Assumption* by Perugino, while the first two chapels contain important frescoes by Andrea del Castagno – *Christ with St. Julian* and the *Trinity with St. Jerome between the Madonna and Mary of Cleofa.*

A door from the left arm of the transept leads to the **Cloister of the Dead**, designed by Michelozzo (1453), and decorated with a fresco cycle of the *History* of *the Order* of *the Servi*, attributed to Maria di Bernardino Poccetti; the series is interrupted in the arch of the church portal, by Andrea del Sarto's *Madonna del Sacco* (1525). On the wall facing the side of the church see the *tomb of Guglielmo di Narbona,* which represents the battle disposition of a knight from the 13th century.

EQUESTRIAN STATUE OF FERDINANDO I DE' MEDICI - It is set at the centre of *Piazza della SS. Annunziata,* and represents the proud Grand Duke. It practically is the copy of the one in *Piazza della Signoria,* which instead portrays Cosimo I. This one also is by Giambologna, and finished by Tacca (1608).

FOUNTAINS BY TACCA - The two fountains are symmetrically placed on either sides of the piazza. They were made by Pietro Tacca (1629) for the port of Livorno, but Grand Duke Ferdinando II had them installed in the Florentine piazza. The two bronze fountains are perfectly 16th-century in style, and reproduce *marine monsters* and *grotesques figures* of outstanding artistic quality.

GALLERY OF THE SPEDALE DEGLI INNOCENTI - The five rooms of this small museum contain important works of the 15th and 16th centuries, including the splendid *Adoration of the Christ Child,* with the sweet serene figures of the worshippers, by Ghirlandaio (1488), the terra-cotta *Madonna and Child* (1488) by Luca della Robbia; the famous *Madonna and Child with St. John* (1460) by Botticelli; and an imposing *Madonna and Saints* by Pietro di Cosimo.

SPEDALE DEGLI INNOCENTI (Foundling Home) - Designed by Brunelleschi, the building was finished by Francesco Luna (1445). A lovely portico runs along the **façade**.
Its nine arcades are decorated with polychrome terra-cotta roundels with *Infants in Swaddling Clothes* (to remember that once this place gave hospitality to the orphans), by Luca della Robbia (1463). Inside is a lovely courtyard and on the first floor there is a collection of detached frescoes and a Picture-gallery.

ARCHAEOLOGICAL MUSEUM - It is one of the most important museums of this kind in Italy for the richness of its collections, which include examples of Egyptian, Etruscan, Greek and Roman antiquities.
The **Egyptian Collection** was begun in 1824 ordered by Leopoldo II, and was enriched by material from Tuscan expeditions directed by Ippolito Rossellini. Some of the most interesting items include the fascinating statue of the *Goddess Hathor nursing the Pharaoh,* the polychrome relief of the *Goddess Hathor with the Pharaoh Sethos I,* the bas-relief of the *Goddess of Truth Maat* and the *funerary statue of the priest Amenemhet.*
The **Etruscan section** contains a great amount of material collected during more than three centuries of search. There are a great number of sarcophagi, cinerary urns, bronzes, weapons and objects of daily use. Among the sculptures stand out the famous *Chimaera of Arezzo,* the statue of the orator known as the *Arringatore,* and the statue of *Minerva.*
The **Greek-Roman section**, although considerably smaller, includes very important pieces: such as the bronze statue known as *Idolino,* a Greek work of the 5th century BC.
Of great interest is the vast **Collection of vases and terra-cottas** of Italic, Etruscan and Greek make (including the famous *François Vase,* a Greek work of the 6th century BC found in an Etruscan tomb), as well as the sections of **Eastern Mediterranean culture and Prehistory**.
The annexed **Garden** contains various reconstructions of tombs of the Etruscan period using the original material, a model of a small temple and other antique architectural elements.

THE LAST SUPPER OF ST. APOLLONIA - This small and well-preserved building houses the fascinating and famous fresco of the *Last Supper* by Andrea del Castagno (1457).
Note also on the left wall, three scenes with the *Crucifixion,* the *Deposition* and the *Resurrection,* also by the same artist. In the two lunettes are a *Pietà* and a *Crucifixion with the Virgin, St. John and Saints,* by an unknown painter.

CLOISTER OF THE SCALZO - Site of an old confraternity – the Scalzo – this well-balanced and elegant little cloister, contains beautiful monochrome frescoes which depict sixteen stories from the *Life of St. John the Baptist.* The frescoes are all by Andrea del Sarto (1514-26), except for two by Franciabigio (1518-19).

Florence, the grand façade of Santa Croce dominates the square.

PIAZZA SANTA CROCE - This vast rectangular square, is one of the largest in the city. Dominated by the imposing structure of the Church of St. Croce, it is surrounded by historical palaces. During the Middle Ages it was considered the ideal place for meetings and preaching. During Renaissance it was used for tournaments, and then, became the field for football matches (*calcio storico fiorentino*), still today played here.

CHURCH OF SANTA CROCE - The church is one of city's largest and has a neo-Gothic **façade** added in the 19th century heavily decorated. The building, attributed to Arnolfo di Cambio (13th cent.), has a majestic **interior** with a nave separated from the two aisles by slender octagonal pilasters supporting the broad pointed arches with a double cornice. At the end of the nave, with its open timber roof, is the transept with the chapels. The internal wall of the façade contains a stained-glass window with the *Deposition,* done from a cartoon by Lorenzo Ghiberti. Below, on the right is the *monument to Gino Capponi* by Antonio Bortone (1876), while on the left, is the *monument to G.B. Niccolini,* historian and poet, by Pio Fedi. On the first altar, in the **right aisle**, is a *Crucifixion* by Santi di Tito (1579), while the famous *Madonna del Latte,* a bas-relief by Antonio Rossellino, is on the first pillar. On the wall are the *funeral monuments to Michelangelo Buonarroti,* by Vasari (1564), *to Dante Alighieri,* by Stefano Ricci (1829); *to Vittorio Alfieri,* poet and patriot, by Canova (1803), and *to Niccolò Machiavelli* by Innocenzo Spinazzi (1787). The octagonal *Pulpit* by Benedetto da Maiano (1475), a sculptural ensemble with *Scenes from the Life of St. Francis,* is at the third pillar. Behind the fifth altar there are remains of frescoes by Andrea Orcagna, while further on, you can admire a tabernacle in *pietra serena* with the *Annunciation* by Donatello (1472-76), a very animated monument; the *tomb* of the historian *Leonardo Bruni,* by Rossellino; the *funeral monument to Gioacchino Rossini* and the one to the poet *Ugo Foscolo* by Antonio Berti (1939).

SANTA CROCE

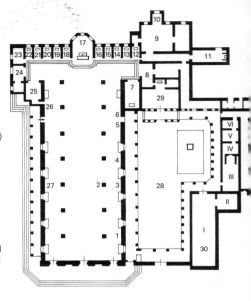

In the **Castellani Chapel**, or *Chapel of the Sacrament*, in the right arm of the transept, is the cycle of frescoes with scenes from the *Lives of SS. Nicholas of Bari, Anthony Abbot, John the Evangelist and John the Baptist,* by Agnolo Gaddi (1385); a fine *Crucifix* by Niccolò Gerini is at the altar, while on the walls are terra-cotta *Saints* from the Della Robbia workshop. Further on, at the head of the transept, is the **Baroncelli Chapel**. Outside is the magnificent *tomb*, in Gothic style, of the Baroncelli family, and a lunette with a *Madonna* by Taddeo Gaddi. Inside, on the right wall, the fine fresco of the *Madonna of the Girdle with St. Thomas*, by Bastiano Mainardi (1490), and the cycle of *Scenes from the Life of Mary*, by Taddeo Gaddi, on the other three walls; on the altar is the fine *Coronation of the Virgin* by Giotto.

Michelozzo's portal, in the right side of the transept, leads to the **Sacristy**, originally built in the 14th century, with *Scenes from the Passion* by Niccolò Gerini on the right wall. From the back wall of the Sacristy you enter the **Rinuccini Chapel**, with scenes from the *Lives of the Virgin and St. Mary Magdalen* by Giovanni da Milano, and a fine altarpiece by Giovanni del Biondo (1379). The Sacristy also leads to the **Medici Chapel** or *Novices' Chapel,* built by Michelozzo for Cosimo the Elder. Here you can admire various works by Della Robbia, including some *busts*, an altarpiece, and a shrine by Verrocchio; to the right is the *monument to Francesco Lombardi* with a magnificent bas-relief that may be by Donatello.

Various chapels with important works of art open off the back of the central part of the transept: the **Velluti Chapel**, with *Scenes from the Legend of St. Michael Archangel,* perhaps by Cimabue; the **Calderini Chapel**, later **Riccardi**, with a lunette-shaped vault with *Scenes from the Life of St. Andrew Apostle* by Giovanni da San Giovanni; the **Giugni Chapel**, later **Bonaparte** with the *monument to Carlotta Bonaparte,* by Lorenzo Bartolini; the **Peruzzi Chapel**, with the magnificent *Scenes from the Life of St. John Evangelist* by Giotto (1320); the **Bardi Chapel**, with the *Scenes from the Life of St. Francis* by Giotto (1318) and, above the external arch, the *Miracle of the Stigmata,* while the *Allegory of Chastity, Poverty* and *Obedience,* and the *Triumph of the Saint* were frescoed on the vaulting by Giotto. On the altar is a panel of *St. Francis* and *Scenes* *from his Life* of Luccan school, late 13th century; then comes the **Sanctuary** with the *Legend of the Cross* (1380) by Agnolo Gaddi. On the altar is a polyptych with the *Madonna* and *Saints* by Niccolò Gerini, and above the altar a *Crucifix* of the school of Giotto; next comes the **Tosinghi Chapel**, with a polyptych by Giovanni del Biondo on the altar; the **Capponi Chapel**, with the *monument to the Virgin Mary and her Dead Son* by Libero Andreotti (1926); the **Ricasoli Chapel**, with two 19th-century canvases of *Scenes from the Life of St. Anthony of Padua;* the **Pulci Chapel**, with a glazed terra-cotta altarpiece by Giovanni della Robbia and noteworthy frescoes on the walls (the *Martyrdom of SS Lawrence and Stephen* by Bernardo Daddi); the **Bardi di Vernio Chapel**, frescoed with scenes from the *Life of Pope Sylvester* (by Giottino) and with two niche-shaped 14th-century *tombs* on the left wall.

At the far end of the left arm of the crossing are the **Niccolini Chapel**, with statues by Pietro Francavilla, paintings by Alessandro Allori (1588) on the altars, and a fine cupola frescoed by Volterrano (1660); the **Bardi Chapel** (the last to the left of the crossing), with Donatello's magnificent *Crucifix* (1425), and the **Salviati Chapel**, with the *Martyrdom of St. Lawrence* by Jacopo Ligozzi (1600) on the altar.

The *tomb-stones* of the humanist *Carlo Marsuppini* by Desiderio da Settignano, and *Galileo Galilei* (1642) by Foggini are in the **left aisle**.

Access to the **First Cloister** is outside through the *Door of the Martello* to the right of the façade. The 14th-century cloister is articulated by fine arcades.

At the back of the cloister, is the marvelous **Pazzi Chapel**, which Filippo Brunelleschi designed on a central plan with a dome and a lantern. Outside, a Corinthian porch is set in front of the façade, with a frieze containing roundels with heads of cherubim, designed by Donatello and executed by Desiderio da Settignano. A fine door designed by Giuliano da

Florence, Cimabue's "Crucifix" (Museo dell'Opera di Santa Croce).

69

Florence, the Pazzi Chapel adjacent the Church of Santa Croce.

Maiano (1472) opens on one of the long sides of the rectangular interior. The ribbed dome and lantern are set above the walls articulated by pilasters. A door in the right-hand corner of the First Cloister, by Michelozzo or Benedetto da Maiano, opens into the **Second Cloister**, or *Large Cloister* designed by Brunelleschi and probably decorated by Rossellino. Entrance to the antique *Refectory* and the **Museum of the Works of Santa Croce**, is on the right of the first cloister.

MUSEUM OF THE WORKS OF SANTA CROCE - Installed next to the Church, the museum consists of six rooms situated in what used to be the convent. The entrance room contains a fine fresco, *Saint Francis distributing bread to the Friars,* by Jacopo Ligozzi. The door on the right leads into a large hall (the old **Refectory**) dominated by a large fresco by Taddeo Gaddi of the *Tree of Life,* a *Last Supper* and various *Episodes from the Life of Christ.* The room also contains Cimabue's famous *Crucifix,* heavily damaged during the flood in 1966, a bronze statue of *St. Louis of Toulouse* by Donatello, and detached frescoes by Andrea del Giusto, Domenico Veneziano and other anonymous Florentine painters. Back in the entrance hall, the doorway to the left leads to a room (the old **Cerchi Chapel**) in which various outstanding Della Robbia terra-cotta figures are on display: particulary interesting are the glazed terra-cotta altarpiece attributed to Andrea della Robbia, the *Madonna and Child* of the school of the Della Robbias, and over the door, the predella of fine quality, also by Andrea della Robbia. In the next room the finest works are two *Busts of Saints,* which emerged from under the plaster in the Pazzi Chapel; a fine detached fresco depicting the *Martyrdom of St. Matthew,* by the school of Andrea del Castagno; a delightful *Madonna Enthroned,* perhaps by the school of Niccolò di Pietro Gerini; the fresco with the *Madonna of Humility,* probably from the circle of Lorenzo Monaco, and other interesting frescoes, most of which come from the Basilica. Noteworthy in the next room is the *funeral monument of Cardi-*

nal *Gastone della Torre* by the great Tino di Camaino. And finally, in the last room, the particularly striking works include, two spandrels with *Angels* attributed to Matteo Rosselli, a detached fresco depicting *Christ in the Garden,* also by Rosselli, and another detached fresco of *Christ in the Garden appearing to the Madonna,* of the school of Giovanni da San Giovanni.

BUONARROTI HOUSE - Bought by Michelangelo himself in 1508 for his nephew Leonardo, it was later frescoed in the 17th century at the request and under the guidance of Michelangelo the Younger. Here the most important 17th-century Florentine painters frescoed a rich cycle of paintings with the *Glories of Michelangelo.* Today the building contains the **Museum** of Michelangelo's early works.

CHURCH OF ST. AMBROGIO - St. Ambrogio was one of the first religious buildings to go up in Florence. Rebuilt in the 13th century, and again more recently, the present **façade** is 19th-century.
The **interior**, 18th-century on an originally Gothic ground plan, is single-aisled with three chapels at the back and eight Renaissance side altars. There were originally a group of 14th- and 15th-century frescoes near the altars, but they were seriously damaged in the flood of 1966 and were therefore detached. Near the Presbytery is the **Chapel of the Miracle**, in which, in a chalice is preserved the blood that in 1230 miraculously appeared to the priest Uguccione while celebrating Mass. The tabernacle, which contains the reliquary, is by Mino da Fiesole (1481-83); the terra-cotta *Angels* nearby, are by the Della Robbia, while the frescoes on the walls, are 15th-century paintings by Cosimo Roselli.

CHURCH OF ST. MARIA MADDALENA DEI PAZZI - This church and the Benedictine monastery connected to it, were first built in the 13th century; the buildings were often remodeled, especially between 1480 and 1492, by Giuliano da Sangallo.
Entrance to the church is through the **Chapel of the Lily**, a 16th-century structure frescoed by Poccetti with scenes from the *Lives of SS. Nereo, Achilleo, Bernard and Filippo Neri,* and the annexed **Courtyard**, with Ionic portico, is by Sangallo.
The **interior** of the church has a single aisle, and the six arches on either side lead into the chapels, which contain various valuable works of the 16th and 17th centuries. The **Chancel** contains two canvases with *Scenes from the Life of the Magdalen* by Luca Giordano, set below the dome frescoed by Dandini. The **Crypt** at the back of the church leads to the **Chapter Hall**, which contains Perugino's fresco with *Christ on the Cross and the Magdalen, St. Bernard and St. Mary, John the Evangelist and St. Benedict.*

MUSEUM OF ANCIENT FLORENCE - Historical and topographical documents of the city, including water-colours, prints and drawings, are included in the museum. In the building there is also a **Permanent exhibition of the works of Ottone Rosai**. Over fifty examples give us a survey of the great Florentine painter's artistic activity from 1930 to 1940.

SYNAGOGUE - The Israelite Temple, in an eastern Byzantine style, was designed by the architects Falcini, Treves, Micheli and Cioni (1874). When the large dome was finally covered with copper, it was inaugurated in October 1882. The construction is interesting, both for the elegant frescoes and mosaics which decorate it inside and out, and for its historical and cultural meaning. It is the symbol of the liberation from the ghetto which was once in *piazza della Repubblica.*

VIALE DEI COLLI AND PIAZZALE MICHELANGELO - The **Viale dei Colli** (Hill Avenue) winds for about six kilometres on the heights around the south side of the city, providing spots with fascinating views. It was laid out in 1868, by the architect Giuseppe Poggi, who also made the plans for the **Piazzale Michelangelo**, an enormous terrace overlooking Florence. In the piazzale are copies of Michelangelo's sculptures: *David* and the four *allegorical figures* on the Medici tombs in the New Sacristy of San Lorenzo. In the background, set above the piazzale, is the **Palazzina del Caffè** (1873), also by Poggi, which partly hides the churches of St. Salvatore and St. Miniato al Monte.

Scenes from the famous Florentine historical soccer.

Florence, the beautiful decorated façade of the Church of St. Miniato al Monte.

CHURCH OF ST. MINIATO AL MONTE - The Church of St. Miniato al Monte, which was built as a chapel in the 4th century, owes its present structure to Bishop Hildebrand (1018). The lower part of the **façade** is decorated with fine arches; the upper part is simpler and has a fine 12th-century mosaic with *Christ between the Madonna and St. Miniato*.

The **inside** is tripartite, with a trussed timber ceiling. The inlaid marble pavement, with *signs of the zodiac* and *symbolic animals*, is of particular interest. On the walls are fragments of 13th- and 14th-century frescoes. The large **Crypt** is closed by a wrought-iron gate dating from 1338. The altar (11th cent.) preserves the bones of St. Miniato; fragments of frescoes by Taddeo Gaddi (1341) are on the vault. Returning from the crypt, see the raised **Presbytery**, which has a fine *pulpit* (1207) and inlaid wooden choir stalls. In the conch of the apse is a large mosaic of *Christ between Mary and St. Miniato* (1277). To the right of the presbytery there is the entrance to the **Sacristy**, completely frescoed by Spinello Aretino (1387) with sixteen *Scenes from the Legend of St. Benedict*. Descending on the left of the presbytery, one arrives at the **Chapel of St. Jacopo**, known as the *Chapel of the Cardinal of Portugal*, designed by Antonio Manetti and decorated with five marvelous tondos by Luca della Robbia with the *Holy Spirit* and the *Four Cardinal Virtues*. The painting over the altar is a copy of a painting by Pietro del Pollaiolo, now in the Uffizi. At the centre of the church is the **Chapel of the Crucifix**, designed by Michelozzo, with a delicate glazed vault by Luca della Robbia.

FORTE DI BELVEDERE - The Forte di Belvedere, or *of St. George*, was commissioned to Buontalenti (1590-95) by Ferdinando I. The building, set on a hilltop south of the Arno, dominates the city and the river from within its star-shaped fortified walls. The protected access is through an entrance hall and reaches the terrace in front of the **Palazzetto**, which is now used for exhibitions and art happenings. An opening in the bastions communicates with the **Boboli Gardens** below.

PALAZZO PITTI - It is the most imposing of the city palaces, and dates from 1457 on a probable design by Brunelleschi; in the 16th century the Medici commissioned Ammannati to enlarge it.

The **façade**, 205 metres long and 36 metres high, consists of rusticated ashlars with some of the single blocks over two metres long. The only decorative elements are the *crowned heads of lions* between the ground floor window brackets.

Access to the **interior** is through the great portal with its central arch leading into a charming Doric atrium by Pasquale Poccianti (1850). This leads to Ammannati's famous courtyard, at the back of which is the *Grotto of Moses,* carved in porphyry by Raffaelle Curradi; antique Roman statues are set under the arcades at the sides, while to the right is the **Chapel** frescoed by Ademollo, with a magnificent mosaic altar and a fine *Crucifix* by Giambologna. The grand staircase, lined with antique busts, begins on the same side of the courtyard; on the landing is the *Medici Genius* by Giambologna; the first floor goes to the vestibule of the **Royal Quarters** and the **Palatine Gallery**. On the second floor is the **Gallery of Modern Art**.

The portico in the right wing of the façade of the palace leads to the **Bacchus Courtyard**, today's main entrance to the Palatine Gallery and the **Museum of Silverware** with the *Fountain of Bacchus* by Cioli, which portrays the court dwarf of Cosimo I. The Palatine Gallery is the second museum in the city, both for size and interest, after the Uffizi, and contains works of art extremely important for the history of art. It was realised by Ferdinando II de' Medici who commissioned Pietro da Cortona to decorate various rooms of the Gallery. As time passed, the collection – a typically 17th-century *picture gallery* with the walls entirely covered with pictures in the fashion of the times – was enlarged by Cardinal Leopoldo de' Medici and, later, by the last members of the Medici family and by the Lorraine Grand Dukes. The Gallery consists of a series of rooms dedicated to gods and mythological figures, represented in the decoration.

The visit begins with the **Castagnoli Room** (decorated by Castagnoli, 1784) which contains Sodoma's *Saint Sebastian,* with the saint mystically meditating on his suffering. Turning right you will find yourself in the **Volterrano Apartments**, dedicated to the painter who frescoed the five *Allegories* on the walls. Next come the **Fine Arts Room**, the **Hercules Room**, the **Aurora Room**, the **Berenice Room** and the **Room of Psyche**, which house works by Tuscan 17th-century painters. Continuing straight ahead from the Castagnoli Room you will enter the **Music Room**, with frescoes by Luigi Ademollo; then the **Poccetti Gallery** (frescoes by Poccetti), which contains paintings by Rubens and Spagnoletto among others; the **Prometheus Room** (ceiling by Giuseppe Collignon, 1842), contains an outstanding three-dimensional *Madonna* by Filippo Lippi. From here, keeping to the right, you will come to the **Gallery of the Columns**, with many works by Flemish painters on the walls; then to the **Hall of Justice**, which contains the *Portrait of a Man* by Titian and various intense *Portraits* by Bronzino; and lastly to the **Room of Flora**. Back in the Prometheus Room you may continue the itinerary with the **Ulysses Room**, which contains Raphael's famous *Madonna dell'Impannata,* Andrea del Sarto's *Madonna and Child with Saints* and other important paintings; on to the **Education of Jupiter Room**, in which Caravaggio's famous *Sleeping Cupid* is to be found; the lovely **Iliad Room** (decoration by Luigi Sabatelli, 1819) houses various authentic masterpieces are on exhibit, including one of Raphael's most famous pictures, the *Portrait of a Woman* known as *La Gravida* (1508), Andrea del Sarto's mystical *Assumption of the Virgin* (1519), the *Portrait of a Woman* by Ridolfo del Ghirlandaio, Titian's intense and introspective *Portrait of a Man* and his *Philip II of Spain,* and the *Portrait of Philip IV of Spain* by Velasquez. The **Saturn Room** (ceiling by Ciro Ferri) contains works by Raphael, including the *Portraits of Angelo and Maddalena Doni,* the austere *Portrait of Cardinal Bernardo Dovizi da Bibbiena,* the witty *Portrait of Cardinal Inghirami,* the softly modelled *Madonna of the Grand Duke,* the engrossed *Madonna of the Baldachin* and the tender *Madonna of the Chair;* particularly noteworthy in the **Jupiter Room** (ceiling by Pietro da Cortona, 1643-45) is the *Madonna del Sacco* by Perugino, Andrea del Sarto's *St. John the Baptist,* the powerful and intense figure of *Saint Mark* by Fra' Bartolomeo, the *Annunciation,* once more by Andrea del Sarto, the charming *Holy Family* by Rubens, and the enigmatic and delicate *Portrait of a Woman,* known as *La Velata,* by Raphael. The **Mars Room** (ceil-

Florence, the majestic Palazzo Pitti among the green park of Boboli.

ing by Pietro da Cortona, 1646) houses Murillo's *Madonna and Child* and *Madonna of the Rosary,* the famous *Consequences of War* by Rubens, the *Portrait of Daniele Barbaro,* a bright painting by Veronese, Titian's *Portrait of Cardinal Ippolito de' Medici* and Van Dyck's *Cardinal Luigi Bentivoglio*; of particular interest in the **Apollo Room** (ceiling by Pietro da Cortona, 1660) is Titian's sensuous *Magdalen,* the dramatic *Deposition* by Andrea del Sarto, the *Portrait of Vincenzo Zeno* by Tintoretto, and Rosso Fiorentino's *Madonna Enthroned with Saints.* The **Venus Room** (ceiling by Pietro da Cortona, 1641-42) houses the *Portrait of a Woman,* known as *La Bella,* by Titian, his *Portrait of Pietro Aretino,* one of the outstanding achievements of the Renaissance, and the lively painting of *Ulysses Returning from the Island of Phaecia* by Rubens.

MODERN ART GALLERY - Situated on the second floor of Palazzo Pitti, it consists of over 2000 works of sculpture and painting by artists active between the beginning of the 19th century up to the early decades of the 20th century. The Gallery covers many rooms: the first of these contain works in neoclassic and Romantic style, with imposing historical paintings; among these art works, mention must be made of the *Bust of Napoleon* by Canova in **Room IV**, the large group of *Cain and Abel* by Duprè in **Room X**, various fine portraits by Antonio Ciseri in **Room XII**, and works by the great Giovanni Boldini in **Room XV**; *The Rain of Ashes* by Gioacchino Toma, *Beach near Barletta* by Giuseppe de Nittis and others are in **Room XVII**. **Rooms XXIII** and **XXIV** contain a rich collection of works by the most important Macchiaioli painters: Silvestro Lega, Giuseppe Abbati, Telemaco Signorini, Cristiano Banti, Edoardo Borrani, Vincenzo Cabianca, Cesare Ciani, to name only the best known. Room XXIII also contains some of the outstanding works by the father of the Macchiaioli movement, Giovanni Fattori.

MUSEUM OF SILVERWARE - You will find it in various rooms of Palazzo Pitti, overlooking the Courtyard of Bacchus. The first three rooms are decorated with allegorical and trompe-l'oeil frescoes by Michelangelo Colonna and Agostino Micheli. The frescoes in the fourth room consist of noteworthy allegories which exalt the *Deeds of Lorenzo the Magnificent.*

The Museum contains examples of household and religious objects in precious metals, bowls and splendid vases in semi-precious stone and rock crystal, as well as marvelous ivories and the vases from the collection of Lorenzo the Magnificent. Particularly striking is the famous *vase in lapis-lazuli* by Bilivert, next to the German ivories from the collection of Prince Mattia de' Medici.

The **Treasure** is exhibited in another room. It includes rare jewels and the jewelley collection of Anna Maria Luisa Ludovica, the last of the Medici. The small room on the mezzanine contains ceramics and porcelain.

PORCELAIN MUSEUM - This small Museum is in the Boboli Gardens in the **Palazzina del Cavaliere** and contains a collection of porcelain – Sevres, Chantilly, Vienna, Meissen, Worcester and other manufactories – some of which belonged to Elisa Baciocchi, Napoleon's sister.

CONTINI-BONACOSSI COLLECTION - The collection was donated to the State in 1969 and is on exhibit in the **Meridiana**, a pavilion to the west of Palazzo Pitti. It is composed of fine majolicas, interesting antiquities, but above all, important paintings, including Cimabue's *Madonna and Saints,* Sassetta's *Madonna of the Snow,* the *portrait of Count Da Porto with his Son,* by Veronese, Goya's touching *Torero,* and *El Aguador de Sevilla* by Velázquez.

BOBOLI GARDENS - The Boboli Gardens comprise the largest monumental green space in Florence. The history of the gardens goes back four centuries. In 1549, Cosimo I de' Medici commisioned them to Niccolò Pericoli, called Tribolo. After his death the work was continued and modified by Ammannati, Buontalenti, and finally Alfonso Parigi the Younger.

Today, entrance to the gardens is through the **Bacchus Courtyard**, beyond which is the charming **Buontalenti Grotto** (1583), an artificial grotto consisting of various chambers covered with artificial incrustations and frescoes.

The first chamber contains *idyllic images* by Poccetti and statues by Baccio Bandinelli; the second, known as **Nymphaeum**, is lined with shells and decorated with mythological paintings; at the centre is the fine sculptural group of *Paris and Helen* (1560) by Vincenzo de' Rossi, and a finely carved basin by Battista Lorenzi. The third chamber, completely decorated by Poccetti, contains a splendid *Fountain with Satyrs* who leer at the *Venus of the Grotticella* (1573) by Giambologna.

The fine alley flanked by Roman statues, leads to the **Amphitheater**, designed by Tribolo, at the centre of which is a large Roman *marble basin* and an Egyptian *obelisk* from Thebes (2nd cent. BC). The two Roman *statues* of *Septimius Severus* and a *Magistrate* near the Amphitheater are particularly fine.

Further up, is a large basin called **Neptune's Pond** with a fine bronze *statue* of Neptune by Stoldo Lorenzi (1565) at the centre. On the highest level, at the back of the park, you can admire the *Statue of Abundance,* begun by Giambologna and finished by Tacca (1636).

Nearby are the old walls, constructed by Michelangelo in 1529, near a bastion with the **Grand Duke's Casino** and the nearby **Garden of the Knight** with the fine *Monkey fountain* by Pietro Tacca. Further downhill is an annex of Palazzo Pitti called the **Meridiana**, a pleasant neo-Gothic building (1832).

An alternative itinerary from Neptune's Pond begins from a steep alley, known as the *Viottolone*, which leads to the *Piazzale dell'Isolotto*. Here, at the centre of a charming garden, is the stupendous *Oceanus Fountain* by Alfonso Parigi (1618), a copy with variations of Giambologna's figure of Neptune, surrounded by statues that symbolically represent the young *Nile,* the adult *Ganges* and the old *Euphrates,* the whole theatrically embellished with other statues emerging from the water, such as *Perseus* and *Andromeda.*

CHURCH OF ST. FELICITA - On the site of an ancient oratory of the 5th century, the church has often been remodeled. Its present appearance is due to Federico Ruggeri (1736).

Under the **porch** are various tombs including that of the merchant *Barduccio Chierichini* (1416) and that *of cardinal Luigi De Rossi,* by Raffaello da Montelupo (1500). The **interior** has a single nave, and is in neoclassic style.Various chapels open off the nave, between the pilaster strips: the first chapel on the right was built for the Capponi family, by Brunelleschi (1425); on the altar is a *Deposition* (1528), one of Pontormo's masterpieces. On the wall to the right, is his famous *Annunciation.* To the right of the transept is the **Sacristy** (1470), in the style of Brunelleschi and of uncertain attribution (Michelozzo or Leon Battista Alberti). On the walls are an *Adoration of the Magi* by Francesco di Antonio (1450), a polyptych, *Madonna and Child with Saints,* by Taddeo Gaddi, and a *Saint Felicity with her Seven Sons* by Neri di Bicci. In the small apse, a fine *Crucifix* by Pacino di Buonaguida, a 15th- century *Pietà* by an unknown painter, and a *Madonna* by Giovanni del Biondo.

CHURCH OF SANTO SPIRITO - The church of Santo Spirito, founded in 1250, received its present form in the 15th century, when it was built from a model by Brunelleschi, who had conceived it as a twin to the church of St. Lorenzo. The **façade**, however, was never finished, and is still only a rough plastered wall with an undefined silhouette at the top.

The fine **dome** was designed by Brunelleschi, while the soaring **Bell tower** is by Baccio d'Agnolo (1503).

The **interior** is one of the finest examples of Renaissance architecture, a Latin-cross with three spacious aisles. The colonnade moves forward in a succession of light arches, supported by 35 elegant Corinthian columns in *pietra serena,* forming an internal portico. The ground plan of the 40 semicircular chapels repeats the semicircular rhythm of the arches.

The **internal façade** is comprised of three large doors and was made by Salvi d'Andrea (1483) on Brunelleschi's design. Behind the high altar is a *Crucifix* that may be an early work by Michelangelo. In the right crossing are various important examples of painting: in the third chapel the *Madonna del Soccorso* by an unknown 15th-century painter; in the fifth chapel, Filippino Lippi's famous *Madonna and Child with Saints.* Other fine works are in the left crossing; in the first chapel a *Madonna and Child with Angels and Saints* by Raffaellino del Garbo; in the second, *Saint Monica Establishing the Rule of the Augustinian Nuns* by Francesco Botticini; in the third, a delicate *Madonna and Child with Saints* by Cosimo Rosselli and, in the fourth, a marble altar by Andrea Sansovino. Other important works are also in the apse chapels: in the first is the *Madonna with Saints* by Lorenzo di Credi; in the third the *Madonna and Child with four Saints* by Maso di Banco.

Entry to the **Vestibule**, by Andrea Sansovino, and to the **Sacristy** is near the organ. The Sacristy has a fine octagonal ground plan by Giuliano da Sangallo and Cronaca (1456). The Vestibule leads to the **First Cloister**, in 17th-century style, with frescoes of the same period. Then comes the **Second Cloister**, built by Ammannati and frescoed by Poccetti (the cloister is not at present open to the public since it is occupied by the recruiting centre). Entry to the nearby **Refectory** is from the square. It contains the imposing fresco of the *Last Supper* by Nardo di Cione.

CHURCH OF ST. MARIA DEL CARMINE - The 14th-century building was almost completely destroyed in a fire in 1771. The present structure is therefore 18th-century and was built by G. Ruggeri and G. Mannaioni on a Latin-cross plan with a single aisle. The works **inside** include Vasari's *Crucifixion* on the third altar to the right. One of the greatest works of the entire Renaissance came through the fire miraculously intact – the **Brancacci Chapel** in the right transept preserves a cycle of extremely important frescoes which have recently been restored. The frescoes were begun in 1425 by Masolino da Panicale, who painted the *Temptation of Adam and Eve*, in the first compartment above right, *St. Peter Resuscitating Tabitha*, in the first scene to the right of the large compartment at the top, and the *Preaching of St. Peter* above, to the left of the altar. The compartment on the right wall, *St. Peter Heals a Cripple*, is in part by the great Masaccio, who also painted the compartment above to the right of the altar, with *St. Peter Baptizing the Neophytes* and the splendid *Expul-*

Florence, the simple façade of the Church of Santo Spirito.

sion *from Paradise,* in the first panel above left. Masaccio then went on to the large compartment at the top of the left wall, with *St. Peter taking the Coin from the Mouth of the Fish* (left), *Jesus Ordering Peter to Fish* (center), and *St. Peter paying the Tribute to the Publican* (right). In the lower tier, the compartment to the right of the altar with *St. Peter and St. John distributing the Goods* and the *Death of Ananias* by Masaccio, as also, to the left of the altar, *St. Peter Healing the Sick with his Shadow;* on the lower part of the left wall, *St. Peter in Cattedra* (left) and part of *St. Peter Bringing back to Life the Son of the Prefect Theophilus of Antioch.* Finally, the last compartment of the left wall, *St. Peter in Prison Visited by St. Paul,* in the lower part of the right wall, the *Angel Freeing St. Peter from Prison* and the double scene of *St. Peter before the Prefect Agrippa* and the *Crucifixion of St. Peter* are by another great artist, Filippino Lippi.

ENVIRONS

The **Charterhouse of Galluzzo** or of *Florence in val d'Ema* was founded by Niccolò Acciaioli when he decided to construct a monastery in Florence that was "*lo più notabile loco a tutta l'Italia*" (the most remarkable place in all of Italy). The monastic complex, which dates from the end of the 14th century, lies on the summit of a hill, where the Ema and the Greve rivers run together. There are two churches and a series of rooms connected to them (cloisters, friars' cells, refectory, chapter room), in addition to the large crenellated building known as **Palazzo degli Studi**, which was intended as a hall of residence for Florentine youths and where they would be prepared in the liberal arts. The **main Church** is a large building with a single nave and cross vaults, slightly pointed, which spring from composite piers "*multipli et uni*" set against the walls, forming a sort of framework which articulates the space in a restrained rhythm. This structure is still visible despite the modifications carried out over the centuries, above all inside, which was literally covered with stuccoes, marble and frescoed intonaco, and in the façade, remodelled at the end of the 16th century in forms that already tended towards the Baroque. The second **Church** of the Charterhouse, Greek-cross in plan, is an extremely elegant example of a typically Florentine Gothic style, which has undergone only slight modifications. Ogival cross vaulting covers the arms of the cross, springing from powerful massive composite piers which have capitals and moldings that are already in line with the pictorial tendencies of Gothic art. The underground chambers of the monastery are preserved intact in their original 14th-century structures. They house the Gothic *arch* containing the mortal remains of Niccolò Acciaiuoli and the 15th-century *sepulchre* of Cardinal Angiolo Acciaiuoli. For the most part, the other rooms of the Charterhouse date from the Renaissance, in particular the **Cloisters**: the one in the centre, with arches on Corinthian columns, and the two smaller cloisters with Ionic capitals in the style of Brunelleschi.

At **Careggi**, now a suburb of Florence but once outside the city, there is the ancient **Medicean Villa**. The villa was bought by the Medici in 1417; in 1457, Cosimo the Elder commissioned to Michelozzo the restructure and enlargement. Michelozzo transformed what was a castle in a pleasant residence for the rich Florentine merchant. The façade is simple, with a linear portal supported by ashlars. On the first floor there are some windows. The inside, visits only with a permission from the Arch-hospital administration, has a small and limited courtyard with an irregular plan, designed by Michelozzo, which connects the two sides with three arches and Renaissance columns, to the remains of the 14th-century part, of which are preserved the octagonal pilasters. The posterior façade, outstanding, develops on two three-arcaded loggias; in the one on the left you can admire a large fresco, probably by Volterrano. From here starts a beautiful Italian garden. The villa also has a great historical and literary importance, since here, at the time of Lorenzo the Magnificent, gathered the most famous humanists of those days.

Environs of Florence, view of the central Cloister of the Charterhouse of Galluzzo.

ABBADIA SAN SALVATORE (Siena)

This locality takes its name from the abbey here founded, in 743, by the Lombard nobleman, Rachis. The abbey was alternately under the guidance of the Benedictines, the Camaldolites, and the Cistercians, and its power grew extremely. Today the **Abbey** has a single large nave with a timber roof, but this is due to a 20th century restoration which attempted to cancel from the structure the 16th-century additions, and restore it to its original forms (dating 1036). The interior contains a remarkable 12th-century wooden *Cross*. The Crypt under the church is also very interesting: the plan is Greek cross with thirty-six columns with beautiful capitals, dating from the early 8th century. The **Borgo**, next to the abbey, was initially subjected to the jurisdiction of the abbey, but it soon became independent, having its period of greatest development when the abbey declined. The village is of exceptional interest to the visitor: the streets and buildings are intact since medieval times. Unfortunately, the religious buildings are the most ruined by time: such as the **Country Church of Santa Croce**, still retaining on the façade elements of the original Romanesque church, but being in such a poor condition that at the end of the 18th century it was remade. Inside, there is a fine 16th-century baptismal font. Beautiful is also **San Leonardo**, recently restored to its original Gothic forms.

ABBEY OF SAN GALGANO (Siena)

This complex of buildings was one of the most important examples of the Gothic-Cistercian style in Italy. The **Church** has a Latin-cross plan and is covered with travertine and bricks. It was built by the Cistercian monks between 1224 and 1238. Its slow decline began in the 16th centu-

A striking view of the ruins of the Abbey of San Galgano.

ry and it had to go through the first restoration in 1577. In the 18th century, the church was partially destroyed when the bell tower and some of the vaults collapsed. The **façade**, incomplete, has four columns and three arched doorways with ogive extrados. The side walls contain beautiful windows with one light, some of which are surmounted by an oculus, as well as the same number of fine ogive windows with two lights. The apse has two tiers of mullioned windows with two lights. Grass now grows over the vast **interior** (almost 70 metres), which has been roofless for decades. The nave and two aisles have sixteen cruciform pilasters with four columns fixed in a third one. The lovely arches are Gothic with double archivolts. The vaulting of the nave does not exist anymore. The transept, still well-preserved, has a nave and two aisles, with the one on the east transformed into four small chapels. Next to the church, there is the **Monastery**, of which nothing is left except for the **Chapter-house** and the **Monks' Hall**, developed along two aisles with piers. On the upper floor, a narrow corridor leads to the **monks' cells** and the **choir**.

ABBEY OF SANT'ANTIMO (Siena)

The Abbey of Sant'Antimo, standing alone in the valley of the Starcia torrent, 10 km from Montalcino, was once one of the richest and most powerful in Tuscany, and the legend says, it was founded by Charlemagne. Unfortunately, the rich archives of the abbey have been destroyed and we know little of its vicissitudes. However, the chapel, now flanking the imposing Romanesque building, with its simple ground plan of a nave and an apse, and with its coarse masonry, as well as the small **Crypt** divided by small columns supporting the cross vaulting without ribbing, certainly dates from the early Middle Ages. The monastic complex has been almost completely lost: there is just part of a wall with a mullioned window with three lights, perhaps part of the chapter-house. Testimony of the grandeur, is the imposing mass of the **Church**, with its bell tower. These date from the 12th century, and were built thanks to the monk Azzo dei Porcari, who is mentioned in a memorial tablet as the promoter and maybe even the architect. But the life of this monastic complex was brief. It had not yet been completed when it began to decline, and in 1291, in full decadence, it was ceded to the Guglielmiti. In 1462, it was suppressed by Pius II, and incorporated in the diocese of Montalcino. Shortly after, the bishop's apartment must have been built, in the right-hand women's gallery of the church. The building, one of the finest expressions of Romanesque monastic architecture, also features French and Lombard elements, and has some Pisan influence. The nave is divided from the two aisles by tall columns and four cruciform piers, and moves around the large apse into an ambulatory with three radiating chapels. The women's galleries run along over the aisles, opened by elegant mullioned windows with two lights, towards the inside. The nave and the apse are covered by a timber roof, and the aisles and ambulatory by cross vaults. The Carolingian chapel, set against the left side of the church and communicating with it, is balanced by the unfinished **Bell tower**; this has four stories with a cornice and blind arches. The **façade**, as well, does not seem finished: the remains of a portico with four blind arches, which should have been formed by cruciform columns set against the wall, demonstrate that the original project intended to have two portals, so the one now existing (probably one of the two) is a makeshift solution; the upper part of the façade also seems very poor, with only a mullioned window with two lights and a smaller one with one light. There is a large mullioned window with two lights on the apse rising above the ambulatory, crowned by a simple cornice on corbels. The radiating chapels, in the form of an apsidiole, fit into the ambulatory, are also crowned by a frame supported by corbels, but also have small columns on high basements set on the wall; in between the chapels, there are large mullioned windows with one light with an arched lintel that start from small columns. Rich is also the interior decoration of the ambulatory, with blind arches in the chapels and in the spaces between them. Corbel arches also decorate the top of the façade and the walls of the aisle; these also have pilaster strips and columns on the side of the building. The ornamental sculpture is of extremely fine quality, above all in the capitals and for one of these, the *Daniel in the*

The Abbey of Sant'Antimo, isolated in the silent Sienese countryside.

Lion's Pit, the artist has been named as the Master of Cabestany. The building material also lends a particular aspect to the structure: it is of travertine stone with varieties, improperly called alabaster or onyx that present golden, white and brown veining, at times almost transparent.

ABETONE (Pistoia)

One of the most famous winter resorts of the Tuscan Apennines is Abetone, 1388 metres high, provided with hotels and facilities for the great number of mountain lovers who come every year. It is crowned by an immense forest of firs, larches, Scotch firs, beeches, maples and birches, and it includes various localities, among which **Boscolungo, Consuma, Le Regine, Chirofonte** and **Serrabassa**. Numerous excursions and climbs can be made from the Abetone. The many fine ski-runs are often used for high level competitions.

Abetone, the ski-runs covered with snow.

ANGHIARI (Arezzo)

HISTORICAL SURVEY - *This pretty hill town lies in an area between the Sovara river and the Val Tiberina. The new city is in the lower part, while the old lies above, on a slope with enchanting views, churches and imposing palaces. The first information of Anghiari dates from the 11th century. At that time the town was the feud of the lords of Galbino, later it passed under the jurisdiction of the Camaldoli and the Tarlati of Pietramala. In 1440, the Tarlati were subjected to the Florentines and Anghiari fell under Florentine dominion.*

CHURCH OF ST. MARIA DELLE GRAZIE - This 18th-century church has a single linear **façade**. The Latin-cross **interior** has a single large nave. In the right wing of the crossing there is a *Deposition* by Domenico Puligo; in the left wing, a panel painting of the *Last Supper* by Giovanni Antonio Sogliani (1531); finally, behind the high altar, a splendid *Madonna of Mercy*, a polychrome glazed terra-cotta figure from the Della Robbia workshop.

CHURCH OF BADIA (OF ST. BARTOLOMEO APOSTOLO) - Its origins date from the year 1000, but the frequent restorations have changed the original structure. Inside, on the second altar to the left, there is an altarpiece that may be by Desiderio da Settignano; on the high altar, there is a lovely wooden *Crucifix* of the 15th century.

CHURCH OF ST. AGOSTINO - Built at the end of the 12th century, the church was enlarged in the 13th century, and numerous modifications were also made in the 15th century. The Romanesque **façade** has a fine Renaissance portal. The **interior**, with only one nave, houses two large 15th-century holy-water fonts in the entrance hall. On the high altar, there is the beautiful triptych of the *Madonna and Child with Angels and Saints* by Matteo di Giovanni; in the choir, the high relief in coloured terra-cotta of the *Adoration of the Shepherds*, dates from the 16th century.

CHURCH OF SANTA CROCE - This small 16th-century church contains a canvas of the *Virgin* by Passignano, on the first altar to the right, and on the high altar, a canvas of the *Discovery of the Holy Cross* by Carlo Dolci.

PALAZZO PRETORIO - This imposing palace dates from the 14th century and has fine decorations on the **façade**, and fragments of 15th-century frescoes in the antrium and in the **Chapel**. Today, it is the town hall.

84

MUSEUM OF POPULAR ARTS AND CUSTOMS OF THE UPPER VALLEY OF THE TEVERE - You will find this exposition in the ancient **Palazzo Taglieschi**, of Renaissance origins. It includes sculptures and detached frescoes from the churches of Anghiari and the Val Tiberina. Some of the famous artists, here represented, include the Della Robbia, Antonio Sogliani, Jacopo Vignali and Matteo Rosselli.

ENVIRONS - Various important religious buildings are situated only a few kilometres from Anghiari; such as **Santa Maria a Corsano** (13th century), with a charming Romanesque façade, and the **Country Church of Sovara** (10th century) with its splendid Romanesque forms.

ANSEDONIA (Grosseto)

Today's Ansedonia, once the Roman city of *Cosa*, dominates the marshy countryside of Orbetello and Mount Argentario. Destroyed by the Barbarians and reconstructed during the late Middle Ages, Ansedonia became prey to the Saracen pirates (10th century), finally falling into the hands of the Sienese. Not far from the old *Portus Cosanus*, you can see the so-called **Tagliata etrusca**, a remarkable example of the work undertaken by the hydraulic constructors of Rome, designed to prevent the silting up of the harbour. Near the **Spacco della Regina** is the **Torre della Tagliata**, once home of the musician Puccini. On the flat-topped hill above, you can visit the ruins of Cosa, which still preserve various constructions (**Capitolium, Acropolis, Temples, Forum** among others).

Ansedonia, a stunning picture of Puccini's Tower of the Tagliata.

AREZZO

HISTORICAL SURVEY - *Arezzo is the furthest inland important city of Tuscany. Surrounded by small mountain ranges, it is situated at the confluence of four fertile valleys: the Casentino, the Valdichiana, the upper Valdarno and the upper Valtiberina. This area seems to have been inhabited in prehistoric times, but it was not until the Etruscans came, that Arezzo rapidly became a flourishing and powerful centre. Together with Volterra, Roselle, Vetulonia and Chiusi, it was one of the most important Etruscan cities of the time, promising also help to the Latin against the king of Rome, Tarquinius Priscus. Under Roman rule, it continued to prosper until the 1st-2nd century AD, when, as a result of irresolvable internal struggles, it rapidly declined. In 575, it fell under Lombard dominion, and then passed to the Franks, until it became part of the Marquisate of Tuscany. In the 11th century, it was a free Commune, and a period of revival began with an incredible increase in building activity. The city contested Florentine supremacy over the region until it was finally defeated by the latter, in the battle of Campaldino, in 1289. Thus, Arezzo fell under the Florentine influence, together with many other cities, forming the Grand Duchy of Tuscany, first ruled by the Medici and then by the Lorraine.*

Arezzo, the apse of the Parish Church of St. Maria and the palaces of the Law-court and of the Secular Fraternity frame the central Piazza Grande.

MEDICEAN FORTRESS - Built in 1500, by Antonio and Giuliano da Sangallo on a previous structure, this fortress is situated near the **ruins of the Etruscan walls**. This powerful fortress with bastions has a star-shaped plan, and is characterised by a high escarpment on top of which there is a small stretch of vertical wall. From various points of the walls, you can admire beautiful views sweeping the horizon all the way to the Pratomagno and the Catenaia Alps.

CATHEDRAL AND DIOCESAN MUSEUM - The **Cathedral** was begun at the end of the 14th century. The **façade**, designed by Dante Viviani, is recent (1901-1914), and is in Gothic style. The portal on the right side is of particular interest: it is Romanesque-Gothic (1319-1337) and is sided by two truncated columns. The portal, also, is surmounted by a fine lunette, with a sculpture of the *Madonna and Child, Saints and Angels*, by Niccolò di Luca Spinelli. The spacious **interior**, divided in a nave and two aisles, but with no transept, has tall piers supporting the cross vaults. The great storied stained-glass windows by Guillaume de Marcillat, which flood the interior with coloured light, are particularly beautiful. Noteworthy, at the end of the right aisle, is the **Tarlati Chapel** (1334) with a fresco, the *Crucifix, the Madonna, three Saints with Ciuccio di Vanni Tarlati di Pietramala*, by Maestro del Vescovado. Near the portal, leading to the sacristy, there is the famous fresco of the *St. Mary Magdalene* by Piero della Francesca, and on the left, the imposing *cenotaph of*

Petrarca's House.

The Parish Church of St. Maria.

87

Arezzo, view of the Cathedral and its tall bell-tower.

Guido Tarlati, completed by Agostino di Giovanni and Agnolo Ventura, probably on a design by Giotto. The Cathedral also contains other outstanding works of art: in the right aisle, fragments of a 14th-century fresco, the *Madonna and Child Enthroned with Saints*, perhaps by Buffalmacco Bonamico; at the third altar, other frescoes, the *Madonna and Child* and *Six Scenes from the Lives of Saint Christopher and Saint James the Greater*, by an unknown painter of the second half of the 14th century. In the left aisle, have a look at the great Renaissance organ set on big marble brackets designed by Vasari; below, there is a fine wooden statue, the *Madonna and Child*, an Aretinian work of the late 1200s. Behind a magnificent wrought-iron gate, you will find the grand **Chapel of the Madonna del Conforto**, late 18th-century. It is formed by a nave, two aisles and an apse, and contains fine works of art, such as *Our Lady of the Assumption*, a terra-cotta figure by Andrea Della Robbia, and, respectively on the right and left altars, the *Crucifix with Saints Donato and Francesco*, also by Della Robbia, and a *Madonna and Child Enthroned*, from the Della Robbia workshop. The sacristy is seat of the **Diocesan Museum**, which contains fine works of art from the Cathedral and other churches in the diocese. The finest include: various detached frescoes by Spinello Aretino and Lorentino d'Arezzo, some terra-cotta sculptures attributed to Michele da Firenze and paintings by Bartolomeo della Gatta, Vasari, Santi di Tito and many others.

CHURCH OF ST. DOMENICO - The church was built after 1275, probably from a design by Nicola Pisano. Throughout the centuries it has often been restructured. In front of the lively **façade** there is a pronaos added later. The large Romanesque portal preserves, in the lunette, a fresco of the *Madonna and Child with Saints Francis and Donato*, by Angelo di Lorentino. The **Bell tower**, in Gothic style, is set next to the façade. The **interior**, with just one nave, is covered by a trussed timber roof, and contains noteworthy works, including a *Crucifix* and *Saints* by Parri di Spinello, to the right facing the façade, and fine *Stories of Saints Filippo and Jacopo*, by Spinello Aretino, to the left. On the right wall, there is *St. Catherine of Alexandria*, again by Parri di Spinello. Beyond a shrine, you will see the frescoes by Spinello Aretino picturing the *Madonna and Child with Saints* and *Lives of Saints Caterina and Lorenzo* (1408). The chapel to the right of the presbytery, contains a stone *Madonna and Child* of the 14th-century Sienese school. Nearby, on the right-hand wall, there is a *Crucifixion* by an unknown 14th-century Aretinian painter. The *tomb of Bishop Ranieri degli Umbertini*, dating from the 14th century, is on the left wall of the apse, and nearby, you will also see, a fresco of a *Madonna and Child with Angels*, of the same period. A splendid *Madonna and Child*, a fresco by Angelo di Lorentino, dating from the early 16th century, is on the left wall of the presbytery. To the left of the nave, there are a *Crucifix between Saints* and an *Annunciation*, perhaps by Giovanni d'Agnolo di Balduccio; a *Madonna with Child Enthroned* and two *Saints* by Giovanni d'Agnolo; *Scenes from the Lives of Saints Jacopo and Cristofano* by Spinello Aretino. An absolute masterpiece towers over the high altar: the *Crucifix* by Cimabue, an early work, one of the first examples of iconography of Christ.

PIAZZA GRANDE AND ITS PALACES - It is known also as *Piazza Vasari*, and is one of the most fascinating in Italy, with its unique layout, irregular and out of balance. Like all other old Italian squares, it is surrounded by fine palaces and tower houses. On the west side, see the imposing apse of the **Country Church of St. Maria**, with its arcades and loggias, followed by the severe **Palazzo del Tribunale**, from a design by Cerotti (17th-18th century). Then there is the **Palazzo della Fraternita dei Laici**, with a magnificent façade, a good mixture of Renaissance and Gothic style. Noteworthy, in the lunette, is the fine *Christ in Pietà with Madonna and St. Giovanni*, a detached fresco attributed to Spinello Aretino. Two niches contain the statues of *St. Donato* and *St. Gregorio*, by Bernardo Rossellino, who also worked on the final version of the façade in 1434. The big and beautiful **Palazzo delle Logge**, built from a design by Vasari,

Following pages:
Arezzo, scenes from the
Giostra del Saracino.

Arezzo, a beautiful view of the medieval buildings of Piazza Grande.

is on the upper part of the square. On the south-east, instead, there is a row of lovely **tower houses**, tall and narrow, the finest of which is the so-called **dei Lappoli**. The square is also the site of the famous *Giostra del Saracino*: this traditional event, dating from the Middle Ages, was revived only in 1930. The first Sunday of September, the four quarters into which the city is divided, participate in this competition. The *Saracen* (a giant wooden bust with a steel plate on his left arm and on the right one a long cut-o'-nine-tails with three leather covered lead balls at the end) is set up on the north-east corner of the square. Each quarter has a knight representing it, whose task is to strike the plate with his lance while dodging the whip that has began spinning wildly. It is a difficult and rather dangerous game, and it attracts enthusiastic crowds of Aretinians and tourists every year.

CHURCH OF ST. MARIA IN GRADI - Originally of the 11th century, this church was almost completely rebuilt with a 16th-century structure (1592). The **interior** has a fine early 18th-century wooden ceiling and stone and wood altars of the 17th century. A splendid cambered terracotta *Madonna del Soccorso* by Andrea della Robbia is on the first altar to the left. On the second altar to the left, there is a wooden 13th-century *Crucifix* and, to the right, a fresco of the *Madonna and Saints*.

CHURCH OF BADIA - Built in the 13th century by the Benedictines from Cassino, this church was enlarged in the 16th century according to a design by Vasari. The **façade** was done again in 1914, and only a large mullioned window with two lights and part of a side portal are original. The **interior** reveals a late 16th-century style and develops in a series of arches and cupolas. The dome was painted by Andrea Pozzo in 1703. Among the various important works, there is a fine fresco of *St. Lorenzo* by Bartolomeo della Gatta (1476) on the inside of the façade to the left of the portal; a *Crucifix* on panel by Segna di Bonaventura is in the crossing, and near the altar, there is a remarkable marble ciborium, attributed to the skillful hand of Benedetto da Maiano. Worth seeing, are also the works by Giovanni Antonio Lippoli, Baccio da Montelupo, Paolo de Matteis, Teofilo Torri and Vasari.

CHURCH OF THE SANTISSIMA ANNUNZIATA - The church was built between 1490 and 1517, from a design by Bartolomeo della Gatta. The **façade**, with its three doorways, is almost intact. The good fresco of the *Annunciation* above the right doorway is attributed to Spinello Aretino. The **interior** is divided into a nave and two aisles, separated by pilasters. The stained-glass windows are by Marcillat. Among the works of art this church contains, there is a *Mary appearing to St. Francis* by Pietro da Cortona, at the fourth altar on the right, and the beautiful high altar in polychrome marble with the precious 15th-century terra-cotta figure of the *Madonna and Child* in a shrine. Niccolò Soggi's *Adoration of the Child* (1522) is on the altar to the left of the presbytery. At the fourth altar on the left, there is a very fine *Annunciation* by Matteo Rosselli (1620) and, finally, by the first altar, there is a *Deposition* by Vasari.

CHURCH OF ST. FRANCESCO - This church was built during the 13th century, but what we see today is the result of a 14th-century renovation. It is made of stone and brick in Umbrian-Tuscan Gothic style. The **interior** has just one nave, typical of the Franciscan churches, with three square chapels at the end. A large **Crypt** spreads out under the nave, almost an underground church, divided into a nave and two aisles by piers, and covered with cross vaults. The church contains remarkable pieces of art, the most interesting of which is the cycle of frescoes to be found in the choir, called the *Legend of the true Cross*, painted by Piero della Francesca between 1453 and 1464; it is considered the most important art work of the 15th century, and among the finest in all the history of art. But the church also contains other good pieces of art: to the right of the choir, in the **Guasconi Chapel**, there are Spinello Aretino's frescoes; on the altar, there is a triptych of the *Assumption of the Virgin and Five Saints*, by Niccolò di Pietro Gerini. To the left of the choir, there is the **Tarlati Chapel**, housing a *Crucifixion* by Spinello Aretino, on the right wall, and on the left wall, an *Annunciation* by Luca Signorelli. Also in the church, works by Michele da Firenze, Lorentino d'Arezzo, Parri di Spinello, Niccolò Soggi and others.

Arezzo, the rough façade of the Church of St. Francesco.

CHURCH OF ST. AGOSTINO - This church was begun in 1257, and reconstructed between the 15th and 18th centuries. The simple linear **façade** is made of ashlars and has a fine rose window. Next to the building there is the high square **Bell tower** dating from the 13th century. The **interior** is Baroque, with 18th century modification.

PARISH CHURCH OF ST. MARIA - This pieve, or parish church, built between the 12th and 14th centuries, is one of the most interesting Romanesque buildings of the region. The beautiful **façade** clearly has some Pisan Romanesque influences. The small galleries, superimposed, are set on five arches on strong granite columns with capitals with smooth leaves, enclosing the main portal and the other two side doorways. The upper part has three tiers of galleries and the capitals, bases and columns are extremely varied in the design. In the lunette of the portal, there is a bas-relief of the *Madonna praying*, and on the sides *Angels* holding her gown and two smaller ones crowning her. The lunettes of the side doorways also have fine bas-reliefs. Elegant is also the high **Bell tower** (14th cent.). The **interior** is divided in a nave and two aisles and is covered by a trussed timber roof: at the back, under the presbytery, there is an austere **Crypt**.

PETRARCA'S HOUSE - The building, 16th-century, rises on a pre-existent medieval house, presumably owned by the Florentine notary, ser Pietro, father of Francesco Petrarca. According to tradition, the great man of letters was born here on July 20, 1304. Today the house is the seat of the **Accademia Petrarchesca** of letters, arts and sciences and preserves a prestigious **Library**.

93

Arezzo, Vasari's Archive.   *Arezzo, Roman Amphitheatre.*

PALAZZO DEI PRIORI - Built in 1333, the palace is today the town hall. To the left of the **façade**, there is a 16th-century relief of a *Madonna and Child* set under a small roof. A tall solid medieval **Tower** (1337) rises up next to it. **Inside**, there is a charming courtyard with portico and loggia. A 16th-century staircase leads to the landing, where you may see a *Madonna and Child Enthroned with Two Saints* by Lorentino d'Arezzo (1483), and above the stairs the effigy of *St. Francis with the Stigmata* by Angelo di Lorentino. Nearby, the magnificent **Wedding Room** (open on request) with two *Portraits of Cardinals* by Vasari. The **Council Hall** is on the same floor; it contains a *Crucifix* and a *Virgin and St. John* by Parri di Spinello, a *Crucifix and St. Donato* by Alessandro Forzori, and an interesting although badly preserved *Portrait of Pietro Aretino* attributed to Sebastiano del Piombo.

PALAZZO PRETORIO - The building is late 14th-century, but was modified during the 16th century. The **façade**, linear and with roof that juts out, is completely covered with armorial bearings of the Florentine vicars who governed the city. The **interior** houses many medieval and Renaissance sculptures, and is also seat of the big **Public Library**, with over 80 thousand volumes, incunabula, illuminated codexes, and other interesting documents.

VASARI'S HOUSE AND ARCHIVE - The House-Museum is completely covered with remarkable frescoes, the majority of which by Vasari, and summarises the late 16th-century Tuscan taste of art. The visit begins in the **Room of Fame**, in which the artist painted the *Allegory of Fame*, the *Four Arts* and the *portraits* of great artists, such as *Luca Signorelli*, *Spinello Aretino*, *Michelangelo*, and *Andrea del Sarto*. Then we come to the **Room of Apollo**, where Vasari continued his work portraying *Apollo and the Muses*, and which also contains a *St. Francis*, by Alessandro Allori and a *St. Girolamo* by Jacopo Ligozzi. The room that follows houses works by Tuscan school, and from here, a short corridor leads to the **Wedding Chamber**, with the ceiling decorated by Vasari. A small study, with a richly decorated ceiling opens off this room. Next to the study, there is the **Gallery**, containing Fra' Bartolomeo's famous *Christ in Judgement*.

ROMAN AMPHITHEATRE AND ARCHAEOLOGICAL MUSEUM - The **Amphitheatre** preserves 1st-century remains, and consists of large blocks of sandstone and brick in two orders of tiers. Of the amphitheatre has remained part of the stalls and some ruins of the ambulatory. The **Museum** is in the 16th-century **Monastery of San Bernardo**, and contains very interesting items dating back to prehistory and to the Roman, and especially, Etruscan period. It also exhibits a fine collection of pottery, that ranges from the 1st century BC to the 1st century AD.

STATE MUSEUM OF MEDIEVAL AND MODERN ART - The museum is installed in the antique **Palazzo Bruni-Ciocchi** in various rooms on two floors. The paintings here exhibited range from the 13th to the 19th century. The remarkable paintings, sculptures and art objects are arranged in 15 rooms. Among the most famous are an ecstatic *St. Francis* by Margaritone d'Arezzo, the beautiful *Madonna of Mercy* by Bernardino Rosselli, some interesting fragments of frescoes, the *Madonna with Angels and Saints*, probably by Luca Signorelli, the *Adoration of the Child* also by Signorelli, and also works by Rosso Fiorentino, Spinello Aretino, Parri di Spinello, Jacopo del Sellaio, Andrea della Robbia, Empoli, Alessandro Magnasco, Lodovico Carracci, Giorgio Vasari, Bernardino Pocetti, Alessandro Allori, Jacopo Vignali, Cigoli, all the way up to the 19th-century Macchiaioli, here represented by Giovanni Fattori, Telemaco Signorini, and many others. Noteworthy, also the collection of majolicas dating from the 13th to the 18th century.

ASCIANO (Siena)

The **walls** that surround the town were reinforced by the Sienese during the 14th century, when they ruled here, to repair the damages caused by an earthquake. The guard towers can still be seen, while the gates leading into town have been destroyed. The small centre contains interesting buildings, such as the **Palazzo del Podestà**, decorated with armorial bearings of the Sienese vicars, and **Casa Corboli**, at the beginning of *Sant'Agostino Street,* with rooms frescoed with *Allegories of the Four Seasons*, in a style similar to the ones of Ambrogio Lorenzetti in the Palazzo Pubblico in Siena. Remarkable, is also the **Collegiate Church of Sant'Agata**, dating back from the 11th century. Next to this, you will find, the **Museum of Sacred Art**, which houses fine examples of 14th and 15th-century painting and sculpture, including a *polypytch* by Matteo di Giovanni, a *St. Michael* by Ambrogio Lorenzetti (from the nearby Abbey at Rofeno) and a *Nativity* attributed to Sassetta. The **Church of St. Francesco**, lying a bit further on, is worthwhile seeing for its Gothic façade. At the opposite end of the town there is the **Church of Sant'Agostino**, Gothic structure, containing a *Madonna and Child*, part of a triptych by Matteo di Giovanni, now divided and in the Museum of Sacred Art.

ENVIRONS - **Rapolano Terme** was also involved in the disputes between the Sienese and Florentines. The 13th-century **Gate dei Tintori** opens in the ancient circular city walls. Interesting is the country **Church of St. Vittore** (13th century). There are two spas: **St. Giovanni** and **Antica Querciolaia**.

BAGNI DI LUCCA (Lucca)

The Commune of Bagni di Lucca is formed by various localities along the Lima and on the hills. Already during the Middle Ages, its waters were famous, but the **Spas** began to be built only from the 15th century. It was Domenico Bertini, who started this work in 1469, as you will see from a commemorative plaque at the entrance to the spas. In the 19th century, the spa was frequented by Ludovico di Borbone, and attracted the nobility and various personalities, including Byron and Shelley, who sojourned, during their stay, at **Casa Bonvisi**. To exalt the spa, the **Casino** was built in 1839 by Giuseppe Pardini. It was used until 1846, then transformed into a ball-room. Among the most interesting buildings for the visitor to see, there is the **Anglican Church**, situated in the suburb La Villa, where also is the Romanesque **Church of St. Pietro**.

BARGA (Lucca)

Although from a geographical point of view Barga was nearer to Lucca, since the Middle Ages it has been politically in conflict with this city, therefore becoming the heart of the Medici Grand Duchy in Garfagnana. The contrast with Lucca started when the Countess Matilde of Canossa granted Barga some privileges and autonomy that Lucca refused to recognise, and moreover, tried to eliminate more than once without success. The Florentines instead, succeeded in subjecting Barga, respecting its autonomy. The town still retains its medieval aspect, especially in the streets: the *Via di Mezzo* crosses the town lengthwise, while the *Via di Borgo* crosses it in its width; the *Via del Pretorio* and the *Via della Sper-*

anza follow the route of the ancient **city walls**; of these, only the gates remain: **Porta Manciana**, **Porta Macchiaia**, and **Porta di Borgo**. Many small alleys, called "carraie" connect the main streets. The religious buildings of the city are particularly interesting: first of all, the **Cathedral**, built and modified in various stages from the 9th to the 20th century. The decoration of the façade is typically Romanesque, with a double series of arches; the beautiful portal is flanked by two lions supporting columns and has an architrave with a low relief illustrating *Scenes of the Vintage*. Inside, there are many valuable art works: a 12th-century ambo, attributed to the sculptor Guido Bigarelli; 12th-13th-century holy-water fonts; elegant Della Robbia terra-cotta pieces; the great *Cross* by Giotto's school. The **Cathedral Treasure** - the access is from the left of the church entrance - contains splendid examples of 16th and 17th-century gold-work. Interesting are also the 16th-century **Church of San Francesco**, containing three fine Della Robbia altars, and the **Church of the Santissimo Crocifisso**, divided in a nave and two aisles, with 17th-century wooden stalls and high altar. Noteworthy are the many **palazzi** on the *Via di Mezzo*, *Via di Borgo* and *Via di Pretorio*, owned by important local families, and the **Palazzo Pretorio**, seat of the Florentine "podestà", and the nearby 14th-century loggia with their armorial bearings; under the loggia, is engraved the old markings of the units of measurement adopted by the city, the "statio" and the "braccio". Interesting for the visitor, is also the *Piazza del Mercato*, with a 16th-century loggia.

ENVIRONS

Among the Apuan Alps, in a beautiful and still untouched area called the "Massiccio delle Piane", and not far from Fornovalasco, lies the **Grotta del Vento**: a big cave that can be visited. Inside you may admire bare channels smoothed by the water, followed by spacious caverns, small pools and vertiginous abysses. All this, decorated by stalactites and stalagmites of incredible purity. You can reach the cave from Gallicano, from which, going up the valley of the Turrite Secca, you arrive to the village of Fornolovasco; from here, there is a carriage road of about two and a half kilometres that takes you right at the cave. Among the thick woods, **Coreglia Antelminelli** is situated on a hill. It contains the 13th-century **Church of St. Michele**, embellished on the façade with a sculpture by Matteo Civitali representing the titular saint. Also worth seeing is the **Town Hall**, of Renaissance construction, the old **Church of St. Martino** (9th century). The **Museum of plaster figurines** gives an idea of one of the oldest craft traditions of the Lucca area.

Barga, a pretty aerial view of the town.

BORGO SAN LORENZO (Florence)

It is the most important town of the Mugello and it contains a few interesting monuments; one of which is the **Palazzo del Podestà**, in *Piazza Garibaldi*, rebuilt in the 20th century, but of medieval origins, as one can see from the armorial bearings of the various Florentine podestà, who ruled here from 1290. Among the religious buildings, the finest is the **Church of St. Lorenzo**, begun in the 12th century, reconstructed later, and recently restored. Inside, you can admire a *Crucifix* by the school of Giotto, and a *St. Sebastian*, from Perugino's circle. Noteworthy is also the **Oratory of the Miracles** originally 18th-century, but built again after the earthquake in 1919. It houses a sculptured *Crucifix*, probably by the school of Giovanni Pisano. The visit will be incomplete without taking a look at the **parish churches** in the surroundings. This area, during the Middle Ages, was on an important connection route between Florence and Faenza; this is why you will find quite a few grand country churches, built during that period. They also served as refuge for the travellers. You should visit **St. Giovanni**, of the 11th century, with inside a Romanesque pulpit, and **St. Cresci**, 9th century, reconstructed after the year 1919.

ENVIRONS - In a pretty hilly landscape rises **Barberino di Mugello**, its 19th-century **Villa** was actually built on the site of a medieval manor-house, destroyed by the Florentines (14th century).

BUONCONVENTO (Siena)

This ancient stronghold of the Sienese Republic, at the confluence of the rivers Arbia and Ombrone, is known for the death of Emperor Henry VII, which occurred here on 24 August 1313. The ancient buildings, among which is the **Palazzo Pretorio,** create the typical atmosphere of a medieval village. The **Museum of Sacred Art of Val d'Arbia** exhibits various objects of ecclesiastic use. Among the artists whose works are exhibited here are Sano di Pietro, Girolamo di Benvenuto, Guidoccio Cozzarelli and Andrea di Bartolo di Fredi; in the 14th-century **Church of SS. Pietro and Paolo**, reconstructed during the 18th century, the visitor can admire the works of Giacomo Pacchiarotti and Matteo di Giovanni.

ENVIRONS - **Murlo** is a typical tiny Medieval village. It is built on an Etruscan site, and in the **Palazzo Vescovile** you will find the **Antiquarium of Poggio Civitate**, in which important Etruscan finds can be seen.

CALCI (Pisa)

The name of the town (Calci, means "lime") refers to the activity once carried out by its inhabitants. During Etruscan times, the people here already worked the stone from the near Mount Pisano, grinding it, firing it and transforming it into lime, which would have been then used for building. Around the year 1000, the ecclesiastic authorities, thanks to hereditaments and gifts, became the owners of most of the land in the area. This was when the remarkable **Parish Church of St. John the Evangelist and Ermolao Martyr** was built. The façade is in Pisan style, with two tiers of arcades and a majestic bell tower. Inside, admire the 12th-century baptismal font with many low reliefs. The **Charterhouse of Pisa** was founded in 1366. Its construction went on until the 17th century, through many difficulties: the work was also controlled by St. Catherine of Siena, worried for the slowness. This imposing complex of buildings includes a church, a guest house and a cloister. The entrance hall leads into a large square dominated by the monastery, with the fine marble **façade** of the church at the centre, with its long double flight of stairs. Further on from the entrance, there is the **Grand-ducal Hall**, decorated with charming stuccoes by Somazzi and frescoes by Pietro Giarrè. Nearby, there is the **Small Chapter-cloister**, by Lorenzo da Settignano, with a well at the centre dating 1614; on the wall, note the fine marble lavabo of the 18th century. From here you can reach the **Refectory**, embellished by a large *Last Supper*, a fresco by Bernardo Pocetti, and other frescoes by Pietro Giarrè. Continuing, you will arrive to the **Capter Chapel**, and

Calci, the great Charterhouse of Pisa.

then to the **Great Cloister**, enclosed in a beautiful circle of arches on marble columns. At the centre, there is a richly decorated *Fountain* dating from the 17th century. Nearby, also is the monks' cemetery.

The **interior** of the **Church** has a single nave divided crosswise by a partition of polychrome marble with a terra-cotta figure, *Christ falling under the weight of the Cross*, by Giuseppe Giacobbi. On the walls there are various frescoes: *Stories from the Bible* (17th-18th century) by the Rolli brothers, and under the dome, frescoes by Stefano Cassiani. The high altar is completely in marble and has a fine altarpiece, *The Certosa offered by St. Bruno to the Madonna* by Baldassare Franceschini, 'Il Volterrano.' On one side of the church there are a series of chapels; in the one dedicated to St. Bruno, there is a beautiful painting by Jacopo Vignali (*St. Brunone kneeling*). Finally, there is the Archive, containing a precious *Illuminated Bible* of 1169.

The Charterhouse, returned by the monks to the State in 1973, can be considered an important **Museum of Art and History**. In 1981 the interesting **Museum of Natural History** was moved here; inside there are collections of Zoology, Comparative Anatomy, Geology, Palaeontology, Mineralogy and Petrography.

ENVIRONS - Mention must also be made of **Uliveto Terme**, which can be found at about 6 km from Calci. It is famous for its bicarbonate-alkaline waters. Inside the spa there is the small Romanesque **Church of St. Martino**.

CAMAIORE (Lucca)

This very old village lies only a few kilometres from the sea. The small historical centre boasts various remarkable buildings.

COLLEGIATE CHURCH - It dates from the late 13th century. The **façade** is simple and has on one side a majestic **Bell tower** (1365). The **inside** preserves many evidences of the past: a fine wooden *Christ on the Cross* (14th cent.), on the third altar to the left; a *Communion of the Apostles* by Piero Dandini is at the end of the left aisle; and, an *Assumption* by Benedetto Brandimarte. The **Baptistery** contains a baptismal font dating from 1387.

CHURCH OF ST. MICHELE - It dates back to the 10th century, although it was heavily damaged during World War II. It was completely rebuilt trying to maintain its original structure.

ABBEY OF ST. PIETRO - Just outside Camaiore you will find the Benedictine Abbey of St. Pietro, dating from the 8th century. It has been reconstructed during the 11th century. The **interior** is divided into a nave and two aisles with a fine apse; it contains a great marble altar on which there is an ancient *Madonna of the Pietà*, and fragments of a 14th-century fresco picturing *Scenes of the Life of Santa Maria Egiziaca*, in the left aisle.

COUNTRY CHURCH OF SAINTS GIOVANNI BATTISTA AND STEFANO - It lies a few kilometres away from the village. This interesting Romanesque building has a tall **Bell tower** with three tiers of fine mullioned windows with two lights. The **interior**, a nave and two aisles, houses a *Roman sarcophagus* (2nd century AD) transformed into a baptismal font; also note the triptych of the *Madonna with Child and Saints* (1443) by Battista di Maestro Gerio.

CAMALDOLI (Arezzo)

At the beginning of the 11th century, St. Romuald, created in Camaldoli, a new congregation, reforming the Benedictine monachism. During the first centuries after the year 1000 this Order, together with the Vallombrosan Order, represented the new monastic spirituality. The congregation developed considerably and flourished particularly during the 12th-14th centuries, after which it declined and went through a series of separations that did not stop until 1935, when the surviving branches were reunited in a single order. The present **Monastery** of Camaldoli, was originally only a guest house of the above hermitage, later enlarged and reconstructed to house the monks. Frequently reduced after fires and pillages, the monastery today consists of a complex of buildings, dating from different periods, distributed around the church and its courtyard. Particularly interesting is the so-called **Cloister of Maldolo**, with arches carried on columns with 13th-century capitals; the **Ex-apartment of the superior-general**, with windows in Gothic style; the delightful small **Cloister**, enclosed on two sides by a portico on columns. The **Church**, with its single nave, is the result of an 18th-century Baroque "modernisation", precursor of the rococo. The interior, frescoed in the vaults and over the high altar by Sante Pacini (active from 1762 to 1790), also contains paintings by Vasari and Pacini. Other works of art can be found in the **Chapter Hall** and the other rooms, where the monks still live: a painting on canvas by Pomarancino, paintings by Lorenzo Lippi, Vasari and his school.

The **Hermitage of Camaldoli** stands on the very site where, in 1012, St. Romuald began his new monastic experience. The **Church of the Hermitage** is dedicated to *St. Salvatore* and dates from the 17th-18th century with a Baroque façade framed by two **Bell towers**. The interior has a reverse Egyptian cross plan, and is an elegant and lively example of Baroque. It contains painting and frescoes mostly of the 17th and 18th centuries. Various monastic quarters are grouped around the church, including the **Chapter House**, the **Library**, the **Refectory**, the **Oratory of St. Romuald**, the **Chapel of the Madonna of the Rosary**, the **Chapel of St. Antonio**. In these you may find some interesting pieces of art, such as a

Camaldoli, the fascinating ancient hermitage.

high-relief of the *Madonna and Child* in the style of Verrocchio by Tommaso Fiamberti, formerly attributed to Mino da Fiesole; and a large glazed terra-cotta figure in the style of Andrea della Robbia. The hermitage itself still retains its original layout formed by isolated small houses, the **cells**, arranged in parallel rows. Every cell is in fact a small house, with bed chamber, a study, an oratory, a woodshed and a washroom, and with outside a tiny porch. The cells are interesting for the history each of one has: they have either been built or have lived in by some famous person, after which they have been named. At the end of the road separating the small buildings, you will find the cell where Cardinal Ugolino dei Conti di Segni, later Gregory IX, stayed, at the beginning of the 13th century. It was transformed into a chapel in the 16th century. Next to it is the picturesque **Cemetery of the monks**. The Camaldoli monks have always had great respect for the forest. This explains their efforts to preserve this patrimony, and the result can be seen in the famous **"Forest of Camaldoli"**, which surrounds the hermitage and the monastery with its magnificent firs, larches, chestnuts, oaks, beeches and linden trees.

CAMPIGLIA MARITTIMA (Livorno)

Typical hill village looking over the Cornia plain and revealing wide views towards the gulf of Follonica and facing the Island of Elba. Ancient feud of the Della Ghelardesca, it belonged to Pisa and to Florence. In the Medieval district, next to the great stone **Tower**, there is the beautiful **Palazzo Pretorio**, studded with armorial bearings of the "podestà". Inside you can visit the **Permanent Mineral Exhibition**. The ruins of an ancient **Fortress** overlook the town, probably built in the 8th century, and rebuilt during the 12th and 13th centuries. Near the cemetery there is the isolated **Parish Church of St. Giovanni** (Romanesque, 12th century). The beautiful façade is covered with marble. The side portal is surmounted by a frieze depicting the *Hunt of Meleagro for the calidonio wild boar* (12th century).

ENVIRONS

On the road to San Vincenzo, it is worthwhile visiting the **Mineral Park of Rocca S. Silvestro** (guided tours), which allows the visitor to understand the ancient activity of mineral fusion of this area, through arranged visits, including the one to the mines and to the excavations of the Medieval village of Rocca S. Silvestro still in progress.

As already mentioned for Populonia and Vetulonia, the mineral area around the Metalliferous Hills has been inhabited since the Bronze Age; this because of its many ore bodies, including copper, lead, zinc and iron; and furthermore, there has always been mining activity in the area: by a wide net of exchanges, mostly by sea, the extracted minerals have supplied most of the metallurgic industry of central Italy for many centuries. Near the mines a certain number of workshops were opened: they either worked with the coarse mineral or were involved in the production of finished objects to be sold on the national and foreign market. In the **Val Fucinaia**, not far from Campiglia Marittima, **ovens** used for the working of copper have been found: they are made of two chambers separated by a horizontal plane with circular holes; the lower chamber was used to put the wood or charcoal to produce the heat, while in the upper chamber the mineral was heated in suitable containers (naturally, the material used to make the oven was heat resistant). It is quite probable, though, that the following stages of work, that is the real fusion, were done in ovens suitable for high temperatures and not in these found in Campiglia.

CAPALBIO (Grosseto)

It is a typical small medieval village. It sits on top of a hill covered with thick woods overlooking the coastal lake of Burano. The **city walls**, well preserved, with **Towers** and **walkable rounds**, are the boast of this locality. If you arrive here you should take a look at the following: the **Oratory of the Providence**, home to a fresco of Pinturicchio's school, the country **Church of St. Nicola**, where you can admire some fine frescoes; the **Sienese Gate** and the **Palazzo Collacchioni**. The latter was built in the place of the fortress of the Aldobrandeschi.

Campiglia Marittima, a delightful picture of the town in Maremma.

Island of CAPRAIA (Livorno)

This small volcanic island is only 8 km long and almost all covered with mountains. The vegetation is scarce, although there are a few extremely rare plants, studied by botanists and nature lovers, that here grow wild. The island was already known by the Greeks and Romans, but it was never very populated. In 1055, it was captured by the Saracens, subsequently by Pisa, Genoa, and after a series of events, it was annexed to the Kingdom of Sardinia, in 1815. The only settlement, today, is **Capraia** (300 inhabitants), a tiny village which seems stopped in time. The beautiful **Fort of St. Giorgio** was built by the Genoese, at the beginning of the 15th century, to defend the inhabitants from the Barbarian incursions. Near the village, there also is a penal settlement dating from 1872, which was closed at the end of the 1980s.

CARRARA (Massa Carrara)

HISTORICAL SURVEY - *The city, situated below the Apuan Alps, is separated from Massa by the hills of Candia. The stream Carrione flows through the city. Carrara is the city of the marble; its inexhaustible quarries have been known for over 2000 years. Today, Carrara is a rather modern city, although there are various important monuments in its historical centre. When it became property of the bishops of Luni after the fall of the Roman Empire, Carrara was already well-known. For a brief time, during the 12th century, it succeeded in proclaiming itself free Commune, but it was soon absorbed in Lucca's sphere of influence, and subsequently in that of the Spinola of Genoa, the Scaligera of Verona and the Viscounts of Milan. In 1442, together with Massa, it became part of the Marquesate of the Malaspina, and from then, the history of these two cities was the same.*

Carrara, "Andrea Doria as Neptune" (B. Bandinelli); in the background the Cathedral.

MARBLE MUSEUM - The exposition is in modern pavilions, and shows a wide range of marbles from the Apuan Alps, as well as a description of the various aspects of quarrying, transportation and working of the marble.

PALAZZO CYBO MALASPINA - It is situated in *Piazza Gramsci*. It is a 16th-century building, but it incorporates a pre-existing medieval castle, of which you can still see the **Keep**.
Various interesting finds are preserved in the pretty **courtyard**: these include sculptures from Luni and a famous Roman marble low relief (an altar), called the *aedicule of the Fontesecchi*. The palace, is also the seat of the **Academy of Fine Arts**, which preserves interesting marble antiquities and a small **Picture Gallery**. Among the most famous is the *aedicule of the Fantiscritti*, another fine Roman altar, this time with inscriptions of great artists of the past, such as Giambologna and Canova, who visited the quarry in which the altar was found.

THE CATHEDRAL - Next to the *Fountain of Andrea Doria*, also called *of the Giant*, a good art work by Baccio Bandinelli, you will find the Cathedral, begun in the 11th century, and completed two centuries later. It is completely covered with grey and white marble, and a part is in Romanesque style and the other in Gothic. The **façade** has a beautiful arcade with a Romanesque doorway sculptured with animal figures. Above, there is a splendid rose window inside a square structure, finely decorated. The 13th-century **Bell tower** is a fine example of Ligurian architecture. The **interior**, a nave and two aisles, is embellished with 12th and 13th-century frescoes, and some important sculptures, including, in the right aisle, a fine 14th-century marble group of the *Annunciation*, and the *sepulchre shrine of St. Ceccardo* (15th century). In the presbytery, there is a *Pulpit* in polychrome marble attributed to Domenico del Sarto and Maestro Nicodemo, and a finely carved marble altar. Next to the Cathedral, there is an **Oratory-Baptistery** that preserves a hexagonal basin carved from a single block of marble, and a baptismal font, both dating from the 16th century.

PIAZZA ALBERICA - The square is surrounded by interesting palaces, particularly the **Palazzo dei Conti del Medico** (17th century) and the **Palazzo delle Logge**. In the centre, is set the *Statue of Maria Beatrice d'Este*, sculptured by Pietro Fontana in 1826.

MADONNA DELLE GRAZIE - The Church of Madonna delle Grazie (17th century) is near *Piazza Alberica*. **Inside**, there are various works in marble, including an interesting high altar by Alessandro Bergamini.

CASCIANA TERME (Pisa)

Among the fertile hills that surround the river Cascina we come upon Casciana Terme, one of the most well-known spas in the province of Pisa. The fortunes of this spa, called by the Romans *Castrum ad Acquas*, date back to the interest of Matilde of Canossa. The original spa, now completely non-existent, was built by the Pisans during the 14th century. A park surrounds today's **spa**, which was rebuilt during the 1960s. Quite a number of treatments are available here: diseases of the veins and of the respiratory system, gastroenteric and hepatobiliary problems as well as those of the gynaecological organs find relief here. Most of the treatments available make use of hydrotherapeutics, possible in one of the spas provided with a swimming pool. The **St. Leopoldo Spring** has a plant for the pouring and bottling of this water.

CASTAGNETO CARDUCCI (Livorno)

This small town, famous for its medieval features, sits on top of a hill looking over the lowlands and the Pisan Maremma coast. It once belonged to the Della Ghelardesca, as testified by the **Castle** which has undergone many transformations; in the **Church of St. Lorenzo**, of medieval architecture, you will find fine frescos and an 18th-century *Madonna*. In the **Oratory of Crucifix**, 16th-century, there is a wooden *Crucifix* of Pisan school (15th century).

Castagneto Carducci, a sunny view of the ancient town centre.

ENVIRONS - Along the coast you will come upon the bathing establishments of **Marina di Castagneto** and **Donoratico**. The amusement park **"Cavallino Matto"** or *Parco Gulliver* is very popular, both for children and adults.

Reminders of the poet Carducci can be found at **Bolgheri**, where his **House** still is, and also the **Castle** of the Della Ghelardesca. A very attractive road, shaded by cypresses, famous for having been mentioned in one of Carducci's poems, leads to the octagonal **Church of St. Guido** (18th century), today beside the new *Aurelia Road*.

CASTELLINA IN CHIANTI (Siena)

The **Tumulus of Montecalvario**, with the four hypogeum tombs dating from the 7th and 6th centuries BC, makes archaeologists assume the existence of an important Etruscan centre, which recent excavations seem to have identified. Moreover, various archaeological and toponymical finds bear witness to the diffusion, around all this territory, of Etruscan and Roman settlements: finds dating from the oriental period at Rèncine, the tombs, similar to the ones in Populonia, at Vignale, and the many land names that derive from Latin names (Grignano, Ligliano, Cispiano, Cignano, Cagnano, and many others). Castellina, like many other places in the Chianti area, entered the Florentine sphere of influence during the second half of the 13th century. It became part of the so-called "League of Chianti", and later was the head of a "Terzi" (third: the League was divided into three parts), the part of Chianti towards the Valdelsa. The Chianti, being on the border of the districts of Siena and Florence, was contended by these two since the 12th century. The Florentine Republic, however, already in 1176, had taken possession of most of the region. Castellina is situated on the ancient ridge road leading to Siena, therefore in a strategic point for Florence in the conflict with Siena. This fact gave importance to this town, that later became chief town of all the territory of the League. In 1397, the castle "strong in site but weak in art" was sacked and burnt by the soldiers of the Duke of Milan, allied with Siena. Therefore, in 1400, Florence decided to build new **fortifications** - the imposing defensive structures whose remains still enclose part of the town, in an irregular hexagon form. Defensive towers were built along the walls at regular intervals (many are still standing, although without the top part). On the southern side, on the highest part of the built-up area, the walls were interrupted with a powerful keep, rectangular in plan, restored about fifty years ago. Underground routes ran all along the perimeter of the fortification, as you still can see from the route by the north part of the wall, called the "street of the vaults". Two gates (both destroyed), were set at one end and the other of the road that ran in the middle of the town, on which there are various late Renaissance palaces (**Palazzo Bianciardi**, **Palazzo Segni-Straccali**). The neo-Romanesque **Parish Church** is a modern construction and it houses a detached fresco of the *Madonna Enthroned* attributed to Bicci di Lorenzo. The territory of Castellina is dotted with the remains of many medieval castles, once owned by important feudal families or that may have played a leading role in the defences of the Florentine Republic. One of these, is the picturesque ruins of the **Castle of Monternano**, that testifies the power of the noble Squarcialupi family, whom the Florentines managed to weaken only in the 13th century. A few ruins, now part of a farm house built later, is all that remains of the great fortification of **Rèncine**, built by the Florentines to oppose the strong Sienese castle of Monteriggioni. A remarkable tower, on the top of a hill on the Pesa river, is all that is left of the **Castle of Grignano**, mentioned since 998 in the donation made by the Marquise Ugo to the Abbey of San Michele in Marturi (today Poggibonsi). Not much is left either of **Pietrafitta**, another castle mentioned in the same document. **La Leccia** was also an important stronghold, and its remains have been incorporated in an imposing villa-farmhouse. The **Parish Church of Sant'Agnese** was also fortified, and was one of the three plebeian churches of the Terzo of Castellina. The church has a nave and two aisles and three apses, and was entirely rebuilt shortly after the Second World War. Part of its original structure, including a doorway, can still be seen on the right side. Its fortification consisted in a strong tower, still existing though in ruins, near the apses. Inside, you may admire a tempera panel by Bicci di Lorenzo of the *Madonna and Child with Saints*. The **Parish Church of Santa Caterina in Lilliano** is a much simpler building, with a single nave; most of it was rebuilt but it still has its Romanesque façade with rows of "alberese". The third Parish church included in the Terzo of Castellina was **St. Leolino in Conio**, in the Fiesole diocese. The church has been often restructured, and only around the presbytery it still preserves its Romanesque apse and two arcades (today closed) which divided the inside into a nave and three aisles. In addition to these Romanesque churches and the castle mentioned, the hills of the Chianti, sloping gently to the Valdelsa and serving as watersheds for the neighbouring valleys of the Pesa and the Arbia, show the visitor many extraordinary examples of country architecture, with its beautiful farmhouses, often built on the site of medieval ruins (see Collelungo, Palagione, La Rocca, La Torre, and others).

A piece of the coast near Castiglioncello.

CASTELNUOVO BERARDENGA (Siena)

The area around Berardenga, took its name in the Middle Ages from Berardo, a nobleman who had his territories here. Siena began to exercise its power on this land during the 12th century, and in 1366, the General Council of the city decided to build a castle that was to become the chief town of the Berardenga, today's Castelnuovo. The visitor can still see the **Tower** and parts of the **Walls**, part of the defensive structure built by the Sienese. The more recent complex of the **Villa Chigi Saracini**, with its grandiose park, contrasts with the medieval part.

CASTIGLIONCELLO (Livorno)

Pleasant bathing resort on the Livorno coast in the middle of a charming environment with sun, sea and pine woods. The rocky and sometimes high shore line is full of pretty little inlets, that together with the many tourist facilities make Castiglioncello a perfect tourist and bathing attraction. The **Museum of Archaeology** preserves many funerary finds of the Etruscan period (3rd-1st centuries BC).

ENVIRONS - **Rosignano Marittimo**, chief town of the Commune, dominates from the top of a panoramic hill. The ancient village surrounds the 13-14th-century **Castle**. In the lowlands, near the coastline, there is the modern town of Rosignano Solvay, which was built and grew around the chemical plant.

CASTIGLIONE DELLA PESCAIA (Grosseto)

Famous seaside resort on the Maremma coast, Castiglione has lovely beaches and cliffs. The picturesque **Port-canal** is always crowded with fishing boats and yachts. Also beautiful is the pine-forest, surrounding the town and that reaches the sea, in many points. On a hillside, enclosed in solid walls, the old medieval town of **Castiglione Castello** is dominated by the fine **Aragonese fortress** of the 14th-15th century.

CASTIGLIONE D'ORCIA (Siena)

Charming village up on the hills, in the so-called "Sienese Maremma", with a feudal past (Aldobrandeschi of Santa Fiora, Salimbeni, Riario) and submissions to Siena and Florence. The **Church of Santa Maria Maddalena** contains a *Virgin with Child and Angels*, by Vecchietta, who was born in this village, and a *Madonna* of the school of Lippo Memmi. The country **Church of SS. Stefano and Degna** has a 15th-century façade, although the basic structure is Medieval. Inside there are many Sienese frescoes and a work by Pietro Lorenzetti: a *Madonna with Child*.

ENVIRONS - The centre of **Rocca d'Orcia** has a very medieval setting. It is situated below the 14th-century **Fortress of Tentennano**, built by the Salimbeni. Paintings of the 14th and 15th centuries can be seen in the **Church of St. Simeone**.

CASTIGLION FIORENTINO (Arezzo)

The origins of this small town are early medieval, as you can see from the **fortified walls**, the 14th-century guard towers and the narrow winding alleys. Since the 10th century, it was strategically important for its position: dominating the valley that goes from the Valdichiana to the Trasimeno. For this reason, it passed alternately in the hands of the Aretinians, the Florentines and the Perugians. The art works that you will find in Castiglion Fiorentino date from the Middle Ages to the 17th and 18th centuries: the **Keep** is the oldest building, dating from the 12th century, while the **Church of St. Francesco**, Romanesque-Gothic, is from the 13th century. The **Palazzo Comunale** is a 16th-century building, restructured at the beginning of this century, the **Picture-gallery** is on the first floor and it houses numerous works of art from the city churches. Worth mentioning is the *reliquary bust of Saint Orsola*, 15th-century, in silver and enamel; the panel painting of the *Madonna and Child* by Taddeo Gaddi; and the various paintings by Luca Signorelli and Bartolomeo della Gatta. Finally, the visitor should also see the **Church of the Madonna of the Consolation**, built during the 16th and 17th centuries. Its design is attributed to Antonio da Sangallo il Giovane. The **Collegiate Church of St. Giuliano**, finished in 1850, is in Neo-classic style. Inside there are panel paintings by Lorenzo di Credi, Segna di Bonaventura and Bartolomeo della Gatta.

CETONA (Siena)

It is a beautifully preserved Medieval village in the Valdichiana inhabited since prehistory, as proved by the rupestrian sites of Belverde and the many caves open on the sides of Mount Cetona. This village is characterised by the elliptical city plan winding round the 12th-century **Fortress**. In the **Collegiate Church** (13th century), there is a painting attributed to Pinturicchio. In the **Church of Sant'Angelo** there is a 14th-century wooden *Virgin*. Boast of Cetona is the **Civic Museum of Prehistory of Mount Cetona**, in which a chronologically displayed exhibition, completed with explanatory posters and dioramas, allows the visitor to understand the area's history, particularly of the Neolithic and Palaeolithic age.

CHIANCIANO TERME (Siena)

Big spas, specialised in treatments for liver complaints, lie in the fertile hills that divide Valdichiana from Val d'Orcia. The spas are situated in the modern part of the town, where there also are many hotels, wide streets and parks. The spas are: **Acqua Santa** (*Parco delle Fonti*), **Fucoli, Sillene** and **Sant'Elena**. The town boasts a history that goes all the way back to the Etruscans and Romans; later it was contended by Florence and Siena: the latter, in the 13th century, managed to rule. You can still see parts of the **City walls** and the **Gates**, some of which were rebuilt. Of interest is the 13th-century **Palazzo del Podestà** decorated with 15th- and 16th-century armorial bearings; the nearby **Palazzo dell'Arcipretura**, built in the 18th century, that houses the **Museum of Sacred Art** on the first floor, with fine Sienese and Florentine works. Among the religious buildings, you should see the **Collegiate Church of San Giovanni Battista**, originally Romanesque but restructured in the 19th century in Neo-classic style; and the **Madonna della Rosa**, a Greek-cross building from a design of Baldassare Lanci, dating from 1585; the **Church of Santa Maria della Stella**. An Archaeological Park and an Etruscan Museum are in preparation (Villa Simoneschi barn).

CHIUSI (Siena)

HISTORICAL SURVEY - *Situated in the hills that close the Valdichiana to the south, present-day Chiusi is a city that does not adequately express its antiquity and the importance it once had. Probably of Umbrian origins, to which the name* Chamars, *how Livy called it, may be connected,* Clusium - *its Latin name, which probably derived from Etruscan - was the most famous town of northern Etruria. In fact, to Porsenna, one of its kings, are attributed legendary feats against Rome, in the years around 520 BC. Chiusi reached its greatest splendour between the 7th and 6th centuries BC, as proved by the richness and quantity of necropolises in the surrounding area. The position of the city, on a tufa hill dominating the valley of the Clanis (Chiana), certainly is the reason for its fortune. The Chiana river was at that time a tributary of the Tiber, and as it was navigable, it favoured communication with the south. The wealth of Chiusi was based on agriculture, being the area extremely fertile. Therefore, although never reaching the wealth of the coastal cities based on trade, the economy of Chiusi was always steady. Chiusi was also in the middle of a variety of cultural influences, thanks to the communication routes that linked the town to the west, with Roselle, Populonia and Vetulonia, through the valleys of the Orcia and the Ombrone rivers, and with southern Etruria through the valley of the Paglia, all the way to lake Bolsena. During the Roman period, Chiusi found itself on the Via Cassia,*

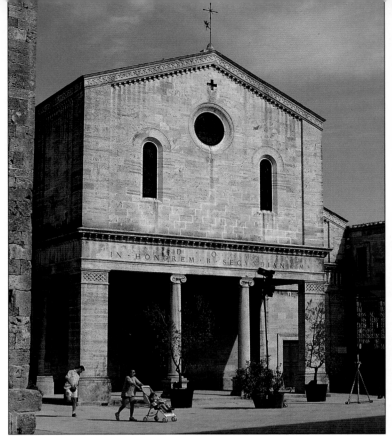

Chiusi, the elegant façade of the Cathedral.

which connected Rome with Arezzo and Fiesole, and later with Florence, Pistoia and Lucca. Unfortunately, not much remains of the Etruscan city which was on the site of modern Chiusi: our knowledge comes from the necropolises plundered of their finest golden and bronze objects since antiquity. The urban structure of Chiusi still retains traces of the Roman presence: in the "decumanus" (east to west), corresponding to the second part of Via Porsenna and Via Arunte, and the "cardo" (from south to north) on the first part of Via Porsenna and continuing in Via Baldetti and Via Lavinia, reaching the gate which has the same name.

ETRUSCAN NATIONAL MUSEUM - It is arranged chronologically, giving the visitor a thorough idea of Chiusi's ancient history. You will see prehistory finds, which are proof of the early settlements in the area, and fine examples of oriental art, such as the *Gualandi cinerary urn*, and the typical canopic vases. These contained the ashes of the deceased, and are composed by an ovoid body and a lid in the shape of a rudimental human head (the head is not a portrait, although one can think it is). The Archaic period is represented by examples of the local production of Bucchero - a black pottery - known as "bucchero pesante", and stone cinerary urns. The museum also contains Hellenistic, Roman and Lombard material, as well as imported Greek pottery. At the museum you can also make reservations for the visit to the necropolis.

CATHEDRAL - In the centre of the town, in the square, which bears the same name, lies the most important monument, the Cathedral dedicated to *Saint Secondiano*. The origins of the church are early Christian: it was founded in the 5th century by the bishop of Florence. It was rebuilt during the 12th century, and heavily restored at the end of the 19th. The large basilican **interior**, is divide in a nave and two aisles, all of these ending in an apse and divided on each side by ten arches. The columns and the capitals supporting the arches come from local Roman edifices.

The rough dosserets over the capitals reveal Byzantine influence. The church has a trussed timber ceiling. The **façade** (restructured) is preceded by a Doric portico with a caisson ceiling. The **Bell tower**, on the left, dates from the Romanesque period, although the ending part is late 16th-century. Among the various works of art inside the church and chapter hall, noteworthy are the twenty illuminated codexes that come from the Monastery of Monte Oliveto Maggiore, and of which some are attributed to Sano di Pietro and Liberale da Verona.

PORSENNA LABYRINTH - From the **Cathedral Museum** you can reach this remarkable system of underground passages, documented from the Etruscan age when it was used as a water channel, and then also used by the Romans. The **monumental Cistern** (1st century BC) situated under the streets at the base of the bell tower, is believed to have been a water supply for the *Collegium Centonariorum* (the "fire brigade" of those times). The excavations that began in the 1920s, carried out by the local archaeological group, enabled the opening of this interesting structure in 1995.

CHURCHES AND PALACES - Various religious and civil buildings in Chiusi stand as witnesses to its past. Among the religious ones, mention must be made of the **Church of Santa Maria della Morte**, 13th century; the former **Medieval Hospital**, of which you can still see the loggia; and, especially, the **Church of St. Francesco**, founded in the 13th century, which has Romanesque elements on the façade and material taken from classical monuments. The **Clock Tower**, in *Piazza XX Settembre*, was rebuilt in the 19th century, when the **Town Hall** was enlarged. You will also find interesting edifices along the *Via Porsenna*, such as the **Palazzo Petrozzi**, attributed to Vignola; the 15th century **Palazzo Bonci Casuccini**; and other 14th century buildings, as for example **Palazzo dei Della Ciaia**.

THE WALLS - Chiusi's city walls, today only in part still visible, were irregular, adapting to the land on which they were built. To the north there is the **Lavinia Gate**, with a round arch, which practically is the only gate left. On the western part of the walls, there is a natural projection containing what is left of the **Fortress**, with two **Towers**. The bell towers of the Cathedral and of Santa Maria della Morte were built using the towers from the city walls.

ENVIRONS

The **Torre di Béccati questo** (meaning, *Tower of You take this*), today partially underground, lies in the environs, opposite, in the southern part of **lake Chiusi**, to the **Torre di Béccati quello** (meaning, *Tower of You take that*), Perugian, not far from Santa Mustiola. The most interesting sights to see in this area, obviously are the ancient findings. The most important are concentrated towards the north: the **Tomb della Pellegrina**, with niche-shaped cells set along a corridor and a number of urns with mythological figures; the **Tomb of the Monkey**, interesting for its paintings; the **Tomb of the Grand Duke**, with a single chamber; the **Tomb of the Well**. Towards the east, instead, there is the **Tomb Bonci Casuccini**, with two chambers and the **Tomb delle Tassinaie**, a later and single chamber tomb. Noteworthy are also the **Catacombs of Santa Mustiola**, which can be dated from the 3rd century AD, like those of **Santa Caterina**, and were brought to the light during the 19th century.

COLLE DI VAL D'ELSA (Siena)

HISTORICAL SURVEY - *Colle, situated in the centre of an area already settled in Etruscan and Roman times, was an independent Commune in 1200, although allied to Florence. In the middle of the 14th century, it was subjected to Florence and, as Siena declined, Colle went through a period of peace and economical prosperity, based on the industries that exploited the hydraulic energy of the Elsa river. The structure of the historical centre of Colle consists of an upper part (Colle Alta) and a lower part (Colle Basso), that developed in the plains during the Middle Ages. The lower part has obviously been influenced by the lay of the territory on which it was built, stretching out along the ridge of the hill and divided into the "Castello" and the "Borgo".*

CASTELLO - The part of the town known as Castello, situated in the eastern part and descending steeply down the hill, develops on a longitudinal line. On this line, lies the principal square with the **Cathedral**, built on the site of an ancient parish church, the **Palazzo Pretorio** and the **Palazzo Comunale**. Further east, the road meets another square, with the **Parsonage of St. Maria**, which may have been the old church of the castle of Piticciano. Not far from here, there is an imposing tower-house, traditionally thought to be the **House of Arnolfo di Cambio**. Moreover, there are many traces of medieval architecture, among which, some smaller palaces recalling the Sienese style. Minor streets, running lower down, flank the main street and are connected by lanes. Large parts of the **walls**, that used to surround the Castello, can still be seen, although often only the lower parts remain. Nothing is left of the gates: the eastern gate has been replaced by a Renaissance bastion, while where the western one was, there is **Palazzo Campana**, lying across the street, which Vasari says to be designed by Giuliano, the son of Baccio d'Agnolo.

BORGO - Through Palazzo Campana and crossing the bridge, the street reaches **Borgo di Santa Caterina**. Borgo is the natural extension of Castello on the crest of the hill, westwards. It develops essentially along the continuation of the road that begins with the Renaissance gateway called **Porta Nuova** (or *Volterrana*), attributed to Giuliano da Sangallo, and flanked by two short cylindrical towers, with sloping bases.

COLLE BASSO - From Borgo, a steep road, running downhill from the **Church of Santa Caterina**, joins it to Colle Basso. This part of the town, developed on the plain during the Middle Ages, has always had a more regular urban layout. Only the southern part of the **City walls** remain, on which opens the **Guelph Gate**, on the ancient *Via Maremmana*. The urban construction of modern Colle is all around this part of the old historical centre. Finally, to complete the lower part of the town, there are the **Monastic Complexes of Sant'Agostino** and of **San Francesco**. The first was built in the plain, in a vast square, which probably also served as market place, in front of the Guelph Gate. The second, rose on a small high ground, north of Borgo, to which it was joined by a daring viaduct. Its position seems to want to connect the city with the surrounding countryside.

Colle Val d'Elsa, the Porta Nuova (or Volterrana).

CATHEDRAL - The various monuments and many works of art are the proof of the intense life in Colle. The most important monument certainly is the Cathedral, a simple late mannerist building, designed by Fausto Bugliesi of Montepulciano. The **façade** was finished only in the 19th century. It is laid on a Latin cross and divided in a nave and two aisles, with side chapels and a large transept. Since construction it was embellished with a number of paintings by Nasini, Manetti, Maratti and others. Later paintings include the *Nativity* by Poppi, and the much more famous *Communication of Saint Mary Egyziaca* by Pollaiolo. Noteworthy also the lectern in bronze by Tacca, the bronze *Crucifix* by Giambologna and the marble *pulpit* (1465), probably by Benedetto da Maiano. Interesting is also the chapel, called **Cappella del Chiodo**, on the right side of the transept: it has a 15th-century wrought-iron gate and preserves a reliquary of the Cross in a marble tabernacle dating from the late 15th century.

OTHER CHURCHES - In Colle Alto, as well as the **Parsonage of Santa Maria** - inside which you may admire an altarpiece by Pier Francesco Fiorentino - there are other interesting religious buildings: the **Conservatory**, founded in the 16th century by the Usinbardi, and the annexed **Oratory of St. Pietro**; the **Church of St. Caterina**, with a fine *Pietà*, dating from the first half of the 17th century, by the "Cieco di Gambassi". In Colle Basso, see the small **Church of the Spugna**, built in the 18th century to remember the famous abbey.

PALACES AND MUSEUMS - In Colle, you can also see worthy examples of civil architecture: two of these are in *Piazza del Duomo*: **Palazzo Pretorio** (next to the Cathedral, said to have been built in 1365) and, facing it, **Palazzo del Popolo**. In addition to these, there are many private palaces still retaining their architectural elements. Most of these can be seen along the main street of Castello, such as the old **Hospital of Colle**. Examples of post-medieval architecture, are present on the road that leads from Borgo to **Palazzo Campana**, after which it is named, and where the **Municipal Palace** is also located. In Colle you may also visit various small museums that exhibit interesting works of art. The **Civic Museum** contains a late 15th-century altarpiece attributed to Pier Francesco Fiorentino, an *Adoration of the Shepherds* by Rutilio Manetti, and a *Madonna and Child* by the school of Perugino. In the **Museum of Sacred Art**, there are frescoes attributed to the Lorenzetti brothers and Cennino Cennini, a *Deposition* by Cigoli, a triptych attributed to Bartolo di Fredi, a panel painting attributed to Luca di Tommè, the so-called "Chalice of Saint Albert" (Florentine gold work of the 15th century) and a number of illuminated choir books from the convent of St. Lucchese, near Poggibonsi. Palazzo Pretorio houses the **Archaeological Museum Bianchi-Bandinelli**. It exposes archaeological finds from various Etruscan tombs of the surroundings, dating from the 7th century BC to the Roman period. Moreover, there is a permanent iconographic exhibition of the works of Arnolfo di Cambio, the most renowned man of Colle di Val d'Elsa.

CORTONA (Arezzo)

HISTORICAL SURVEY - *This very old city lies about 500 meters above sea level, and the ancient quarter has remained almost intact. Its historical centre can be considered as the most interesting in Tuscany. Crowds of tourists come here every year, especially for the beauty of its churches, palaces and squares. Cortona was already inhabited during Etruscan times, and in the 4th century BC was allied with Rome. During the first centuries of the Christian era, it was taken over by the Goths, and in the 13th century it became a free Commune, only to be occupied by Arezzo at the end of the same century. After various political changes, that did not however influence its economy and artistic development, the city passed under the rule of the Casali family. In 1411, it entered the dominion of the Florentine Republic, and in the following centuries was part of the Grand Duchy of Tuscany.*

CATHEDRAL - Probably built on the remains of the pre-existing Romanesque Church of *Santa Maria*, the cathedral was designed and realised by the great Giuliano da Sangallo. The severe **façade** is in stone; in front of the right side there is a Renaissance porch. The **Bell tower**, next to the façade, built in 1566 by Francesco Laparelli, has two tiers of mullioned windows with two lights. The **interior**, a nave and two aisles, was also probably designed by Sangallo, although it was heavily restructured during the 18th century. The Cathedral preserves various interesting works of art: in the apse, there is a fine *Madonna and Saints* by Cigoli; the *Crucifix* and the *Doubting Thomas* by Signorelli's school; and the *Madonna and Saints* by Alessandro Allori. In the last chapel on the left aisle, there is the *Communion of the Virgin* by Salvi di Castellucci, and on the left wall, a fine marble ciborium by Ciuccio di Nuccio (1491).

CHURCH OF ST. MARIA NUOVA - Vasari was involved in the construction of this late Renaissance edifice.
The **interior** is on a Greek-cross plan, and it houses, on the first altar to the right, a *Nativity of the Virgin* by Alessandro Allori, and on the second altar, a fine *Annunciation* by Empoli. Noteworthy is also the high altar by Bernardino Radi.

CHURCH OF ST. FRANCESCO - It is one of the best churches in Cortona. It dates from the middle of the 13th century and the **façade** is simple and linear, with a remarkable portal.
The **interior** contains fine works of art including, on the fourth altar to the right, a *St. Anthony of Padua*, a beautiful painting by Cigoli; a *Nativity* by Raffaele Vanni is on the fifth altar to the right; a touching *Annunciation* by Pietro da Cortona, on the third altar to the left; and a dramatic *Martyrdom of St. Lucia* by Sagrestani, on the second altar to the left. The precious marble tabernacle (1629) by Bernardo Radi, on the high altar, contains a *Reliquary of the Holy Cross*.

CHURCH OF ST. NICCOLÒ - This pretty church, with a Ionic porch in front of the **façade**, was built during the 15th century. The rectangular **interior** has a remarkable 18th century coffer ceiling. Among the works of art, you must not miss the *Madonna and Child with Saints*, a fresco by Luca Signorelli, which you will find on the left wall.

SANCTUARY OF ST. MARGHERITA - This interesting little church dates from 1856. In the **interior**, a nave and two aisles, you will find statues of *Saints* on the piers; in the chapel to the right of the presbytery, there is a 13th-century wooden *Crucifix*. The silver urn, on the high altar, contains the mortal remains of Saint Margaret. Tabernacles of the *Via Crucis*, with mosaics by the modern artist Severini, line the way that leads to the Sanctuary.

CHURCH OF ST. DOMENICO - The building, with its simple ashlar **façade** and the fine Gothic portal, dates from the early 15th century; admire the magnificent fresco of the *Madonna and Child between Dominicans* by Fra' Angelico.
The **interior** has a single nave and houses remarkable works of art: a wooden 16th-century *Crucifix*, on the first altar to the right; a *Madonna and Child with Angels and Saints* by Luca Signorelli, in the right apse; a large triptych of the *Coronation of the Virgin* (1402) by Lorenzo di Niccolò Gerini, on the high altar; and on the third altar to the left, an *Assumption* by Palma il Giovane.

CHURCH OF ST. AGOSTINO - This small religious edifice dates from the late 13th century, and underwent numerous restorations during the 17th century. **Inside**, you may admire a fine *Madonna and Saints* by Empoli, on the second altar to the right; and another *Madonna and Saints* by Pietro da Cortona, in the chapel to the left of the presbytery.

CHURCH OF ST. FILIPPO - It is a 18th-century well proportioned edifice by the architect Antonio Iannelli. The **interior** has a Greek-cross plan and houses, on the altar in the left transept, a *Holy Family with two Saints*, a masterpiece by Piazzetta.

PALAZZO COMUNALE - This imposing building dates from the first half of the 13th century. Before the **façade**, surmounted by a solid tower, there is a stairway. Interesting **inside**, is the **Council Hall**, with a big 16th-century fireplace.

PALAZZO PRETORIO - It dates from the thirteenth century, although the rough façade was added in 1613. The inside courtyard, with the elegant loggia, is pretty to see. The edifice, once *Palazzo Casali*, is the seat of the **Museum of Etruscan Art**, the **Public Library**, the **Public Historical Archive** and the **Etruscan Academy**.

MUSEUM OF ETRUSCAN ART - It contains an important collection of Etruscan, Roman and Egyptian finds, together with numerous paintings and objects dating from the 13th to the 19th century. Among the most interesting, you should see the bronze lamp of Etruscan manufacture (5th century BC); the beautiful *Crucifix*, a panel painting; the Egyptian funerary boat; the charming Etruscan *statuettes* in bronze; and the fine paintings by Niccolò di Pietro Gerini, Pinturicchio, Ghirlandaio, Bicci di Lorenzo, Piazzetta, Pietro da Cortona, Empoli, and Alessandro Allori.

DIOCESAN MUSEUM - Its seat is in the former **Church del Gesù**, in front of the Cathedral. There are very interesting collections, especially those of the Tuscan school. Here, you can admire one of the masterpieces of Fra' Angelico, the *Assumption*. Also noteworthy, the big *Crucifix* on panel by Pietro Lorenzetti; the remarkable triptych of the *Madonna and Child with four Saints* also by Fra' Angelico; the *Madonna and Child* of the school of Duccio da Buoninsegna; the *Assumption* by Bartolomeo della Gatta; and other works by Lorenzetti, Sassetta, Signorelli and Giuseppe Maria Crespi.

MEDICI FORTRESS - Also known as the *Girifalco Fortress*, it is situated on the top of a hill, dominating the town. It was built in 1556 by Gabrio Serbelloni, and is now used for exhibitions and festivals.

PALACES IN CORTONA - In the historical centre there are various interesting patrician palaces: **Palazzo Mancini Sermini** has a fine façade with three orders; the 16th-century **Palazzo Mancini**; the 15th-century **Palazzo Fierli-Petrella**; the 17th-century **Palazzo Venuti**; the 18th-century **Palazzo Ferretti**; and the very ancient **Palazzo Cinaglia**.

CHURCH OF THE MADONNA DEL CALCINAIO - This 16th-century church was designed by Francesco di Giorgio Martini. It is built on a Latin-cross plan and has a beautiful dome. The **interior** is structured with only one nave and is admired for its clean lines. It preserves remarkable works of art: on the high altar, there is the fine image of the *Madonna del Calcinaio* (14th century); on the first and second altar to the left, *Immaculate Conception* and *Epiphany*, both by Papacello. The church is embellished by beautiful stained-glass windows by Marcillat (16th century).

TANELLA DI PITAGORA - It was originally an Etruscan hypogeum (maybe 4th century BC), with six loculi where the cinerary urns were kept, under a barrel vault.

CONVENT DELLE CELLE - It was built by request of Saint Francis between 1211 and 1221; the small **Church** dates from 1573.

ETRUSCAN TOMBS OF CAMUCIA - At the feet of Cortona there are various Etruscan tombs; among which, **Melone di Camucia**, oriental tumulus (7th century BC) made of two separate tombs of which only one can be visited. Not far from this one, you will find the **Melone del Sodo**, other tumulus of more or less the same period, formed by various funerary chambers; it can be visited, although part of it is being restored.

ENVIRONS

Abbey of Farneta, built during the 9th and 10th centuries, once was made up of many other edifices. Today, only the church remains, an example of Romanesque art in the Aretinian area. The interior has a nave with transept and has a beautiful trussed roof. On one of the walls, there is a remarkable fresco of the *Madonna and Child with Saints Sebastian and Rocco* by an unknown 16th-century painter. The *Crypt* is probably the most interesting thing to see, which can be reached from the transept: it has a unique plan, divided into three cells with barrel and cross vaults.

Island of ELBA (Livorno)

HISTORICAL SURVEY - *The largest island of the Tuscan Archipelago lies about 10 kilometres from the mainland. The coast, with its gulfs and bays, is particularly beautiful. The island has also many mountains, the highest of which is Mount Capanne (1019 metres). The island's economy is practically all based on tourism (exploded in the last decades), while the once traditional activities, like fishing and agriculture have become of secondary importance. Farm holidays have opened new horizons, while the once rich mineral industry has left many archaeological sites. Very good and refined is the wine, produced in various types: red, white, muscat and "aleatico" (a sweet red wine). Elba was already known by the Greeks who had discovered the iron ore; later the Etruscans came here, and, to follow, the Romans who left remarkable traces of their presence: splendid villas and pretty towns, such as Pomonte and Capoliveri (Caput Liberum). In the early Middle Ages, it was invaded by the Lombards. In the 11th century, it passed under the dominion of Pisa, which managed to defend it from the attacks of the Saracens and the Genoese until the end of the 15th century. After various events - it was ruled by the Medici, and then contended by Spain and France - the island was occupied by the English and three years later fell into the hands of the French, who made it become part of Tuscany. From 1814 to 1815, during which it was independent, Napoleon passed here his exile. In 1815, it was annexed to the Grand Duchy of Tuscany, and in 1860, to the Kingdom of Italy.*

PORTOFERRAIO - It is the chief town of the island. Its old district is small and surrounded by a strong 16th century **fortification**. Portoferraio is also the main port of the island, as well as a popular tourist attraction.

A picturesque view of the coast on the island of Elba.

114

Among the historical buildings, the most interesting are the 16th-century **Parish Church**, and the **Town Hall**, with *inscription* on the façade dedicated to Napoleon's stay on the island and a beautiful courtyard with a Roman *sacrificial altar* in the centre. The mansion is the seat of the **Communal Library Foresiana**. Also noteworthy is the **Church of the SS. Sacramento**, with a *Madonna of the Assumption* by Giovanni Camillo Sagrestani on the ceiling; the **Church of the Misericordia**, Renaissance, that houses a *Madonna and Child* attributed to Tino di Camaiano and from which the tourist can reach a small **Napoleonic Museum**. Nearby, there is a monastery, seat of the **De Laugier Centre** and of the **Picture-Gallery Foresiana**, that houses a large collection of various objects and paintings dating from the 16th to the 19th century; the **Stella Fort**, built from 1540 to 1548; the **Fort Falcone**, of the same period, in square plan, in which the Emperor of France spent his brief period on the island. This house, very beautiful, has many rooms: the *Emperors Study*, the *Reception Room*, the *Valets' Rooms*, the *Cloak-Room*, *Napoleon's Bedroom*, the *Officers Hall*, and the *Library*. The **Napoleon Villa of St. Martino**, is situated six kilometres from Portoferraio. This summer house was the residence of the Emperor's court; it contains interesting frescoes. Near here, you will find the **Villino Demidoff**. In the area around Portoferraio, interesting are the **Roman Villa delle Grotte** (1st century BC - 1st century AD), the **Church of St. Stefano alle Trane**, Pisan Romanesque (12th century), and the remains of the very ancient **Castle of Volterraio**.

CAPOLIVERI - It is a charming village, lying on a terraced hill, dating from Roman times (*Caput Liberum*). From it, you can reach the beautiful cliffs overhanging the sea.

PORTO AZZURRO - This attractive coastal town surrounds the small picturesque port; it is one of the most popular bathing resorts of the island. The large **Fortress of Portolongone**, dating from the early 17th century, dominates the town from a small promontory. Nearby, you can visit the 18th-century **Sanctuary of the Madonna di Monserrato** and the emerald-green small **lake of Terranera**.

RIO MARINA - It is tiny village, at the centre of the ancient mineral district. The **Town Hall** is the seat of the **Elba Mineralogical Museum**. Also part of the territory of the Commune of Rio Marina are the **Isolotto dei Topi** (Island of the Mice), a rock north of Capo Castello near Cavo, and the small **Island of Palmaiola**, east of Cavo in the Channel of Piombino. The Appiano had a small fortress built on the peak of Palmaiola, which at the beginning of the 19th century was still inhabited by a garrison to defend the navigation in the channel. The small **Island of Cerboli**, an uninhabited rock, lies to the south of Piombino. The tower, of which only the ruins remain, was built here during the Appiano rule.

MARCIANA MARINA - It is a picturesque sea-town, popular among tourists, with a small, but capacious port. On the mole there is a cylindrical **Tower**, called **Medici** or **Saracen Tower**, built by the Pisans during the 12th century. Not very far, there is the picturesque **Rione Cotone**.

MARCIANA - This very interesting town is probably the prettiest of the whole island. It develops around the ancient district, full of traces of its medieval and especially Medici past. It is also a fine tourist resort, situated among forests of chestnuts, under Mount Capanne, the highest peak of the island (1019 m, cable way for the top). On the highest point of the town there is the ancient **Fortress of the Appiani**, built by the Pisans. Also interesting is the **Archaeological Museum**, containing Greek, Etruscan and Roman material found on the island.
Near Marciana you will come upon the picturesque village of **Poggio**, the **Sanctuary of Madonna del Monte** (16th century) and the **Church of St. Lorenzo**, Pisan Romanesque (12th century).

MARINA DI CAMPO - Famous bathing resort, Marina di Campo lies in a wide plane surrounding a gulf. At the port, there is the ancient **Medici Tower**. Not far from Marina di Campo there are pretty villages: **San Piero in Campo**, and **Sant'Ilario in Campo**; also see the **Tower of St. Giovanni**, Pisan, and the **Church of St. Giovanni**, of the same period, but originally early Christian.

FIESOLE (Florence)

HISTORICAL SURVEY - *Today's territory of Fiesole is very different from what the city used to control in ancient times. Numerous finds of the Etruscan civilisation have come to light in the vast area, north of the Arno, between the Sieve and the Ombrone rivers: among these finds are the so-called "Fiesole stelae", which date from the 6th century BC. In addition to these, finds from pre-history, of the early Iron Age and of the Copper and Bronze ages, have been unearthed. It is thought that the Etruscan settlement of Fiesole was at the centre of a populated area overlooking the Florentine valley. The prosperity of Etruscan and Roman Fiesole was probably due to the fortunate geographical position: near a point of the Arno that could easily be forded (Florentia also would have been built near here) and close to the Apennine passes that connected this area with the Valley of the Po. It is supposed that the territory of the Roman* Municipium *of Fiesole extended mostly to the north of the Arno, while the "colonia" of Florence to the south. It was occupied by the Ostrogoths and the Byzantines, and from the 6th century was the site of a Lombard settlement, as documented by the remains of a necropolis. In 1125, after three military campaigns, Florence conquered Fiesole, destroying part of the ancient walls.*

THE RUINS OF ANCIENT FIESOLE - Traces of this period include various parts of the strong **city walls** and the ruins of a one cella **Etruscan Temple** with wings and two columns in the pronaos. Since part of it is till standing, it can be considered as one of the finest examples of this kind in Etruria.

Fiesole, the Roman Theatre.

A considerable number of interesting finds from the Etruscan period - *urns, bucchero*, clay and bronze *statuettes* - together with Roman objects can be seen in the **Museum** near the archaeological site. Fiesole was invaded by the Gauls in 225 BC and captured by Marcus Porcius Cato in 90 BC; in 80 BC it was occupied by Silla and turned into a military colony.

This was when Fiesole became a Roman city (*Faesulae*) with a forum, temples, theatre and baths. In the **Theatre**, which is still well preserved, you can sometimes assist to classical plays and it can hold about 3000 people. It dates from the beginning of the Imperial age and it was embellished during the periods of Claudius and Septimius Severus. The **Baths** also belong to that period and were restructured by Hadrian. The remaking of the Etruscan **Temple** is of Republican times (1st century BC).

CHURCH OF ST. DOMENICO - All the roads that from Florence lead to the hill of Fiesole converge on the terrace where the Church of St. Domenico stands, annexed to the convent founded in 1406.

The Renaissance layout of the edifice was in part transformed between the 16th and 17th century by Dosio (tribune and choir) and by Matteo Nigetti (porch in front and bell tower). In this religious complex you will find many works of art, among which some paintings by Fra' Angelico, who sojourned in the convent. Saint Antonine, Bishop of Florence during the first half of the 15th century, also stayed here, as well as friar Domenico Buonvicini, who, together with Savonarola, was sent to the stake in 1498.

BADIA FIESOLANA - This abbey stands on the site of the old Cathedral of Fiesole dedicated to Saint Peter, on the steep road that from Ponte alla Badia, on the *Faentina Road*, climbs to St. Domenico.

The Camaldolites replaced the original church with another, of which we can still admire the **façade**, decorated in green and white marble in a style similar to the one of San Miniato al Monte. The monastery (12th century) passed to the Benedictines until 1439, when it was transferred to the Augustinian canons of the congregation of Saint Frediano of Lucca; and, lastly, to the Piarists. From the middle of the 15th century, thanks to the generosity and will of Cosimo the Elder, the church and most of the complex were restructured. The religious edifice is today an example of early Renaissance architecture. It has a Latin-cross plan covered with barrel vaults and with side chapels. The plastered surfaces are outlined with "pietra serena" (a grey stone). Cosimo himself lived in the **Convent**, which has an elegant *Cloister*. He had his personal quarters built, and collected rare illuminated codexes, which passed to the Laurentian Library, in 1778, when the convent was suppressed. In 1753, it became the seat of the Georgofili Academy, the first in Europe dealing with agriculture.

CATHEDRAL - Fiesole, set between the two hills of San Francesco and Sant'Apollinare, is, today, one of the most admired places in the environs of Florence. Among the city's historical edifices, the most remarkable is the Cathedral, dedicated to *Saint Romulus*. It was begun during the 11th century, and finished and enlarged later. During the 19th century, it was restructured and restored, especially the façade and the tower.

The **interior** is on a basilican plan, with a nave and two aisles divided by round pillars - some have salvaged Roman capitals - and a large semi-circular apse. The presbytery is raised for the existence of a big **Crypt** beneath it - this same structure can be observed in the Basilica of San Miniato al Monte, near Florence.

PIAZZA MINO DA FIESOLE - To the left of the Cathedral is the **Rectory**, originally 11th-century, but rebuilt during the first half of the 15th century. The **Palazzo Vescovile** was also begun in the same period, but completed in the late 17th century, from which also dates the nearby **Seminary**.

The large square, named after *Mino da Fiesole*, is closed by **Palazzo Pretorio**, set on a slight high ground, and, to the east, by the **Church of Santa Maria Primerana**. The first is a picturesque edifice, prevalently 15th-century in style, and with a slender porch with architraves. The church has a 16th-century porch in front.

Fiesole, the small church of the Convent of St. Francesco.

SANT'ALESSANDRO - The ancient Basilica of Sant'Alessandro lies almost at the top of the steep road leading to the summit of the hill of San Francesco. Originally, it was the site of an Etruscan temple, then replaced by a Roman one, and finally, by the Christian church. Its origins are said to go back to Theodoric and it may have inherited the capitals and columns of the Roman temple. The pre-Romanesque origins are almost certain, although the church was restored during the 11th century and remodelled during the 16th and 18th centuries. The neo-classical **façade** was added at the beginning of the 19th century. Recent restorations have brought back to light the Romanesque structures, among which the columns in oriental cipolin with Ionic capitals and bases.

THE CONVENT OF ST. FRANCESCO - It stands on the summit of the hill. This was once the site of an Etruscan necropolis, followed by a Roman one, and later the site of the medieval fortress destroyed by the Florentines in 1125. Founded at the beginning of the 14th century, as the headquarters of the Florentine hermits, it passed to the Franciscans in the early 15th century. They enlarged the **Church** - which today has a long narrow nave with barrel vaults - and the **Convent**, of which Saint Bernadino of Siena was abbot.

BANDINI MUSEUM - In Fiesole there also is a picture gallery with numerous paintings, especially Florentine , dating from the 14th and 15th centuries. The paintings were collected by the canon Angiolo Maria Bandini during the end of the 18th century (the Museum takes his name), who made a bequest to the Chapter of Fiesole.

At **Pratolino**, on the hills north of Florence, there is **Villa Demidoff**, once a Medici villa. Designed by Buontalenti in a sober space setting, it consisted of three blocks, without a courtyard, on elevated grounds, these should have contained the grottoes; but the best part of the whole construction, is the park.

Montaigne, a great traveller and a man usually sparing of praise, when visiting the villa, in 1580, when the work at the great statue of Apennine was not yet finished, described the park in his *Journey to Italy*: "... with the action of water, not only can you create music and harmony, but you can give movement to many statues and gates, to the animals diving in to drink. Move a single device and the whole grotto will be full of water: all the seats will sprinkle water on your buttocks, and if you flee up the stairs of the castle, every two steps will sprinkle - for those who enjoy this amusement - a thousand spurts, wetting you all the way up to the top of the building".

All this was possible with a complex hydraulic system, using the water from 12 spring of Monte Senario. Among the marvels of the park, mention must be made of the great *Avenue of the Fountains*, flanked by jets of water crossing in a fantastic iridescent gallery, at the end of which was the The *laundress' basin*, with a statue of a woman wringing wet clothes; and also the *Monte Parnaso*, with a water organ in memory of the divine harmony of the Muses; and, moreover, *Cupid's grotto*, with its "artifices" and "deceptions" played on the visitors. But the greatest marvel of the park of Pratolino, certainly is the huge *Apennine*, 19 metres high, with fantastic underground grottoes, still today in excellent condition, and the great aviary. In any case, the villa, or better its park, reflects the love for alchemy and technology in general, of Francesco I, who in fact commissioned it.

During the Medici period the Villa of Pratolino was in full vogue: Händel and Scarlatti passed through its theatre. But the non-maintenance of the complex hydraulic system produced irreparable damages to the foundations of the villa. Ferdinando III of Lorraine, during the Romantic period, commissioned Fricks to restructure the park. In 1870, the Lorraine sold what was left of the property to the Demidoff, who restored part of the park and turned the old *Paggeria* of Francesco into their villa. Today the park has been restored, although without the devices it once had, and is open to the visitors.

GAIOLE IN CHIANTI (Siena)

Gaiole was already an important centre in the Middle Ages, thanks to its position: near the route that went from the Chianti to the upper Valdarno; for this reason in the 11th century, all of the markets of the nearby castles moved to Gaiole. The city's fortune regressed only in the last years of the Medici dominion, and in the 18th century, agriculture gave the town new impetus. From an artistic point of view, of interest is the **Country Church of St. Maria a Spaltenna**, near the town, built during the first half of the 12th century, although it has been restored during the 18th century. The grand **Castle of Meleto**, a fine example of fortified medieval farmhouse, is situated about two and a half kilometres from Gaiole, towards Siena.

Island of GIGLIO (Grosseto)

It was once inhabited by the Etruscans, as proved by the remains of a wreck found in the waters of Giglio Porto. The Romans built here **Villa degli Enobardi**, at **Castellari**. Various reconstructions and hypotheses, advanced by historians and based on what remains, seem to indicate that the villa had rooms with barrel vaults, decorated with marble and stuccoes in various colours. It also seems to have had a complex system of piping which carried the water to the rooms. Next to the edifice there was a *cetaria*, a fish pond.

Other remains of Roman buildings have been found near Giglio Castello, further proof of the fact that the island was inhabited by a fairly large number of persons. This is not surprising, because the island was full of

Wild coasts and blue sea transparency of the island of Giglio.

granite, a stone widely used in Roman times to build and decorate the palaces and the villas of the richer families. In 1362, the island of Giglio passed from the Pisans to the Genoese, and in 1447 it became a Florentine possession.

The brief journey (about 6 kilometres), that from **Giglio Porto** goes to Giglio Castello, is among the most fascinating ones in the Archipelago. The road starts from Giglio Porto, a small centre clustered around its bay, and leads steeply upwards among the terraced vineyards, which produce the famous Ansonaco wine (limited in quantity).

Continuing upwards, you will come upon the imposing **Tower of the Lazzeretto**, and further on, the **Old Lighthouse**. After a few curves, in which the vegetation suddenly changes from the typical Mediterranean grapevines and olive groves, to a typical mountain vegetation, made of chestnuts, the tourist will be able to see the rough and severe village of **Giglio Castello**. It is completely enclosed in the grey **medieval walls** with cylindrical and rectangular towers, and at the highest point, there is the 14th-century **Fortress**. Entering the walls is like going back in time 500 years. The stone houses are very small - the largest have two stories - and each have exterior stairs topped by picturesque arches. The streets are extremely narrow, and the only transportation consists of silent donkeys.

Although the town of Giglio Castello can be considered by itself a work of art, particular interest should be given to the **Parish Church**, restored, but still revealing its 14th-century origins. It contains an ivory *Crucifix* attributed to Giambologna; two 14th-century statues and a silver reliquary with the forearm of Saint Mamiliano, patron saint of the island.

From the asphalt road that connects Giglio Porto to Giglio castello, you can reach **Campese**, tiny village popular among skin divers for its limpid waters and the variety of fish. Next to the village there is the **Tower of the Campese**, built during the reign of Francesco I, Grand Duke of Tuscany.

ENVIRONS - **Giannutri**, the small island also part of the Commune of Giglio, and which today counts only seven inhabitants, was already known in Roman times. There are numerous ruins of the period, including those of a big **Villa**, dating from the 1st century AD.

120

GREVE IN CHIANTI (Florence)

With its 10.000 inhabitants Greve is the largest agricultural town in Chianti. It is situated on the banks of the river Greve, in an area surrounded by olives and vineyards. Greve is a prosperous town thanks to its vineyards and the production of Gallo Nero wine. Every year the famous Mostra Mercato (a fair) of Chianti Classico is held here: an exhibition of the wines from the area of the Chianti, sold throughout the world. The town once was around a powerful castle, destroyed, in 1325, by Castruccio Castracani. Today the whole town extends around the lovely **Main Square** known as "*Mercatale*". The square is characterised by a unique asymmetrical form and fine terraced porticoes. At the back is the façade of the **Church of Santa Croce**, a building completely remade in the 19th century: inside there is a *Madonna and Saints* by the so-called Maestro di Greve and a charming tryptych, the *Annunciation*, by Bicci di Lorenzo. Near the square there is also the small **Oratory of San Francesco**, with a fine glazed terra-cotta group of the *Deposition with the Three Maries and Three Saints*, dating from the beginning of the 16th century.

ENVIRONS

About one and a half kilometres west of the town lies **Montefioralle** (hamlet of Greve), a very old medieval village at the top of a hill and developed around the **Castle** which takes the same name. At the hightest point of the hamlet is the **Church of St. Stefano**, of medieval origins and containing outstanding works of art: on the first altar to the left is the fine *Madonna and Child with Two Angels*, a 13th-century panel attributed to the Master of Bagnano or the Master of Greve; in the presbytery, you can admire the panel by an anonymous painter, perhaps of the school of Neri di Bicci or Andrea del Castagno, the *Trinity and Four Saints*. Noteworthy also on the left, the *Annunciation with Saints John, the Baptist, and Stephen*, dating from the early 15th century and presumably by the school of Lorenzo Monaco. The hamlet also has a fine medieval house where apparently the navigator Amerigo Vespucci was born. Finally, the tourist should visit the small Romanesque **Parish Church of San Cresci** a few hundred metres from Montefioralle. The fine façade is original in its lower part.

Greve in Chianti, a view of the Mercatale.

121

GROSSETO

HISTORICAL SURVEY – *Grosseto lies in the heart of the Maremma, near the right banks of the Ombrone river which winds its way throught the vast plain. It is about ten kilometres from the sea. This prevalently modern city has spread around the small compact historical centre marked by the old Medici bastions. The first historical data comes from a document, dated 973, refering to a castle which had ties with the powerful Aldobrandeschi family and was situated on the present site of the city. In 1138, Innocent II transferred there the episcopal chair from impoverished Roselle and from that point the castle became a town, no longer subjected to the contrasts between the power of the bishop and that of*

Grosseto, Piazza Dante with the side of the Cathedral, the Monument to Leopold II and Palazzo della Provincia.

the despotic Aldobrandeschi family. With difficulty it managed to become a free Commune, but the continuous clashes with powerful Siena limited its freedom and, in 1336, after various vicissitudes, it passed under Sienese hegemony. In 1559, it entered the Medici sphere of influence, and while on the one hand this limited its freedom, on the other it made the town prosper, for the Medici also started the great reclamation operations (in the course of the centuries malaria had literally exterminated the population of Grosseto), and built the magnificent bastions which surrounded and protected the city. The town once more declined in the 18th century, but with the advent of the Lorraine things went better. In the 19th century, further reclamation works finally led to a demographic stability.

CATHEDRAL – As proved by an inscription, the Cathedral was begun in 1294 and finished early in the 14th century by Sozzo di Pace Rustichini, known also as Sozzo di Rustichino. The Cathedral was probably built on the remains of a Romanesque church: this is thought because of the pilasters with engaged columns set against the interior of the façade and the pilaster strips outside on the side walls. The **façade,** restructured in the 19th century, has three portals and an elegant loggia with a rose window above. The right side has a fine low-relief portal surmounted by a splendid sculpture by Cesare Maccari (1800) and above, two Gothic mullioned windows with two lights. The **interior** has a nave divided from the two aisles by solid compound piers. At the end of the second bay is the apse, semi-circular on the outside but square inside. Of particular interest in the second bay, is a fine baptismal font by Antonio Ghini (1470) on the left and, in the left arm of the transept, a lovely altarpiece, also by Ghini, with a splendid Assumption (15th cent.) by Matteo di Giovanni.

Grosseto, from the porticos of Piazza Dante a view of the Cathedral façade.

Grosseto, part of the Medicean Walls.

ARCHAEOLOGICAL AND ART MUSEUM OF THE MAREMMA – The Museum has a rich artistic and archaeological collection. The **Prehistoric section** is installed on the ground floor and has material from the palaeolithic to the Prehistoric period. The **Etruscan section** exposes finds from the excavations of ancient settlements including Talamone, Vetulonia, Cosa, Sovana, Castro, Vulci, Pitigliano, Saturnia, Magliano and, above all, Roselle, where excavations are still undergoing in the ancient urban area. The upper floor contains the **Topographical section** where the material is arranged according to the river basin it comes from (Ombrone, Fiora, and others). There is also a rich **Collection of religious art** on the second floor, including paintings of the Sienese school dating from the 13th to the 17th century. Of particular interest is a magnificent *Last Judgement* by Guido da Siena or his circle; a charming *Madonna and Child* by Segna di Bonaventura; a good number of works that can be attributed to the circle of one of the above mentioned masters; a touching *Crucifixion* (first half of the 13th cent.) which is of such high quality that the name of Simone Martini comes to mind; the famous *Madonna of the Cherries* by Sassetta; and the two *Saints*, once wings of a polyptych, by Sano di Pietro. The collection also contains works by many other renowned masters, such as Girolamo di Benvenuto, Pietro di Domenico, Riccio, Vanni and Rutilio Manetti, as well as a fine *Collection of ceramics*.

CHURCH OF ST. FRANCESCO – This austere 13th-century church is in Gothic style. The gabled brick **façade** is embellished with a portal with lunette and a fine rose window. The convent buildings were on the left side. Still standing is a **Cloister** with the so-called *well of the "bufala"*,

124

built by Ferdinando I towards the end of the 16th century. Another well lies outside the church opposite the hospital. The **interior** has a single large nave with a trussed timber roof and a fine chapel at the end. It contains a valuable *Cross* set behind the high altar, perhaps an early work by Duccio da Boninsegna (1289), and a lovely wooden *Crucifix* (16th cent.) of Sienese school. The interior is in part lined with frescoes.

COMMUNAL LIBRARY CHELLIANA – This Library has its seat in the Palazzo del Liceo. Founded in 1860 by Giovanni Chelli, it was badly damaged during the last war. It contains about 118,000 volumes, as well as about 30 precious incunabuli and hundreds of "*cinquecentine*".

WALLS AND MEDICI FORTRESS – The fortified walls have a hexagonal ground plan and completely surround the historical centre of Grosseto. The Grand Duke Francesco I (1574) ordered them to be built, and they were designed by Baldassare Lanci. In 1835, the terraces and bulwarks of the walls were transformed into boulevards and gardens. At one corner of the walls is the **Medici Fortress** which incorporates the old Sienese keep (a solid structure composed by two distinct parts, with a strong escarpment bordered by a stone ridge). A fine view of the old town can be admired from the fortress.

LA VERNA (Arezzo)

From the 13th century this tiny settlement, which had risen *ex nihilo* on exclusively religious grounds, asserted its authority on all other attempts of settlements in the territory. It was one of the greatest centres of Franciscan spirituality, abounding in natural beauty and art, as well as memories and legends of the figure of the "Poverello". The rocky mountain top ("the rude stone") donated to St Francis by Count Orlando dei Catani, was a wild uninhabited place when, in 1215, the friar erected the first hut for himself and his companions. The place was par-

La Verna, view of the overhanging cliffs supporting the sanctuary.

The precious Della Robbia sculptural group is one of the most remarkable ornaments inside La Verna.

ticularly dear to the saint: he often stayed there and received there the stigmata, in 1224 ("He now received from Christ that final seal", Dante, *Paradise* XI, 106). The first hermitage was built at the southern base of the enormous boulder that juts out from the ridge of the mountain. In 1264, at Count Simone da Battifolleis expense, a new convent (il Conventino) and the Church at the Stigmata, were being built. Then, in 1348, when La Verna was already the mecca of crowds of pilgrims, a larger church, Santa Maria degli Angeli, was built. It took its name from the first small church St. Francis himself had built. Further additions and enlargments followed.

Today La Verna, still the site of a flourishing **Convent of the Order of the Minor Friars**, consists of a vast complex of buildings some of which built recently, which harmonise beautifully with the setting. The original entrance is marked by a large vault with a depressed arch, set under the building that serves as **Guest house**. The first building you will encounter on entering the Sanctuary is the small 14th-century **Church of St. Maria degli Angeli**, with the armorial bearings of Pope Eugene IV, of the Florentine people, of the City of Florence and the Wool Guild on the simple **façade**. The **inside** has a single nave covered with a pointed barrel vault divided by arches. It contains two altars with glazed terra-cotta sculptures by Giovanni della Robbia representing, respectively, the *Deposition* and the *Adoration of the Child with St. Francis* and *St. Anthony of Padua*. The choir is surrounded by Renaissance wooden stalls of Florentine inspiration; at the main altar is the *Madonna of the Girdle*, one of Andrea della Robbia's most harmonious works, carried out in 1486. The high magistrates of the Florentine Wool Guild gave the Della Robbia workshop great thrive with the many commissions for the Sanctuary.

A number of other works, by the Della Robbia brothers and their workshop, are scattered throughout the sanctuary: two charming altarpieces by Andrea, white figures on a blue ground set in sandstone shrines are to be found in the **Major Church** (or *Basilica of St. Maria Assunta*). One represents a marvelously clear *Annunciation*, the other an *Adoration of the Child* which recalls Fra' Filippo Lippi in its composition. The same church also contains a *Madonna and Child Enthroned with Saints* from the Della Robbia workshop, as well as three other works by Andrea: two high reliefs with *St. Francis and St. Anthony Abbot* and an imposing arched altarpiece with the *Assumption*.

The Major Church of La Verna has a simple structure: a single vast nave with deep side chapels, on a design that dates from the 13th century. The building was modernised already in the 15th century, in its ending chapel; and then, again, in the 16th century, the portico on the front and right side was added. Lastly, in the 17th century, the **interior** was constructed in its present form. In addition to the Della Robbia terra-cotta figures, the church has a number of precious reliquaries (including one from the 15th century in gilded copper and shaped like a Gothic temple), a fine wooden choir dating from 1495, formed by two tiers of carved and inlaid stalls, and an interesting collection of church vestments. The portico, which runs around the Major Church, continues in the so-called **Corridor of the Stigmata**, entrance to which is through a small opening to one side of the **Chapel of the Count of Montedoglio**, dominated by a large *Pietà*, a polychrome low relief dating from 1532 circa, by Giovanni della Robbia. A series of 17th century frecoes with scenes from the *Life of St. Francis* (restored in 1840 and integrated in 1933 by the painter Baccio Maria Bacci) are on the walls of the corridor. A number of small rooms, full of atmosphere, which often recall facts and legends related to the life of St. Francis, are grouped together at the end of the corridor: the **Loddi Chapel**, with a 13th-century wooden *Crucifix*; the **Chapel of the Cross**, with a 19th-century *Statue of St. Francis* by Graziani di Faenza; the **Chapels** dedicated to **St. Bonaventura**, **St. Sebastian** and **St. Anthony of Padua**. Lastly, there is the **Chapel of the Stigmata**, with carved and inlaid 16th-century wooden choir-stalls along the walls and, on the altar, a large glazed terra-cotta altarpiece of the *Crucifixion* by Andrea della Robbia (above the door there is also a *Madonna and Child* by Luca della Robbia). The corridor also leads to a **cave** in the midst of boulders, once St. Francis' cell, and to another cell used by the saint; nearby is the so-called **"Sasso Spicco"**, an enormous rock wich seems detached from the mountain and hanging in mid-air forming a grotto.

The **Convent** itself lies behind the two churches, the Major Church and St. Maria degli Angeli, and comprises various buildings (**Guest house**, **Refectory**, **Dormitory**, **Library**, and others) surrounded by the lovely forest of secular beeches and firs, and enclosing several cloisters. Among the many pieces of art preserved in the cloister, mention should be made of the *51 portraits of Saints and Blessed of the Order*, painted above the cells between 1501 and 1509 by Gerino da Pistoia, and terracotta figures by the Della Robbia brothers, among which a *Madonna and Child* by Andrea della Robbia, in the large severe refectory.

ENVIRONS – On one side of the Catenaia Alp you will come upon the ancient village of **Caprese Michelangelo**, famous for the man who gave his name to this hamlet, born here on 6th March 1475. Also worth visiting are the **Buonarroti Home-Museum**, the **Country Church of St. John Baptist** (13th century), and the ruins of the 14th-century **Castle**.

LIVORNO

HISTORICAL SURVEY – *The city, today one of Italy's main ports, is situated a few kilometres south of the mouth of the Arno, at the edge of a plain that was once marshy. Its origins are uncertain: probably the area where the city lies was already inhabited in neolithic times, as proved by various finds. The Ligurians may also have had interests in the area, and, in Roman times, it seems that a small port and a tiny settlement were on the site. But the actual birth of the city is relatively recent. After the fall of Pisa, caused by the Florentines (1405), Livorno passed under Genoa, which a few years later ceded it to Florence for 100,000 florins. On 28 March 1577, the first stone of the modern Livorno was laid, with the intent of making it the new port of Pisa, since the old Porto Pisano had silted up. This was the beginning of the city's prosperity. The population quadrupled, and it rapidly became a very important port. This was when the large Medicean Port was built – a fine structure which added lustre to the city. In the 17th and 18th centuries, the fame of the port of Livorno increased even further, thanks to the preferences of the Medici first, and then of the Lorraine, becoming a connection point for international trade. With the union of Italy, it lost its status of free port and became the regional port of Tuscany. During World War II, Livorno was heavily bombed and some of its most important monuments were lost.*

CATHEDRAL – Built at the end of the 16th century on a project by Alessandro Pieroni, the cathedral was later enlarged in the 18th century. The simple **façade** is entirely covered with marble. In front, there is a porch on Doric columns, topped by a charming terrace. The **Bell tower**,

Livorno, the Old Fortress.

Livorno, the Mascagni Terrace on the sea promenade.

Livorno, Piazza della Repubblica.

which rises up behind the façade, is square and made of brick. The Latin-cross **interior** has only a nave. Three enormous canvases fill the ceiling: the *Triumph of Saint Julia* by Jacopo Ligozzi, the *Madonna of the Assumption* by Passignano, and *St. Francis Receiving the Child from Mary* by Empoli. The interior also has various fine *monumental tombs*, such as the one dedicated to the Marquise Marco Alessandro del Borro and Count Ginori.

CHURCH OF THE MADONNA – This religious edifice is by Pieroni (1599). The **façade** is simple and well-balanced. The single-nave **interior** contains fine works of art, including a bronze *Crucifix*, perhaps by Ferdinan-

Livorno, the Four Moors.

Livorno, the statue dedicated to Ferdinand I de' Medici, known as the Four Moors ("I Quattro Mori").

do Tacca, on the first altar to the right; a fine painting on canvas of *St. Louis of France*, by Matteo Rosselli, on the second altar to the right; and on the third altar, another lovely painting on canvas of *St. John and the Madonna* by Volterrano. From the inside, you can enter a small delightful **Cloister**, part of the **Convent of the Minor Friars**.

GIOVANNI FATTORI CITY MUSEUM – The museum is situated in a small palace at the centre of the park of **Villa Fabbricotti**. It was founded at the end of the 19th century when the decision was taken to order in a single museum the numerous collections donated to the city by Enrico Chiellini. These included prehistoric, Etruscan, and Roman archaeological material and, later, various works by Giovanni Fattori together with numerous other Macchiaioli artists. The coin collection is also of interest.

OLD FORTRESS – This imposing fortification in brick was built by Antonio da Sangallo the Younger, between 1521 and 1534. In the inside there is the small **Church of St. Francesco** and archaeological material from the old Roman *castrum*. The fort is composed of three bastions and has a double entrance: one is named after *the duke Alexander*, and the other is from where Marie de' Medici, queen of France, departed.

STATUE "I QUATTRO MORI" – The monument is situated in *Piazza Giuseppe Micheli* and is dedicated to the Grand Duke Ferdinando I de' Medici, whose statue, made in 1595 by Giovanni Bandini, is at the centre of the group. But the real masterpiece of sculpture is a group of four figures, the *Four Moors*, or the four barbaric pirates in chains. The four statues were added in 1626, and are by Pietro Tacca, a fine sculptor who worked for a long time for the prestigious Medici family.

MEDICEAN PORT – The big Medicean port starts from the *Piazza Micheli*, continues along the street named after the *Molo Mediceo*, on which the old **Small Fort of the Sassaia** is situated, and reaches the **Mole "of Cosimo"** (so-called because it was finished by the Grand Duke Cosimo II de' Medici, in 1620) with the remains of the fort once guarding the entrance to the port. On the other side of the mole there is a vast basin with a large dam called the **Curvilinea**. Further north, there is the **Dam of Marzocco**, which takes its name from the **Marzocco Tower**, built by the Florentines in 1439. Lastly, between the mole and the dam Curvilinea, on the rocks you will see the lovely **Torre del Fanale** (a light house) similar to the original 14th century construction, which may have been built by Giovanni di Nicola Pisano.

PROGRESSIVE MUSEUM OF CONTEMPORARY ART – It is situated in **Villa Maria** and has a collection of works by many of today's artists, including Cappiello, Guttuso and Rosai. A museum dedicated to **Mascagni**, the famous musician of Livorno, has been set up in the Villa's annex. Not far from Villa Maria there is the **Y. Marini Jewish Museum**.

ENVIRONS

What has made **Montenero** unique among Catholics is the worship that a countless number of people have dedicated to the mysterious and miraculous image of the *Madonna*, brought to high grounds by a lame sheperd who was healed when he found it. The initially incredulous ecclesiastic authorities could not ignore the prodigious event. To begin with, they gave their *placet* to the construction of a small oratory, replaced, in 1455, by a larger church entrusted to the Gesuiti (an order of St. Girolamo). Then, it passed to the Benedictine monks of Vallombrosa. In 1720, the majestic **Monastery** we still see, and which took fifty years to build, was begun. The Baroque richness of the **Church**, centred around the miraculous effigy of the *Madonna and Child*, attributed by the critics to followers of Giotto (although it is traditionally said to come from Greece), in a different way continues in the adjacent **Rooms**, covered with a great number of *ex-voto*. In addition to the usual gold or silver hearts, and drawings or paintings (some of which by known artists) representing the circumstances in which the donor was miraculously saved, there are crutches, eyeglasses, plaster casts, weapons, helmets, stones, steering wheels, fragments of bullets – an indescribable variety of relics which prove, according to a modern psychologist, how strong faith can be, when it goes together with an ingenuousness sense of the supernatural. In the portico, at the entrance, there are the tombs of famous citizens, which make this a memorial chapel of the Livorno culture. You should not forget the visit to the **Gallery of the Tuscan Communes** (the Virgin of Montenero is the patron saint of the region), the **Grotto Madonna**, the **Pharmacy** and the underground **caves**.

Environs of Livorno, the "Madonna with Child" inside the Sanctuary of Montenero.

LUCCA

HISTORICAL SURVEY – *Lucca was founded on a level and alluvial ground stretching from the last offshoots of the Tusco-Emilian Appenines to the northern high grounds of Monte Pisano, not far from the river Serchio. This ancient noble city has many picturesque towers and churches, Renaissance palaces, quaint streets, and squares with their neat structure. The oldest part of the city is enclosed by walls, still in good condition, which give the city its typical medieval aspect. Not much is known of its origins, but they go far back in time: the site was first inhabited by the Ligurians and then by the Etruscans. Its name seems to derive from the Celtic-Ligurian* luk *which means "swampy area". In Roman times it was an important* municipium *and the city certainly reached a considerable authority, as it was chosen for the stipulation of the famous triumvirate of 56 BC. Todays* Via S. Gerolamo, Via Beccheria, Via S. Lucia, Via del Moro, *correspond to the ancient cardo; the decumanum ran along the Via S. Paolino and the Via S. Croce. Further important evidence of Roman times is the amphitheatre and what little remains of the Roman walls. The city then was taken by the Goths and subsequently by the Lombards, under whom it prospered.*

The Via Francigena *and the other important roads date from this period, and allowed the flourishing of Lucca's commerce and the economic growth of the entire city. It was in fact in the period of Lombard domina-*

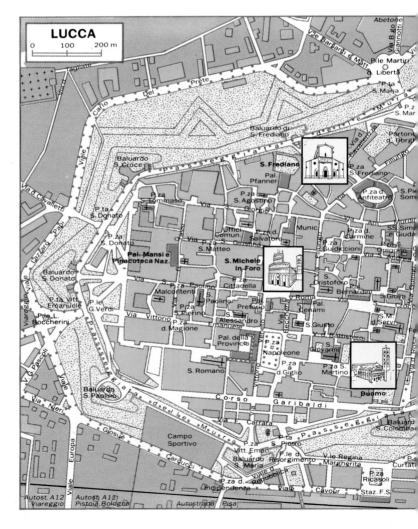

tion that Lucca became the capital of Tuscia. The Lombards were followed by the Carolingians and by the first German emperors who elected Lucca as their main seat when the Marquisate of Tuscany was founded. After a period of harsh struggles, in 1119, the city managed to become a free Commune. This was the beginning of an extremely important period for the city's economy and art. The fame of the silk industry spread throughout the world. Banking activities enriches the city and raised the standard of living. Lucca became the centre for pictorial activity, influencing many other schools in Tuscany. In 1314, the city fell into the hands of the tyrant of Pisa, Uguccione della Faggiola, followed by the government of Castruccio Castracani, which conferred prestige and power to the city. When Castracani died, Lucca went through a period of contrasting dominions, until, finally, in 1369, Charles IV conquered the city and gave it independence. But that fortunate season of the Communes was over, and gradually Lucca lost the primacy achieved with difficulty. After three rather uneventful centuries, in the 19th century, Lucca once more became a rich and powerful city, thanks to the fine figure of Maria Luisa of Bourbon of Parma. When Napoleon fell, Lucca was first subjugated to Naples, and then to the Austrians, who gave the city as a duchy to Maria Luisa of Bourbon (1817). From her it passed to her son, Charles Louis, who, in 1847, abdicated in favour of Leopoldo of Tuscany. With the plebiscite of 1860, Lucca became part of the Kingdom of Italy. Today, the city is an important tourist centre, with an active industry (textile, mechanic, food). Among the agricultural activities, the olive oil cultivation is still of great importance.

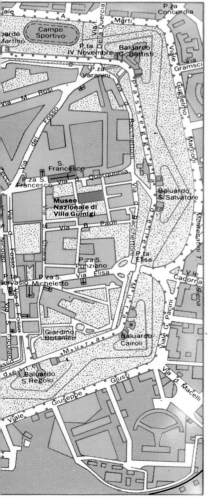

CATHEDRAL OF ST. MARTINO – Founded in 1060, by the bishop Anselmo da Baggio, it was begun in the 12th century in Romanesque style, but the Gothic style we see today is the result of a complete restructure done in the 14th-15th centuries. The **façade**, however, is Romanesque, and has three large different arches at the bottom, supported by composite piers, and three tiers of loggias above. There are various interesting Romanesque reliefs under the porch, set next to the portals and in the lunettes. Among these, a *Nativity*, in the left lintel, and in a lunette, a *Deposition*, probably by Nicola Pisano. The **interior**, a nave and two aisles, has women's galleries, and contains numerous remarkable works of art: in the first chapel of the left transept, there is the statue of *St. John Evangelist* by Jacopo della Quercia. The Sacristy (admission after payment), now houses the beautiful *tomb of Ilaria del Carretto*, one of Jacopo della Quercia's greatest works. In here, also admire the *Madonna and Saints* by Ghirlandaio. The right transept contains a fine *altar of Saint Regolo* by Civitali; in the nave, the *pulpit*, also is by Civitali; on the third altar of the right aisle, there is a magnificent *Last Supper* by Tintoretto. The famous **Shrine of the Holy Face** (*Volto Santo*, 1484) by Civitali, is in the left aisle. It contains the wooden 11th-12th century *Crucifix* mentioned by Dante in

Lucca, the apse of the Basilica of San Frediano with the Bell tower.

his *Hell*. The **Cathedral Museum,** next to the Cathedral, houses the **Treasure**, a collection of many religious objects in gold and silver from the 14th and 15th centuries.

CHURCH OF ST. MICHELE IN FORO – Begun in 1143, and not finished until the 14th century, the church of St. Michele is one of the finest examples of Pisan-Luccan Romanesque style. The **façade** has four tiers of small loggias and outstanding decorations in marble. Particularly striking is the statue of *St. Michael Killing the Dragon*. The robust **Bell tower**, has on each floor small thick arches. The **interior** of the church, a nave and two aisles, has a perfect semi-circular apse. The interesting works in the church include: on the first altar to the right, a glazed terra-cotta figure by Andrea della Robbia; in the left transept, in a niche, there is a beautiful panel painting of *Four Saints*, by Filippino Lippi; there also is a *Madonna and Child* by Raffaello da Montelupo; and finally, on the high altar, a Luccan 13th-century *Crucifix*.

BASILICA OF SAN FREDIANO – Once a Longobard basilica (6th century), the church was begun in 1112 and finished in the 13th century. The marvelous tripartite **façade** is decorated with a mosaic of the *Ascension* of the school of Berlinghieri. The **interior** has a nave and two aisles, with Renaissance and Baroque chapels. Particularly interesting works of art include: to the left, on the **inside façade**, a *Visitation* by Domenico del Ghirlandaio, and, to the right, a *Madonna and Saints* by Aspertini; in the right aisle, a Della Robbia terra-cotta figure, a lovely baptismal font by

134

Civitali, and a Romanesque holy water font dating from the 12th century. An interesting series of reliefs can be seen in the last chapel on the left, including the famous polyptych of the *Madonna and Saints* by Jacopo della Quercia, while there is a cycle of frescoes by Amico Aspertini in the second chapel on the left.

CHURCH OF ST. GIOVANNI – This unique church is the result of the union of two pre-existing churches: the church of St. Reparata and the Baptistery. The building dates from the 12th century, although it has been restored often. Remains of the original building include the portal, flanked by two columns which have on top two *lion statues*. The frieze in the architrave, with the *Madonna between Two Archangels and the Apostles*, made by Master Villano in 1187, is outstanding.
The **interior** has the plan of a basilica, and consists of a nave and two aisles with columns and fine Romanesque capitals. The church contains various interesting works, including the *Crucifix and the Madonna* by Francesco Vanni; the *Madonna Enthroned and Saints*, a fresco of the 14th-century Tuscan school; and several noteworthy *sarcophagi*. Adjacent to the church is the **Baptistery** built during the 14th century. It has a spacious Gothic hall on a square ground plan; fine Gothic arches on

Lucca, the beautiful Pisan-Romanesque façade of the Church of St. Michele.

composite columns are set under a high wedged dome. The baptistery contains the remains of a baptismal basin and another one, known as *new basin* of oval form dating from the end of the 15th century. The *statues of the Evangelists* by Cosimo Fancelli are also interesting.

CHURCH OF ST. PAOLINO – Begun in 1522, by Baccio da Montelupo, the church has a long flight of stairs leading to the fine Renaissance **façade**. The **interior** has a single nave and a transept. The scenic vista of communicating chapels, framed by two stories of pilasters and a row of smaller pilasters with architraves on top, is fascinating.

The chapels contain works of considerable interest: on the second altar on the right side is a *Madonna and Child with Saints* by Alessandro Ardenti (1565); on the third altar is *St. Ansano*, a wooden sculpture by Francesco di Valdambrino (1414); on the fourth altar the *Martyrdom of St. Theodore* by Pietro Testa. See in the chapel to the right of the presbytery, a *Deposition of Saints* by Angelo Puccinelli, and, in the facing chapel, a lovely oil painting of the *Virgin and Saints* by Lorenzo Zacchia (1585).

On the altar in the presbytery there is an *early Christian sarcophagus*, which probably contained the body of Saint Paolino. On the walls there are large frescoes by Gherardi (17th cent.) and Certosino (18th cent.). In the chapel leading to the **Sacristy**, you can admire a *Coronation of the Virgin* and, below, representations of medieval Lucca (Anonymous). Finally, an unusual 14th-century sculpture of the *Madonna and Child*, stands on the third altar of the left aisle.

Lucca, Piazza dell'Anfiteatro is situated where the Roman theatre was.

THE WALLS – About 12 metres high, with 12 curtain walls and 11 bastions (some of which are used for exhibitions and meetings), the walls were built between the 16th and the 17th century as an extension and restructure of the preceding circuit of walls. They are about five kilometres long and are completely practicable.

PALAZZO PRETORIO – The building of Palazzo Pretorio dates from 1492. It was designed by Matteo Civitali, and then enlarged at the end of the 16th century. On the ground floor there is a vast loggia with above, large mullioned windows with two lights decorated with small pilasters. At the centre the **façade** has an antique 17th-century clock. The loggia contains various important works of art: the *Statue of Matteo Civitali* by Arnoldo Fazzi (1893), the *Statue of the sculptor Vincenzo Consani* made by Urbano Lucchesi, the *memorial monument of the Garibaldian* by Tito Strocchi, and above all, a *Madonna and Child with Saints Peter and Paul*, a 17th-century fresco by Paolo Guidotti.

GUINIGI HOUSES – This group of medieval palaces and towers dates from the 14th century. They include a palace entirely in brick dating from the second half of the 14th century, with a lovely and elegant façade with mullioned windows with three and four lights. The highest tower, on top of which some holm-oaks have grown, has become one of the most known symbols of Lucca. Facing the palace is another of the same period, with a magnificent portal on the ground floor and elegant mullioned windows with two and three lights above.

PIAZZA DELL'ANFITEATRO – The name of this square derives from the fact that it lies on the site of a **Roman amphitheatre** dating from the 2nd century AD, and some of the arches can still be seen. The square is one of the most picturesque in the city, enclosed by a ring of old houses, some low and broad, others high. Up until a few years ago, a picturesque coloured market, which gave its name to the place, was held here in the piazza (which was once the arena).

VILLA GUINIGI – Built in 1418, this imposing building has a unique long shape. The central part of the **façade**, has a scenic gallery supported by solid pilasters, and in the upper part there are fine mullioned windows with three lights with trilobate arches. Since 1968, it is the seat of the National Museum.

NATIONAL MUSEUM OF VILLA GUINIGI – The Museum is divided in various **sections**, ranging from the **Archaeological** one, which houses Etruscan, Roman and Ligurian material, to the prestigious **Painting section**, with its rich collection of paintings, sculpture and minor arts, almost all of Luccan school. Among the most interesting, you should not miss the sculptures by Civitali and Baccio da Montelupo; the paintings by Puccinelli, Aspertini, Pompeo Batoni, Zacchia the Elder and the whole group of painters working in Lucca between the 13th and the 18th century, which give the visitor an outline of Luccan painting.

NATIONAL PICTURE-GALLERY – The National Picture Gallery was founded in 1819 by Maria Luisa of Bourbon and further enriched by Leopoldo II. The numerous rooms of the 17th century **Palazzo Mansi** contain works by important Italian and foreign artists, ranging from the Renaissance to the 19th century. Among the most prestigious names there are Salvator Rosa, Luca Giordano, Morazzone, Bronzino, Paolo Veronese, Tintoretto, Dolci and Sustermans.

ENVIRONS

At **Marlia**, you can admire **Villa Reale**, built by the Buonvisi, then passed to the Orsetti, and finally to the Government of Lucca, that gave it to the Princes Elisa Buonaparte and Felice Baciocchi. These last tenants built the last floor and commissioned the pictorial decorations inside, by the Tofanelli of Lucca. However, since it was used as a summer residence by the court, it was the park that received the greatest arrangement: it was disposed similar to the park of the royal palace of Versailles. It has a *Theatre,* embellished with masks of the Italian Comedy, caves, fountains and nymphaea, but most interesting is the use of the waters of the Fraga

Lucca, a striking view of the roofs of the city centre.

stream, to create water-works, small lakes and waterfalls. Among the peculiar whims of the princess, there was the breeding of merinos sheep, but the villa was also meeting point of intellectuals and artists, such as the famous violinist Paganini.

At **Massa Pisana** there is **Villa Matteucci**, formerly Buonvisi, an imposing structure with two splendid avenues at the base of a hill. **Villa Cheli**, now *Marraccini,* lies downhill from the Convent of St. Cerbone and all its monumentality can be admired from the gate, on the *Via Pisana.* **Villa Antonioli** (now *Lazzareschi*) is a solid building embellished by two splendid loggias, while **Villa Rinaldi** is a 16th-century adaptation of a precedent edifice. **Villa Bernardini** is a fine 16th-century structure, as is **Villa Pagliaia**, while **Villa Principessa** is the earliest Luccan villa we know of, built in 1318 by Castruccio Castracani, but transformed in the 19th century.

138

Two kilometres from Lucca, near the river Serchio, at **Monte San Quirico** visit the **Parish Church**, inside which you can admire a terra-cotta *St. Sebastian* by Civitali, and an ancient astylar *Cross* from the 14th century. Nearby, there is **Villa Paolina**, named after Napoleon's sister who bought it, and created a magnificent park; and the **Villa Buonvisi** (now *Spada*), one of the most interesting examples of a "palazzo in villa" with a beautiful porch and a refined loggia.

In **Segromigno in Monte**, on the slope of the Pizzorne, there is **Villa Mansi**, built at the beginning of the 16th century and owned by the Cenami family. Before it passed to the Mansi, in 1675, it was restored by Oddi, in 1635, and, later, embellished with gardens, by Juvara, between 1725 and 1732. In 1742, a loggia with sculptures was added, and during the 19th century the park went through great transformations. Today it is severe in the small woods of fir-trees, elms and ilexes, but brighter in its architectural arrangements, sculptures, fountains and the big Baroque basin. The park and the villa (decorated, in the hall, with late 18th-century paintings representing the *Myth of Apollo,* by Tofanelli; and, in the gaming-hall, with tapestries with scenes from *Gerusalem Liberated*) often accommodated important guests: one of these was the King of Denmark Frederick IV, who had a love story with a young woman of Lucca, who later became nun. This story has inspired a few novels, such as the *Letter of a nun to Frederick IV,* by Pindemonte, and *Young girl of Lucca,* by Jansen.

In Segromigno there also is **Villa Mazzarosa**, 17th-century, for which Juvara had designed an exedra (not carried out). The small *temple,* a memorial to "the representations and works by famous citizens of Lucca" (written on a memorial tablet) was ordered by the owner of the villa, Mazzarosa. Not far from here, there is **Villa Orsucci**, built in the 18th century, on the more ancient Villa Arnolfini, where Gioacchino Murat seems to have sojourned; the beautiful interior contains paintings of the *Deeds of Orazio Coclite* and the *Rape of the Sabine women.*

LUCIGNANO (Arezzo)

Ancient Aretinian possession and, before that, originally Etruscan, it passed under the dominion of Florence (16th century) after a dispute with Siena. The town plan is elliptical and has many Medieval features.

The 13th-century **Church of St. Francesco**, Romanesque, displays a number of frescoes representing Sienese scenarios and by Bartolo di Fredi. The 15th-century **Oratory of the Mercy**, with a Renaissance interior, preserves an *Annunciation* and an *Archangel Gabriel* by the Della Robbia brothers. Inside the **Palazzo Comunale** (14th century) there is the **City Museum** and the **Picture-gallery**. Among the various works, furnishings, Sienese and Aretinian frescoes, the most striking is the *Tree of St. Francesco,* a precious 15th-century late Gothic reliquary.

ENVIRONS

The 16th century **Sanctuary of Madonna delle Querce** was probably designed by Vasari; the interior is attributed to Giuliano da Sangallo. The **Medicean Fortress** (16th century), not far from Lucignano, is an interesting place to visit.

At **Sinalunga**, remarkable for its Medieval setting, there are some interesting churches to see: the **Collegiate Church of St. Martino** (with works by Sodoma, G. del Pacchia and Benvenuto di Giovanni), the **Church of the Madonna delle Nevi** (where you may see a painting attributed to Benvenuto di Giovanni) and the **Church of Santa Croce** (inside, a painting by Luca Signorelli).

Trequanda, and its hamlets **Castelmuzio** and **Petroio**, is a very picturesque Medieval village. It is overlooked by the **Castle of the Cacciaconti**, and the Romanesque **Church of St. Pietro** houses paintings by Sodoma and Giovanni di Paolo.

The ancient origins of **Torrita di Siena** are testified by the **Church of the Madonna dell'Olivo**, built on Roman-Etruscan ruins. The village still preserves Medieval gates; the 14th-century **Church of Saints Flora and Lucilla** is a small picture-gallery: here you can admire works by Lorenzetti, Andrea di Giovanni, Taddeo di Bartolo, Benvenuto di Giovanni, Bartolo di Fredi, and of Sodoma's pupils.

MASSA (Massa Carrara)

HISTORICAL SURVEY – *Situated on one of the low hills closing the narrow valley of the stream Frigido, at the foot of the Apuan Alps, Massa is about five kilometres from the sea. The city contains various interesting examples of medieval and Renaissance architecture. The first document in which Massa is mentioned dates from the 9th century. In the 12th century, it became a possession of the Obertenghi and, at the end of that century, passed under the dominion of the Marchesi Pallodi. But the town really began to take form around the castle of the Malaspina, a noble family that held the power between 1442 and 1741. In the 13th, 14th and 15th centuries, it was often contended by the Florentines, Luccans and Pisans. In 1741, with the marriage of Maria Teresa Cybo Malaspina to Ercole III d'Este, Massa was annexed to the Duchy of Este. In 1796, it became part of the feud of Elisa Baciocchi. In 1815, after the Congress of Vienna, it was once more under Este control. In 1859, it became part of the Kingdom of Sardinia, and then of the Kingdom of Italy.*

PALAZZO CYBO MALASPINA – The palace was begun in 1557 on the remains of a pre-existing Malaspina villa. The elegant polychrome **façade**, is embellished with finely carved busts. The large inside **courtyard** with two floors of loggias is by G.F. Bergamini.

CATHEDRAL – Originally 14th-century, the cathedral has been rebuilt and heavily restored over the years. The **façade** was remade in 1936, and is entirely of marble, with two tiers of superposed arches. The pleasant Baroque **interior**, has a single large nave flanked by a row of side chapels. A 13th-century wooden *Crucifix* is to be found in the left crossing, and in the presbytery there are six stupendous candelabra in bronze, by Pietro Tacca. The **Chapel of the Holy Sacrament** consists of a Baroque altar by Alessandro Bergamini, at the centre of which is a lovely fresco of the *Madonna* by Pinturicchio, as well as a *triptych* attributed to the school of Lippi and a *Nativity* by Benedetto Buglioni. The **Sepulcher of the Cybo-Malaspina** can be reached from the church. It is an enchanting underground chamber in which the sepulchral urns of the princes and dukes of Massa were kept.

Massa, the modern façade of the Cathedral.

HISTORICAL MUSEUM OF SACRED ART – The museum of religious art, annexed to the Cathedral, contains precious church ornaments, goldwork and various important paintings, including the lovely *Madonna of the Rosary*, in silver, dating from the 17th century, and a fine *Crucifix* by Pietro Tacca.

CHURCH OF THE CARMINE – The church, dating from the 18th century, contains valuable 16th century choir books and a beautiful panel painting of the Lombard school of the 15th century, representing the *Madonna del Carmine*.

LA ROCCA – Everyone now calls it "La Rocca", although the real name is **Malaspina Castle**. The plan is more or less triangular and has an older central part where the windows and cornices have fine polychrome marble decorations. The palace is surrounded by a system of **fortified bastions**, and a **loggia** connects it to the medieval part of the city. Long walks along the perimetral walls provide a fine view of the city. Inside, you can visit the **Castle Museum**, with finds from the Palaeolithic to the Roman age.

CHURCH OF ST. ROCCO – This old church has undergone various changes throughout the centuries. At present, the simple **façade** has a few fine decorations. The **interior** contains a lovely *Crucifix*, thought to be by the young Michelangelo.

MASSA MARITTIMA (Grosseto)

HISTORICAL SURVEY – *This lovely town clinging to the hill overlooking the open plain has many interesting traces of its past in the historical centre. The town is now divided into the "old city", situated higher up than the "new city", further down, consisting mainly of modern buildings. Massa Marittima is probably of Etruscan origin, but it became very important in the 9th century, when it was chosen as bishop seat. In 935, it was almost completely destroyed by the Saracens. The city, however, quickly recovered, and in the Middle Ages became one of the most flourishing free Communes, thanks to the exploitation of the copper and silver mines nearby. Wars with Pisa and Siena were frequent, and, in 1335, it was conquered by the latter. In 1555, it passed under Medici rule and, thereafter, followed the Medici fortunes.*

CATHEDRAL – This beautiful church in Romanesque style dates from the first half of the 13th century. It was then enlarged in the area around the presbytery and the apse between 1287 and 1304. The splendid **façade** has seven blind arches decorated with rhombs in the lower part. The architrave of the fine portal has a relief with five *Episodes from the life of St. Cerbone*. The upper order consists of a loggia with five arches resting on slender columns. The gable is decorated with a series of ten arches in diminishing height resting on columns. The right side of the church is also skilfully decorated and the left side, with two portals, is embellished by 13 blind arches in an elegant pattern. The **Bell tower** with its various tiers of windows is as fine as the church. Travertine columns with Corinthian or composite capitals decorated with leaves or figures of animals divide the **interior** into a nave and two aisles. It contains various remarkable works of art. At the beginning of the right aisle there is the **Baptistery**, consisting of a rectangular basin sculptured with *Events from the Life of St. John the Baptist*, marvelous reliefs by Giroldo da Como (1267). At the centre of the basin there is a fine marble shrine with small statues of the *Patriarchs and Prophets* and, on top, the statue of *St. John the Baptist* (1447). Nearby you can admire a lovely late 13th-century marble holy water stoup. Near the baptismal font is the **Chapel of the Crucifix** with a fine *Crucifix*, a panel painting by Segna di Bonaventura, and a fresco of *Saint Lucy, Saint Agatha and the Good Shepherd*, from the second half of the 14th century. There are many paintings in the left aisle: a touching *Annunciation* by Raffaele Vanni (1643); a festive fresco of the *Arrival of the Magi*, probably by a follower of Bartolo di Fredi; a *Madonna and Child with Saints*, a fresco in the manner of Taddeo di Bartolo; and another fresco, under an arch, a *Madonna and Child with Saints Francis and Catherine*, from the beginning of the 14th century. At the altar, in the left transept is a magnificent panel painting of the *Madon-*

na delle Grazie, painted in 1316, by Duccio di Buoninsegna or one of his followers. A door to the left of the high altar leads down to the **Chapel of the Relics**, which contains the *Reliquary of St. Cerbone*, Sienese work of the 14th century, and a *Reliquary cross* in silver foil by Meo and Gaddo Andreassi (15th cent.). Below the apse is the famous *Arch of St. Cerbone*, a splendid sculpture of the Sienese school, done in 1324 by Goro di Gregorio.

CHURCH OF ST. AGOSTINO – This Romanesque-Gothic church dates from the early 14th century. The bare **façade** is in travertine and has a solid doorway with a finely decorated rose window above. Next to the façade is the **Cloister** and the embattled square **Bell tower**, dating from 1627. The **interior**, with a nave only, contains outstanding works of art, including two 16th-century holy water stoups, one on either side of the entrance; on the right wall, a *St. William* by Antonio Rasini, the *Flight into Egypt* by Lorenzo Lippi, *Madonna and Saints* by Rutilio Manetti, and an *Annunciation* by Empoli. On the left wall, there is a lovely *Visitation* by Rutilio Manetti. To the right of the presbytery, is the **Chapel of St. Lucy** (1348), entirely lined with 16th century frescoes. Lastly, in the chapel to the left of the presbytery, on the altar, is a terra-cotta *Madonna and Child* of Florentine school, 15th century.

PALAZZO PRETORIO – Once the residence of the *Podestà*, today the palace houses public offices. This solid severe building in travertine dates from the first half of the 13th century. The two upper floors, with the row of mullioned windows with two lights, brightens the edifice. Here you can visit the **Archaeological Museum** with its interesting material from Etruscan tombs; and the **Museum of the Mine** (reconstruction of the mining activity, exhibition of the tools and machines, collection of rocks and minerals).

PALAZZO COMUNALE – This imposing Romanesque edifice in travertine has a fine series of mullioned windows with two lights, arranged on three floors. The building, dating from the 13th-14th century, is actually the result of the fusion of several medieval tower-hóuses. The central part is an original structure by Stefano di Meo and Gualtiero del Sozzo (14th cent.). The part to the right of the palazzo, known as **Tower of the Bargello**, dates from the early 13th century. **Inside** there are numerous frescoes, including the *Creation of Adam and Eve* and the *Expulsion from Paradise* by an anonymous 16th-century painter. These frescoes are in the town mayor's office. A lovely *Maestà* by Ambrogio Lorenzetti, *Saint Gabriel* by Sassetta and a *Madonna and Child* by Sano di Pietro can be found in the **Commune Picture Gallery**.

OTHER MONUMENTS OF THE CITY – Among the other monuments of interest mention must be made of the imposing **Sienese Fortress**, built around 1335 (inside there is an exhibition of ancient papers and documents describing the mining activity); the **Palazzo Vescovile**, completely rebuilt in 1814; the lovely **House of the counts of Biserno**, a fine Romanesque structure; the **Palazzo dell'Abbondanza**, which dates from the late 13th century.

Massa Marittima, a picturesque view of the town towards the massive structure of the Cathedral.

Montalcino, a view of Poggio alle Mura.

ENVIRONS

Another mining locality is the one near **lake dell'Accesa**, not far from Massa Marittima. Here, excavations have brought to light an Etruscan mining settlement dating from the 6th century BC, made of various houses with rooms, which originally had roofs with rectangular tiles. During the excavations, not much material was found, so it is thought that the abandonment of the site was neither traumatic nor sudden, but done with the necessary calmness; the reasons of the abandonment, though, are unknown. The houses, however, did not belong to the minors, who usually were slaves or war prisoners, but to persons of a higher social class carrying out the technical operations for the conduct of the mine. Evidence of the presence of an aristocratic class comes from the objects (local and imported vases, iron weapons and bronze personal objects) found in the tombs near the lake and which should date from the 7th to the 6th century BC.

MONTALCINO (Siena)

HISTORICAL SURVEY – *Montalcino was already an autonomous Commune in the 12th century and for a long time was divided between the sphere of influence of Florence and that of Siena. After the middle of the 14th century, it fell under the control of the latter, and from 1555 on, it was the seat of the exiled government of the Republic of Siena. Under the French crown in 1559, it was then annexed to the Grand Duchy.*

THE FORTRESS – The **Fortress of Montalcino**, begun in 1361 by Mino Foresi and Domenico de Feo, is a castle-enclosure, on a pentagonal ground plan with three perpendicular sides and a tower at each corner. The south-east tower is polygonal and is flanked by a large building which served as the keep. The **rounds** on the wall are supported by corbel tables while in the **towers** the arcading is supported by rounded corbels shaped like overturned pyramids. **Inside** the Fortress, near the north tower, is what remains of a **Church** which had a nave and two aisles, but was then reduced to the nave alone, and served as the chapel of the castle. In front of the towers facing south, is a wide bastion of the Medici period. Little remains of the city walls towards the valley, but a good stretch still stands on the opposite side, with rectangular towers at intervals. The Fortress now houses a wine cellar for the tasting of "Brunello", the wine of the territory of Montalcino. It also contains the *Standard of the Republic of Siena* by the school of Sodoma.

PIAZZA DEL POPOLO – The city centre of Montalcino is the *Piazza del Popolo*, with a 14th-15th century **Loggia**: it has two Gothic arcades with arches and bars in stone and four round-headed arches in brick. Opposite, set between two streets, is the **Palazzo Comunale**, formerly *Palazzo dei Priori,* built in two distinct periods. The oldest part, uphill, has rough masonry, while the other, downhill, with more precise masonry and wider openings, and with a loggia covered with two cross vaults, is more recent. Towards the square is the **Tower**, in sandstone up to the first balcony and then with corbel tables, the only Sienese feature among the many Florentine characteristics, while the summit, with the aedicula and crowning arch in brick to the battlements, seems to be a 15th-16th century addition. Walking along the side of the Town Hall, you will reach the square with the **Church of St. Egidio**, built by the Sienese in 1325 to replace an older building, with Gothic features on a Romanesque layout. The church has a single nave with a trussed timber roof, and was completely restructured in the 17th century; it contains some fine paintings of the 15th and 16th centuries. The **Church of St. Agostino**, on the road leading from the Fortress to the Cathedral, also has Romanesque-Gothic characteristics. The simple gabled façade has a marble portal and a rose-window. The inside, with a trussed timber roof, holds various frescoes of the Sienese school of painting, dating from the 14th century.

OTHER MONUMENTS – On the highest part of the hill is the **Cathedral**, dedicated to the *Saviour*, like the Romanesque parish church whose place it took. It is an imposing Neo-classic structure built between 1818 and 1832 by Agostino Fantastici. Lower down, near what remains of the old **Gate al Corniolo**, is the **Church of the Madonna del Soccorso**, which conceals Baroque structures with fine altars, behind a modern façade. On the opposite side of the town is the **Church of St. Francesco**, of 13th-century origins but restructured at the end of the 16th century and altered in the 18th century. The sacristy contains frescoes by Vincenzo Tamagni, while on the left side of the church is a 16th-century cloister, with fresco fragments, incorporated into the old **Hospital of St. Maria della Croce**.
Situated in a 16th-century building on the *Piazza Cavour*, there is the **Public Library**, with more than a thousand volumes, manuscripts and incunabuli.
The **Archaeological Museum** is installed in a hall frescoed by Vincenzo Tamagni, inside the adjacent building, the antique **Farmacy of the Hospital of St. Maria della Croce**. The Museum contains prehistoric and Etruscan finds from the surrounding area, especially from the so-called **Fossa del Tesoro**, a 3rd-century BC tomb near Sant'Angelo in Colle, and from the **Buca di Sant'Antimo**. The ex-chapter hall of the convent, near the **Church of St. Agostino**, which also houses the **Seminary**, is the site of the **Diocesan and Civic Museum** which preserves a *Painted cross* of the 12th-13th century from Sant'Antimo, one of the oldest examples of painting in Sienese territory, and various paintings by Girolamo di Benvenuto, the school of Duccio, Domenico Beccafumi, Bartolo di Fredi, Ambrogio Lorenzetti, and Sodoma. Outstanding also are the polychrome wooden statues by Francesco di Valdambrino, Turino di Sano, and Domenico di Niccolò dei Cori. There also are church ornaments of great value and terra-cotta works from the Della Robbia workshop as well as majolicas dating from the 14th and 15th centuries, made in Montalcino (one of the oldest centres for the production of ceramics in Tuscany), and the *Bibbia Atlantica*, with fine miniatures dating from the second half of the 12th century, from the Abbey of Sant'Antimo. Among the civil architecture a special place has the **Palazzo Pieri-Nerli**, in the *Via Ricasoli*, a 15th-century building with a fine internal courtyard, while various other building still retain medieval elements.

ENVIRONS – In the environs of Montalcino there is the complex of the **Osservanza**, in a marvelous setting of cypresses and olive trees. Founded in the 15th century, the church which has a porch, is in 18th-century Baroque style inside. Mention should be made of at least one of the works of art it houses – the *San Bernardino* by Sano di Pietro.

144

Montecatini Terme, marble and architectural ornaments embellish the spa complex.

MONTECATINI TERME (Pistoia)

HISTORICAL SURVEY – *The city lies in a vast plain at the far end of the Valdinievole. It is famous for its spas and has eight springs of prevalently sulphate-alkaline water, an authentic cure-all for disorders of the liver and the digestive apparatus. These springs were already known in antiquity. In 1583 they became the property of the Medici and then, in the 18th century, of the Lorraine. But it was not until the beginning of the 20th century that the spas began to be known nationally and in Europe, and the town of Montecatini grew up around them.*

PARK OF THE THERMAL WATERS – The large green park actually separates the more recent Montecatini from the old. Among the many spas, most of which in neo-classical and liberty style, these are worth mentioning: **Excelsior**, **Terme Leopoldine**, **Tamerici**, **Regina**, **Tettuccio**, **Torretta**, **Rinfresco**, **La Salute**, **Redi**.

BASILICA OF ST. MARIA ASSUNTA – Octagonal Church designed by Tognoni (1962), it houses a 16th-century *Madonna*, attributed to Fra' Bartolomeo della Porta, a *Crucifix* by Cavallini and glass windows by Scalco.

ART ACADEMY – The Academy, situated in front of the Regina spa, was named after D. Scalabrino, and among many others you can admire works by Fattori, Messina, Guttuso, Annigoni, Dupré, Mirò, Viani and Dalì.

MONTECATINI ALTO – In this old castle town situated on a hill behind Montecatini Terme, there is the **Church of St. Pietro**, a Baroque remake of a very old country church. Inside there are various fine works, including a sculptural *Ascension* by Santi di Tito (1595), in the choir, and a *Martyrdom of Saint Barbara*, probably by Jacopo Ligozzi, on the third altar to the left. Next to the church is a small **Museum** with paintings and minor arts.

MONTE OLIVETO MAGGIORE (Siena)

The origins of this monastic settlement are bound to the religious experience of the Sienese nobleman Giovanni Tolomei (1272-1348), who, together with Ambrogio Piccolomini and Patrizio Patrizi, retired from the world, in 1313, to lead the life of a hermit near Chiusure. Shortly thereafter he created a new monastic congregation, essentially based on the Benedictine rule, which was to be lived in its original rigor. The scope of the new "olivetan" order was thus that of reform. A whole series of foundations, dependent on the mother house, were promoted, and from the beginning, particular stress was laid on study, and Monte Oliveto soon became an important centre for culture, art and books. A few hundred metres before the monastic complex, stands a powerful 14th-century **Keep**, of rectangular ground plan which is a sort of fortified outpost for the abbey. Built entirely of brick and preceded by a moat, the massive building is crowned by projecting battlements, set on concentric arches, supported by brackets in the shape of reversed pyramids. On the arches of the entrance gates, at the beginning and end of the corridor crossing the building, there are two large glazed terra-cotta figures of the school of the Della Robbia, representing the *Madonna and Child with two Angels* and a *Blessing Saint Benedict.*

The **Abbey Church**, at least on the outside still preserves many features of the late Gothic structure, built by Abbot Ippolito di Giacomo from Milan in 1399-1417. The building is in brick with a Latin-cross plan and a single nave. The piers supporting the vaulting are set against the walls, thrust counteracted on the exterior by buttresses. The **façade**, framed by two pilasters at the corners, is crowned by a cornice of bricks arranged in a saw-tooth pattern, that continues on the sides. The portal, flanked by pilasters and small columns supporting the depressed arch archivolt, is topped by a gable, in the pediment of which, is a shaped rose-window. A large round window, surrounded by a terra-cotta cornice, is set in the upper part of the elevation. Near the tribune, the robust **Bell tower** of the abbey is built in brick. Gothic mullioned windows with three lights decorate the belfry, and the tower is capped by a conical spire, unusual for Tuscan bell towers, and revealing Lombard influence. The **interior**, remodelled in Baroque forms in 1772 by Giovanni Antinori, has a beautiful wooden choir stall, carved and inlaid by Fra' Giovanni da Verona in the early 16th century, a gigantic lectern by Fra' Raffaele da Brescia, a wooden *Cross* of the 13th century, and frescoes and paintings of various periods. To the right of the church, lies the so-called **Large Cloister**, built in two phases (1426 and 1474), and with the walls covered by the famous fresco cycles of *Events from the Life of Saint Benedict*, painted by Luca Signorelli and Sodoma. Among the other rooms part of the monastic complex, mention should be made of the **Middle Cloister**, enclosed by a portico with octagonal piers (it contains Sodoma's odd portrait of the "*Friar-cook*"), the **Small Cloister**, also with arcade on octagonal piers; the **Refectory**, an enormous room with a vaulted ceiling, decorated with 17th-century frescoes; the **Library**, built in 1518, by Fra' Giovanni da Verona, with three aisles articulated by columns with Corinthian capitals; the **Pharmacy**; the **Chapter Hall**, and still more. All these rooms are richly decorated with frescoes, ceramics, furniture and wooden furnishings, mostly of the 15th and 16th centuries, which together with the about 40,000 volumes, illuminated codexes and incunabuli in the Library, form the inestimable cultural patrimony of the famous Benedictine coenoby.

MONTEPULCIANO (Siena)

HISTORICAL SURVEY – *The urban structure of this noble little city is in part medieval and in part Renaissance. The numerous palaces, the narrow streets running from one of the large arteries to the other, the churches full of history, are all picturesque and enchanting. Already inhabited in Etruscan times, it was contested by Siena and Florence, and finally in 1208 became a free Commune. After various vicissitudes it passed under the jurisdiction of the Medici.*

CATHEDRAL – It was built between 1592 and 1630, on a design by Ippolito Scalza. The simple **façade** rises above a flight of stairs and has three fine portals and three windows. Next to the façade is the **Bell tower** dating from the second half of the 15th century. The Latin-cross **interior** has a nave and two aisles divided by piers. Two frescoes are to be found in the right aisle – a *St. Domenic* (15th cent.) and a *Redeemer* (16th cent.). On either side of the high altar, are the statues of *Faith* and *Science*. Above the altar is the *Assumption*, a fine triptych by Taddeo di Bartolo (1401). In the chapel to the left of the presbytery, is a lovely *Deposition*, of the Flemish school. In the left aisle, between the fifth and fourth chapels, is a beautiful *Madonna and Child* by Sano di Pietro; in the third chapel the *St. Sebastian* from Andrea del Sarto's workshop; and, in the first chapel (now the **Baptistery**) is the glazed terra-cotta *Annunciation and Four Saints* by the school of Andrea della Robbia.

CHURCH OF ST. AGNESE – The modern **façade** (1926) still has a fine 14th-century portal from the time when the church was first built. The **interior** has a single nave and contains various outstanding works: a *Madonna*, fresco by a follower of Simone Martini (first chapel to the right); the *Martyrdom of St. Biagio*; a 17th-century painting on canvas by Giovanni da San Giovanni (right wall); the *Madonna del Latte*, fresco by an unknown 14th-century painter (second altar to the left); a fine *Crucifixion* of the 13th century (first chapel on the left).

Montepulciano, a beautiful picture of the turreted and embattled Town Hall.

CHURCH OF ST. AGOSTINO – Designed by Michelozzo, it is divided by pilasters above which are elegant niches. Particularly lovely is the portal, with a terra-cotta relief of the *Madonna with Sts. John the Baptist and Augustine* in the lunette, by Michelozzo. The **interior** has a single nave. Among the most important works are the *Ascension* by Cesare Nebbia, and the prestigious *Madonna of the Girdle* by Barocci, over the entrance; on the first altar to the right, *Resurrection of Lazarus* by Alessandro Allori; on the third altar to the left is a *Crucifixion with the Madonna and the Magdalen* by Lorenzo di Credi.

THE HOUSE OF POLIZIANO – A fine 14th-15th century building in brick which has frequently been altered in the course of time.

CHURCH OF ST. MARIA DEI SERVI – The church dates from the 14th century, and has a Gothic **façade** and a fine pinnacled portal. The richly decorated **interior** is by Andrea del Pozzo and contains an important 14th-century Sienese fresco, the *Madonna della Santoreggia*, at the second altar to the left, and a prestigious panel of the school of Duccio di Buoninsegna, a *Madonna and Child*, on the third altar to the left.

PALAZZO COMUNALE – This powerful Tower Hall has three floors and a well-preserved battlement on top. The palace dates from the second half of the 14th century, but the **façade** built later, may be by Michelozzo. Inside, the beautiful **courtyard** with superposed loggias, has been restored. The palazzo faces onto the scenic *piazza Grande*, enclosed in austere buildings in pure medieval and Renaissance style, and adorned by the beautiful **Pozzo de' Grifi e de' Leoni** (a well), a valuable piece from the Renaissance. In the cellar of **Palazzo Contucci** (16th century, A. da Sangallo il V., B. Peruzzi) there is a well-known wine cellar. Here, as in many other wine cellars of the area, the best wines of this part of land are presented to the public, among which the "Nobile di Montepulciano" is probably the best wine of this area.

PALAZZO NERI-ORSELLI AND CIVIC MUSEUM – The **Museum** contains important works from various periods. Among the most interesting works are the two altarpieces by Andrea della Robbia, the *Madonna and Child with St. John* by Sebastiano Mainardi, the touching *Nativity* by Rutilio Manetti, the intense *Portrait of a Woman* by Spagnoletto, the two *Portraits* by Sustermans, the famous *Portrait of the Knight of Malta* by Paris Bordone, and the *Portrait of the Knight of St. Stephen* by Santi di Tito, as well as works by Pinturicchio, Filippino Lippi, Cigoli.

CHURCH OF ST. LUCIA – The fine baroque **façade** in travertine, was designed by Flaminio del Turco (1653). The **interior**, with a single nave, has important, works: to the right of the entrance is the *Madonna of Mercy*, a masterpiece by Luca Signorelli, and on the high altar, is a wooden *Crucifixion* by G.B. Alessi.

ENVIRONS – At the feet of the Politian hill, near the charming cypresses by which it is framed, you will find the **Temple of St. Biagio**, it is of Renaissance architecture by Antonio da Sangallo the Elder. 5 km away from the town, at **Sant'Albino**, there is the modern spa **Terme di Montepulciano**.
In Valdichiana there is **Lake Montepulciano**, rich with fish.

MONTERIGGIONI (Siena)

The village of Monteriggioni clings to a small hillside, enclosed in the impressive circuit of **walls**. From a distance, the first impression is that time has stood still, and we are in the Middle Ages, especially if one glances from one four-sided **tower** to the other (there are fourteen set along the walls).
The village was built in 1203, by the Sienese, who used it as an outpost against the Florentines, and as a result of its strategic position, it often changed hands. The walls went up between 1213 and 1219, and extend for about 570 metres, encircling the tiny but compact charming village, which has a fine **Parish Church**, a compact building in a traditional Romanesque-Gothic style.

Monteriggioni, the ancient walled town dominates a green hill.

MONTE SAN SAVINO (Arezzo)

Monte San Savino is known as the home town of the architect Andrea Contucci, know as Sansovino. He was active here, where he left numerous works, and in Florence, Rome and Portugal. In Monte San Savino the design for the 16th-century **Church of St. Agostino** is attributed to him, although it was then built by Domenico di Nenni. The terra-cotta statue of *Saint Sebastian* in **St. Chiara** also seems to be his. The building is particularly interesting for the many Renaissance masterpieces it contains, including a terra-cotta *Madonna and Child with Saints*, modelled by Sansovino and glazed by Giovanni della Robbia. It is not certain whether Sansovino or Antonio da Sangallo the Elder designed the **Loggia dei Mercanti**, an elegant piece of architecture in front of the **Palazzo Comunale**.

ENVIRONS – You will easily feel the Middle Ages at **Gargonza**, a tiny village of ancient stone houses and churches, enclosed in partially conserved city walls.

ORBETELLO (Grosseto)

The town is at the centre of the lagoon of Orbetello, which is about 27 square kilometres, with two strips of sand known as "tomboli". An artificial dam, built in 1842, joins it to the promontory of the Argentario. A visit to Orbetello can begin with the **Gate Medina Coeli**, which was part of the old circuit of walls. The gate leads into the *Piazza Quattro Novembre*, surrounded by the **Spanish fortification** built when it was part of the Spanish garrisons: these fine examples of military architecture were begun by Philip II and continued by Philip III in the 17th century. The 14th-century **Cathedral** is also lovely, although it was remodelled in the 17th century. Inside is a fine marble altarpiece of pre-Romanesque art. The **Palazzo della Pretura** houses the **Antiquarium**, a museum with archaeological material from Etruscan and Roman times from all over the city territory. Particular attention should be paid to the archaic *Sphinx* of the 7th-6th century BC, various amphorae and fine sculptures.

PESCIA (Pistoia)

HISTORICAL SURVEY – *This ancient city, known in all the world for its flowers, is full of signs of the past. It was a free Commune at the end of the 12th century, and passed under the dominion of Florence in 1339. It prospered under the Medici and was granted the title of city, in 1699.*

CATHEDRAL – The church is a 17th-century remaking of the old Country Church of St. Maria, of which evidence remains at the sides and in the **Bell tower** of 1306. The **façade** was redone in the 19th century, by the architect Giuseppe Castellucci. The **interior**, with one nave, contains interesting works of art: to the left of the entrance, is a 16th-century holy water stoup; nearby is the *funeral monument to the poet Giuseppe Giusti*. To the right of the presbytery, is the lovely **Turini Chapel**, by Giuliano di Baccio d'Agnolo, with Piero Bandini's copy of Raphael's famous *Madonna del Baldacchino*. Entrance to the **Hall of the Chapter Library** is from the interior. In the hall there is a statue of *St. Giovannino* by the school of the Della Robbia, the *Coronation of the Virgin*, probably by Bicci di Lorenzo, and five panels with *Saints*, also by Bicci di Lorenzo.

CHURCH OF ST. FRANCESCO – This Gothic building dates from 1298, and is the result of a transformation of a pre-existing oratory. The simple **façade** has frequently been restructured. The **interior** contains various extremely interesting works, such as the fine panel painting, on the third altar to the right, with the *Events from the Life of Saint Francis*, a rare example of Romanesque painting, dating from 1235, by Bonaventura Berlinghieri. The first chapel to the left is the splendid **Orlandi-Cardini Chapel**, with a fine wooden *Crucifix* of the 15th century, behind which is the large fresco by Neri di Bicci of the *Patrons of the chapel with their Protector Saints*, and Giovanni Martinelli's *Miracle of the Mule*. The chapel to the right of the high altar, contains the fine *Stories of the Virgin*, frescoes attributed to Bicci di Lorenzo, and, in the chapel, to the left, a tender triptych of the *Madonna and Child, St. Anne and other Saints*, attributed to Angelo Puccinelli. Other outstanding works are the *Martyrdom of St. Dorothy* by Jacopo Ligozzi (1595) in the left transept, a *Madonna and Child*, a 15th-century wooden sculpture, and the *Deposition*, a 16th-century painting on canvas, in the Baroque chapel in the left wall.

CIVIC MUSEUM – The museum houses works that come from the numerous churches in the surroundings, and from private collections, and is situated in Palazzo Gaelotti. Here you can see a collection of Etruscan archaeological material, illuminated antiphonaries, numerous prints by great artists, and various remarkable paintings by artists such as Lorenzo Monaco, Bicci di Lorenzo and others. The **Geo-palaentologic Museum** is in *Piazza Leonardo da Vinci.*

PIENZA (Siena)

HISTORICAL SURVEY – *In August 1458, Cardinal Aeneas Silvius Piccolomini was elected pope with the name of Pius II. This event produced unexpected effects on the castle of Corsignano: within a few years it not only completely changed its urban layout, but was elevated to the dignity of city, becoming the bishop's see. In 1459, the pope's architect, Bernardo Gambarelli da Settignano, known as Rossellino, began the total restructuring of the castle, in which Pius II was born, and had passed his youth. Three years later very much had already been accomplished, therefore, by papal bull of August 13, the pope elevated the castle to city, changing its name to Pienza, "ad memoriam nostri pontificalis nominis". In addition to the church of Santa Maria Assunta, which was then to become the Cathedral, the Palazzo Piccolomini, and the other main buildings, Pius II had twelve houses built under the direction of Porrina. The premature death of the pontefix (1464), slowed down the work, and some of the buildings were never finished. However, the town continued to be fairly important. Then, in the 16th century, it was subjected to a series of sieges and destruction. The walls, which had been in large part rebuilt in the 15th century and reinforced in 1552, were almost demolished during the last incursions. Their original rectangular circuit can still be traced, despite the restoration and fragmentation consequent to*

Pienza, Palazzo Piccolomini, jewel of Renaissance architecture.

their destruction, in the 16th century. The town seems to have stopped in time within the perimeter of the walls, and is a unique example of 15th-century town planning, based on the concept of the ideal city of the humanist culture. The stylistic unity of the architecture is remarkable, and is evidence of the existence of a single plan in the formative process of the urban fabric, and of the coordinating role played by Rossellino, who was defined by Aeneas Silvius Piccolomini as the leading architect of his time. The piazza named after Pius II is in the heart of the city, and the most important buildings surround it: the Cathedral, Palazzo Piccolomini, the Bishop's Palace with the House of the Canons, and the Town Hall.

CATHEDRAL – Dedicated to the *Virgin of the Assumption*, the Cathedral, Rossellino's major work, was consecrated by the Bishop of Ostia on August 29, 1462. Pius II himself consecrated the high altar, after having promulgated an excommunication bull, for anyone who dared to change the form of the building (the bull was revoked by Gregory XIII, in 1583, since restoration work was required). The church has a solemn **façade** in travertine, divided into three parts by pilasters flanked by a double order of columns, and crowned by a broad fastigium, adorned at the centre with Pius II's coat of arms. **Inside**, the nave and two aisles of equal height, as in the *Hallenkirche* north of the Alps, are divided by composite piers with capitals, each of which is topped by a low abacus, on which is another very high one, terminating in a cornice, from which the cross vaults spring. The aisles, near the presbytery, fuse into a sort of ambulatory, with five radiating apsidal chapels, illuminated by large Gothic windows that flood the interior with light, turning it into a "*templum cristallinum*", the expression used by Pius II in his *Commentarii*. To one side of the church, on the left, is a small **Bell tower**, with a spire in travertine, once more recalling Gothic forms. The **Crypt** (the **Temple of St. Giovanni**) stretches out under the presbytery, like in the Baptistery of Siena, and it contains an elegant font designed by Rossellino, and various fragments of Romanesque sculpture from the old church of St. Maria, that was in the castle of Corsignano. Among the many works of art the Cathedral contains, these are the most remarkable: the *Assumption of the Virgin* by Vecchietta, a gold-ground tempera painting, which is perhaps the artist's masterpiece; various panel paintings by Matteo di Giovanni, Sano di Pietro and Giovanni di Paolo; a marble altar with a silver reliquary, perhaps by Bernardo Rossellino; wooden Gothic choir stalls in two tiers.

BISHOP'S PALACE, HOUSE OF THE CANONS AND DIOCESAN MUSEUM – The **Bishop's Palace** lies to the left of the Cathedral, it has a façade in rows of sandstone and two tiers of Guelph-cross windows. It was built by Cardinal Borgia (later Alexander VI) adapting a precedent Gothic building, of which the traces can still be seen. Next to the palace is the **House of the Canons**, in sober Renaissance forms. The façade was once adorned with graffiti paintings. At present, it is the seat of the local **Cathedral Museum of Sacred Art** which holds works of art from the Cathedral and other churches in the diocese of Pienza. Outstanding is the collection of church vestments and religious objects in gold and silver, mostly from the 15th and 16th century. Among all these art works, remarkable for their refinement are the silver 15th-century *pax*, in the form of a classic temple, the sumptuous gilded silver pastoral given to the Cathedral by Pius II, and the famous cope of Pius II. The cope is a 14th-century English work, given to the pope by Thomas Paleologue. It is semi-circular in form, and decorated with marvelous embroidery in gold and silk on linen, consisting of 150 figures part of various scenes: the *Life of the Madonna*, the *Articles of the Credo*, the *Lives of Saint Margaret of Antioch and Saint Catherine of Alexandria*. The Museum also contains illuminated choir books by Sano di Pietro and Pellegrino di Mariano (1462), 16th-century incunabuli and prints, a collection of eleven 15th-16th century tapestries of Flemish school, and various panel paintings by Sienese painters of the 14th and 15th centuries, including a lovely *Madonna of Mercy* by Bartolo di Fredi, dated 1364. Lastly, in a small room annexed to the museum, there is a collection of Etruscan-Roman cinerary urns, amphoras, chalices, and other material from excavations, mostly from the necropolis of Borghetto.

PALAZZO PICCOLOMINI – Obviously inspired by Alberti's Palazzo Rucellai in Florence, the **Palazzo Piccolomini**, Rossellino's masterpiece, occupies one entire side of the main square, to the right of the Cathedral. It is an imposing building, almost square in plan, with an extremely regular masonry facing of rusticated tufaceous stone, smooth and with canalisations at the edges. Two travertine frames run all around the palace and separate the three floors, articulated by pilaster strips, in between which are set harmonious mullioned windows with two lights. The portal opens onto the inner courtyard, surrounded by a colonnade with rich Corinthian capitals, and leads to the **Hanging gardens**, on which the back of the building overlooks, with a lovely three-tiered loggia from which a magnificent view of the Val d'Orcia can be admired. A brilliant touch by Rossellino is the fine **Well** in a corner, in front of the palace. The well has two columns with Corinthian capitals supporting the architrave with a double cornice set over the basin. The **interior** of the palace is also an example of 15th-century elegance, with the furnishings of the rooms, the wooden coffered ceilings, the library, and the many weapons, musical instruments and objects of art.

TOWN HALL – The square is completed, on the side opposite the Cathedral, by the Town Hall, restored and integrated in 1900. At its base, the building presents a Ionic porch and there are four mullioned windows with two lights above. On the right, it is flanked by a pre-existing crenellated brick **Tower** two stories high.

THE OTHER PALACES – The *Corso Rossellino*, the city's main street which leads into *Piazza Pius II*, is flanked by palaces, most of which retain their original architectural features, especially of the 15th century. One of the major buildings is **Palazzo Newton**, built for the cardinal of Pavia, Giacomo Ammannati, whose three magnificent coats of arms in stone decorate the façade, partially raised like a tower, and which has two levels of windows, the upper Guelph, like the ones on the first floor of the **Palazzo Simonelli** that once belonged to Cardinal Gonzaga. Among the other buildings, interesting are the **Casa Cittadini** and the **Palazzina of the Cardinal Atrabatense**, with mullioned windows with two lights, that are still Gothic in style. All these minor palaces, severe and elegant, together with the typical 15th-century houses, constitute the town of Pienza, giving it the unique Reinassance feature.

ENVIRONS – If you come out from the **Gate al Ciglio**, it is worth taking a short deviation towards the ancient **Country Church of Corsignano**, a jewel of Romanesque architecture (11th century), with its cylindrical **Bell tower**.

PIETRASANTA (Lucca)

HISTORICAL SURVEY – *This old town is famous for the working of marble. It was founded in 1255, by the podestà of Lucca, Guiscardo Pietrasanta, and around the 14th century its urban development began. In the 15th century, it passed under the dominion of Genoa, then under that of Lucca. In 1513, it was admitted to the Medici Grand Duchy, and was lastly governed by the House of Lorraine. The charming historical centre has medieval streets, squares and historical buildings.*

CATHEDRAL – The cathedral dates from the 13th century, although it was considerably enlarged a hundred years later. The tripartite **façade** has a large richly decorated rose window in the centre, and three portals below, all of which have reliefs by Pisan school in their lunettes. Next to the central portal is a fine bas relief of *St. John the Baptist* by the 15th-century sculptor Stagio Stagi, who was born here. The **interior** has a nave and two aisles divided by columns, and contains outstanding works, including two large holy water fonts by Stagio Stagi near the main entrance; two paintings on the altars in the transept, the *Madonna of the Rosary* by Matteo Rosselli (1649), and the *Nativity* (1677) by Piero Dandini. The two stupendous marble candle-holders on the high altar, are by Stagi, who also carried out the 24 marble choir stalls. To the right of the high altar is the **Chapel of the Madonna of the Sun**, with a marvelous late Gothic painting of the *Madonna between Saints John the Baptist and John the Evangelist*. Mention should also be made of works by Matteo Rosselli, Jacopo Vignali and Fabrizio Boschi, all fine 17th-century painters.

BAPTISTERY – This small charming building is set near the Cathedral. The precious baptismal font is by Donato Benti (1509), and the late 14th-century marble basin is probably by Bonuccio Pardini.

CHURCH OF ST. AGOSTINO – The church dates from the 14th century and has a sober **façade** in marble, with three blind arches and small Gothic arches on columns above. The single nave of the **interior** has a fine trussed timber roof. The cloister of the annexed convent, houses the **Museum of Sketches** (Museo dei Bozzetti, moulds and tests of marble works of contemporary artists).

OTHER CITY MONUMENTS – The *Column of Liberty*, in *piazza del Duomo*, is by Donato Benti; it is in front of a fountain, by the school of Benti, and was commissioned by the Medici, to satisfy the water requirements of the population. On one side of the square, there is **Palazzo Pretorio**, built during the 14th century, decorated with armorial bearings, in memory of the period when Pietrasanta became a vicarship. On the opposite side of the square, there is **Palazzo Moroni**, 15th-century, once seat of the Medici chancellery, and today, of the **City Library**, **Historic Archive**, and the **Archaeological Civic Museum of the Versilia**, with Etruscan, Roman and medieval finds. Also on the square is the **Tower of the Hours**, built in the 16th century, but later altered. In antiquity, under the portico surrounding the square, there was a market and the shops. Apart from some Renaissance and Baroque buildings in the streets adjacent the Cathedral, in Pietrasanta you can admire the **Fortress of Sala**, built during the Lombard period, and then connected to the city walls with two long bastions. In *piazza Matteotti* there is a sculpture of the famous contemporary artist Botero.

PISA

HISTORICAL SURVEY – *Pisa lies 13 kilometres from the sea on a vast alluvial plain, protected on the northeast by Monte Pisano where the lower Valdarno joins the coastal plain. It is a swampy humid area, but in the past it connected the coast and inland settlements. A crossroad, in other words, an obligatory stop for trade and commerce. Today the visitor can see Pisa in all its beauty, enclosed in the small, but remarkable historical centre which preserves some of the finest examples of Ro-*

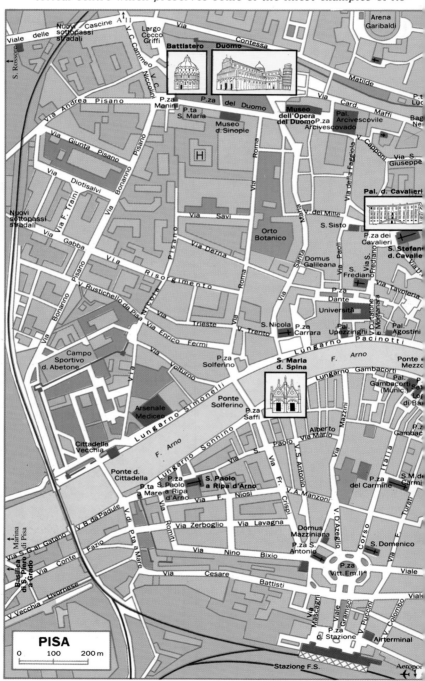

manesque architecture, together with marvelous examples of Renaissance and 17th-century buildings. The origins of Pisa are still now uncertain. Some Latin historians, including Livy, claim that it was founded by the Ligurians. Others, including Servius, state it was built by Phocaean merchants. Recent archaeological findings, in various parts of the city north of the river, have confirmed an old hypothesis: Pisa was a prosperous Etruscan centre between the 6th and 3rd centuries BC. Whatever the case may be, Pisa does not seem to have fully developed until Roman times, when it was allied with Rome in the Second Punic war, a Roman city in 89 BC, and a flourishing colony in the times of Augustus (Colonia Julia Pisana Obsequens). Under the Carolingian dynasty it be-

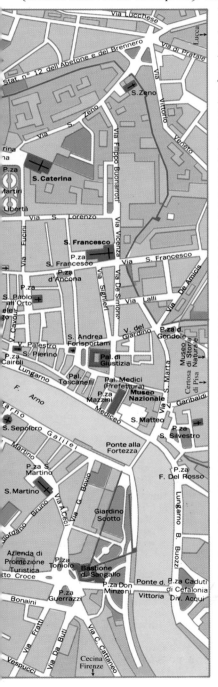

came part of the Marquisate of Tuscany, but although a subjected city, it was actually autonomous enough to succeed in becoming a free Commune at the beginning of the 11th century. This was the beginning of an extremely prosperous period of its history, which lasted almost three centuries. The city became a powerful centre thanks to the control of the seas by its powerful fleet. In this period Pisa became an ally of the Normans and helped them in their conquest of Sicily; participated in the first Crusade with 120 ships, and founded numerous merchant colonies in the East, expanding its commercial dominion. In the 12th century, the city was at the apex of its fortunes. Pisa won a great victory over the Muslim fleet, and later defeated its rival Amalfi. The power of the Maritime Republic was by then consolidated in the Tyrrhene Sea, the ships hoisting the Signum rubicundum controlled the Archipelago, Corsica, Sardinia, and the Balearic Islands, and arrived all the way across the Mediterranean Sea to the eastern ports (Constantinople). Evidence of this fortunate period are the many religious and civil buildings which were built in the city. Work on the Cathedral was begun and the urban growth led to a restructuring of the city walls. Artistically too, Pisa became a great cultural centre, above all thanks to the genius and personality of sculptors such as Nicola Pisano, his son Giovanni Pisano, and Arnolfo di Cambio, who together with a fine group of other great artists, created schools that served as example throughout Italy. A slow but inexorable decline began with the 13th and 14th centuries, caused by the continuous clashes on land, with neighbours Lucca and Florence, and on sea, with its harsh rival Genoa. By the latter defeated at the Meloria (1284), in the 15th century, Florence, ever more powerful, set its eyes on Pisa, and after various struggles and vicissitudes Pisa became subject to the

Medici city (1509). In addition, the building of the port of Livorno destined to substitute the silted up Portus Pisanus, *deprived the city of its link with the sea.*

But Pisa was not a city to be overcome. Defeated on a military and political level, it reconfirmed its status as a great city of culture, one of the most important university centres. In fact, it was no less a figure than Galileo Galilei, who initiated a prestigious scientific tradition which then continued under the Lorraine dynasty. During the Medicean age, under the insignia of the Order of Knighthood of St. Stefano, the Pisans took part in the victorious battle of Lepanto (1571) against the Ottomans. In 1848 volunteers from the University of Pisa fought the Austrians at Curtatone and Montanara. In 1860 Pisa became part of the Kingdom of Italy. Badly damaged by the bombs of the Second World War, injured by the flood of the Arno (1966), Pisa today is a small and walkable town concentrated around its centre. It is rich in cultural activities, favoured by an integrated transportation system (G. Galileo Tuscany Airport, Florence-Pisa-Livorno motorway, railway and motorway network), by a fairly good industry and by a never ending tourism.

THE WALLS – The walls of Pisa were begun under the consulate of Cocco Griffi, in 1155. For a long time it was assumed that this was the first and last circuit of walls built in Pisa. But recent investigation has revealed the traces of a late Roman and medieval circuit, along a line that is basically parallel to what is now the axis of the Borgo streets. Work began in July-August of 1155, with the excavation of the moats of the *civitatem Pisanam*, the city north of the Arno, and the suburb of *Kinticam*, included in the loop of the river, to the south.

At the same time, the walls were begun between the tower of the Lion and the tower on the bridge over the Auser, the stream which was the moat on the north side of the city. The circuit was finished around 1161, even if the masonry continued to be improved for years. The fact that the construction of the walls was begun in the area of the Duomo, testifies to the importance of the northwest corner of the city, in the urban layout. This was where the most important monuments began to take shape. The rows of ashlars used to face the walls are generally more carefully laid in the lower levels, while further up the work is hastier. The name of Bonanno has been made for the project of the walls of Pisa, but there is no real evidence. Nor is there anything in the structure, from a technical or architectural point of view, that would justify the presence of such an outstanding designer.

The four gates completed in 1161 (*"et quattruor portas volverunt et compleverunt"*) probably are the **Legazia** and **Calcesana Gates**, which resemble each other and are still extant, Spina Alba, which no longer exists but documented in old pictures, and the **Parlascio**. This was the loveliest gate in the whole wall, decorated with sculpture, and connected the Via del Borgo with the road that leads to Lucca. Built into the bastion that went up after 1435 (the name of Filippo Brunelleschi has been suggested for the project) the Parlascio gate (known also as *"to Lucca"*) is now being restored. Nearby, you will see the **Bagno di Nerone**, Roman baths of the 2nd century AD.

Of the other gates opened in the city walls, mention can be made of the **Gate of the Lion**, the **Postern Gate of St. Stefano**, the **Gate of St. Zeno**. The building of the walls in 1155, was for Pisa the logical conclusion of an urban expansion, which was the result of successive additions to the oldest nucleus and was not, as was the case in other Tuscan cities of Roman origin (see Lucca, Florence, Pistoia), streched out along the basic communication routes. Moreover, the solution for future urban development had also been indicated, although the precocious political and demographic decline of the city would have not allowed further enlargement.

PIAZZA DEL DUOMO – The Piazza del Duomo in Pisa, known also as the *Campo dei Miracoli*, and so called by D'Annunzio, is known by the tourists as *Piazza dei Miracoli* (Miracle Square). Situated in the northwest corner of the city, near the Gate of the Lion, it can be considered one of the most outstanding examples of medieval town planning, as well as being incredibly well preserved. From the early Middle Ages this was where the baptismal church of Pisa and the Bishop's residence had risen, probably in correspondance to a suburban villa set on the old *Via*

Pisa, a striking aerial view of the famous Piazza dei Miracoli.

Aemilia Scaurii. Excavations carried out between 1939 and 1951, in the area between the Cathedral and the Cemetery have brought to light the foundations of buildings including those of an octagonal baptistery with a semicircular apse. The Square gradually took shape between the middle of the 11th and the middle of the 14th century – when the Bell tower was finished – but work continued even after the middle of the 19th century. Buscheto's original architectural concept was continued by various architects: Rainaldo, who lengthened the Cathedral, Diotisalvi, who started the Baptistery, and Nicola Pisano, who finished it, Bonanno who laid the foundations for the Bell tower, and Giovanni di Simone, who carried the work almost to the top and who also delimited the long sides of the Square with the Cemetery and with the Hospital, which was begun in 1257. Despite this alternation of personalities, who were among the most outstanding figures of Romanesque culture, the monumental and urban complex of Pisa has retained an incredible unity. Everything in Piazza del Duomo is arranged in function of the Cathedral, not according to symmetry, "but by that taking into account the composition of harmonious groups, at times static, other times converging towards pre-ordained points." (P. Sampaolesi). The various buildings not only constitute a whole unity, but also well blend with the surrounding area.

Pisa, the Leaning Tower beyond the southern transept of the Cathedral.

CATHEDRAL – The construction of the *Cathedral of St. Maria Assunta* is said to have been determined by the victory over Palermo in 1062, and the resulting increase in wealth of the city. The presence of a bishop in Pisa with strong a personality, as was Guido of Pavia, must have been as Buscheto. Buscheto not only designed a building in "snow white marble which has no equal", but created what can only be called the "Pisan Romanesque" style. The building of the Cathedral of Pisa was carried out in the second half of the 11th century, and considerably committed all the city. In fact, it is interesting to recall the episode of the excommunication the bishops directed, in 1095, against those who diverted the blacksmiths from their work on the *Primatial Church*. This was probably finished in 1118 – or at least well towards being finished – when it was blessed by Pope Gelasius II, while in 1136, when a Council was held there, it must already have had its present façade.

The vicissitudes of the Cathedral of Pisa lasted much longer, and in 1167, the pulpit by Guglielmo, was installed. Later it was transferred to the Cathedral of Cagliari, when Giovanni Pisano's new pulpit was installed at the very beginning of the 14th century. After a disastrous fire, in 1595, this pulpit was removed, and not until 1926, was it recomposed with integrations. In 1186, the bronze doors, in which Bonanno represented scenes from the *Life of the Virgin and of the Saviour* were put in. But they too, were destroyed in the above mentioned fire and were reconstructed shortly thereafter by followers of Giambologna. Between the 13th and 14th century the façade was finished with the rampant big cats and the statues, while towards the end of the 14th century the cupola had its loggia of gabled aediculae. As well as the portals, the fire

158

of the end of the 16th century destroyed the ceiling, which was replaced with the coffered ceiling it has now. Much of the marble decorations were also damaged, therefore capitals, cornices and architraves had to be replaced, and the various parts were still being restored in the middle of the 19th century.

The Cathedral of Pisa was certainly for its time the most imposing grandiose church in the Christian west. The **interior** has a nave and four aisles, like the largest early Christian basilicas in Rome, but with a projecting three-aisled transept. Women's galleries run along over the side aisles and an octagonal dome is set at the intersection of the nave and transept. A large **apse** is at the end of the nave and also of each arm of the transept. Originally the church must have had a trussed timber roof. Tall columns articulate the nave, interrupted by four piers which support the drum on which the dome rests, while the women's galleries above look out on the nave through broad mullioned windows with two lights. The interior of this large church is luminous, enlivened by the vivacious polychrome decoration, as well as by the play of shadows and lights determinated by the complex spatial organisation. The classic decoration of the capitals in Buscheto's part of construction differ from the more Romanesque ones, with their various decorations, that belong to the 12th-century prolongation of the Cathedral. One of the most outstanding works of art that enriches the Primatial church of Pisa is the *pulpit*, made by Giovanni Pisano in the first decade of the 14th century, to replace the one by Guglielmo sent to Cagliari. The pulpit is on a circular base, and is carved with *Stories from the Lives of St. John the Baptist and Christ* in the panels, which are divided by figures of *Prophets and Saints*. It is one of the finest expressions of Italian Gothic sculpture. There is also a lovely ivory statue of the *Madonna* by Giovanni, in the Treasury of the Cathedral. The Cathedral also contains the *tomb of Arrigo VII* by Tino di Camaino, worthwhile mentioning both as work of art as well as for the light it throws on Pisa's philo-imperial policy. Worth seeing is also the *tomb of Saint Ranieri* – patron saint of Pisa – that together with the *Madonna di sotto gli organi* constitutes the object of devoted veneration. It is impossible to name here all the works of art that make the Cathedral of Pisa a real museum. These are some of the most famous artists: P. Tacca, G.B. Tempesti, A. del Sarto, G.A. Sogliani, S. Conca, B. Ghirlandaio, Beccafumi, Sodoma, D. Cresti, and G.B. Cignaroli.

It is however on the **exterior** that "the splendour of multicoloured marbles" reaches its most. With the exception of the façade, the side walls and the clerestory form an uninterrupted succession of three tiers encircling the monument. At the bottom, blind arcades lie lightly along the walls, circumscribing windows, sunken rhombs and circles, while the next tier is articulated by a tighter rhythm of slender pilaster strips, which support a robust cornice marking the roofing of the aisles. In the clerestories, the design of blind arcades returns, set, however, on small columns. These features also appear in the apses, with slight variations, although in the eastern apse the decorative pattern of the galleries, already appeared on the façade and which was repeated in the Bell tower, is at the top. The solution of the superposed galleries, carried out by Rainaldo, over the ground floor order of blind arcades which house the portals, easily adapted itself to the features used in the other parts of the building. The **façade** also preserves testimony of the principal creators of the Cathedral. In the first arch is the *sarcophagus of Buscheto*; above the central portal on the right, an *inscription* recalls Rainaldo, who began the façade; in the left pilaster, on the level of the sidewalk, is the *sepulchral inscription of Master Guglielmo*, the sculptor famous for the first pulpit of the Cathedral – a model followed for a long time – and who, with his workshop, finished the upper part of the façade. Bonanno, the architect of the Bell tower, also made the doors of the façade, which were later destroyed, and the *door of St. Ranieri*, in the right arm of the transept. The panels of this door consist of twenty *Scenes from the Life of the Redeemer* and *Scenes of Theophany*, where Bonanno, by some claimed to be the major Tuscan artist of the Romanesque period, achieves movement and a feeling for space that is extremely evocative. Another outstanding feature of the Cathedral of Pisa is that "marble, the material of the great architecture of antiquity, here makes its comeback, with all its splendour and its weight" (Sanpaolesi), a material which had not been used for centuries. But in addition to the marble and the limestone of the Verruca, other materials include granite from Elba, Giglio

and Sardinia, for the large and small columns, and "*panchina*" from Livorno for the fill-ins. The Cathedral of Pisa is without doubt the highest expression of Pisan Romanesque. Thanks above all to the genius of Buscheto, the elements of the classic tradition, handed down by Early Christian architecture, fuse with Lombard and Byzantine features, as well as what may have arrived in Pisa from contacts with the Arab and Norman world.

THE LEANING TOWER – An ancient *Cronaca* informs us that in the "*Anno Domini 1174 indictione sexta idus Augusti campanilis Sanctae Mariae, rotundus fundatus est. Sequenti anno factus gradus unus in circuitu*". Around the middle of the 18th century, during work to uncover the base of the Bell tower – which led to an accentuation of its tendency to lean – a broken urn with the name Bonanno was found. The artist, already well-known as sculptor, thus also appeared to be the architect of the tower. It is supposed that when it was founded, Bonanno had prepared a design, which was followed throughout the long building history, even though the height had to be reduced (70 metres had been planned). At first, the tower must simply have sunk down into the ground, but later it began to lean, perhaps as a result of attempts to remove infiltrations of water in the foundations. Therefore, in 1185, when the tower had arrived halfway up the third story, the work was interrupted. Building began again in 1275, under the direction of Giovanni di Simone (who had already built in Pisa the bell tower of St. Francesco), and in only nine years, another three and a half floors were raised. But the unbalance increased again, and work was once more suspended, coinciding with the heavy defeat of the Pisan fleet at Meloria, where Giovanni himself may have died. What ever the case, the incline of the tower, from the few centimetres of the part Bonanno had built, was now more than 90 centimetres and, in 1392, the *Primatial Institution* commissioned Giovanni di Nicola and Guido, son of Giovanni di Simone, to measure the inclination of the tower. However, around the middle of the 14th century, Tommaso Pisano was entrusted with finishing the tower with the present belfry, after having leveled off the floor corresponding to the seventh cornice. It can be demonstrated, that at this point, the incline must have been as much as 143 centimetres. Recent studies by Sanpaolesi, have shown that the situation then stabilised, but it worsened again in the first half of the 19th century, when Gherardesca began excavation to uncover the basement of the bell tower, causing a temporary hydrological alteration in the water-bearing stratum. The disastrous collapse of the bell tower of St. Mark's in Venice in 1902, once more focussed attention on the tower of Pisa, and a commission was constituted for systematic measuring. Around 1935, the basin at the base of the tower was cemented, so that it would not be flooded when the Arno overflowed and thus require the water to be pumped out. In the late 1950s, the movement of the tower had once more slowed up and the difference between the base and the top was then 5 metres and 17 centimetres. From then on the overhang has increased by about a millimetre per year. The inauspicious collapse of the Civic Tower at Pavia (17 March 1989) has dramatically re-proposed the security problem of the Leaning Tower. The last "Committee" instituted in 1990 to decide on the urgent operations to be carried out to protect the monument, is composed of experts of various countries. The committee, that should actually conduct the conservative restoration of the monument and define once and for all the aged and thorny issue of the stabilisation of the Tower foundations and of the consolidation of the soil on which they rest, has approved and realised a number of preliminary steps towards what should be the final operation for the consolidation. It is predicted, however, that all this will take quite a long time. Such steps, temporary and reversible, have brought (May 1992) the application of 18 steel rings, covered with a special plastic, at the height of the first gallery and under the first frame of the mon-

Pisa, a beautiful picture of the Leaning Tower.

ument. Such rings (6 to 10 cm thick) should prevent a possible collapse of the material and the giving in of the Tower masonry, in those parts most susceptible to the pressure caused by the effect of the lean, with consequent collapse of the Tower. Finally, in order to temporarily stabilise the foundations of the Tower and to stop the progression of the inclination, the committee agreed to put 600 tons of lead on the north side of the foundations. Beginning in July 1993 the "blocks" of lead were dislocated from a half-moon shaped platform, connected to the Tower basement through hoopings. Both the rings and the "blocks" of lead should eventually be taken away and replaced with invisible but just as safe protection once the inclination has been reduced. In September 1995, while operating on the basement under the lean, a new and unexpected increase of the inclination imposed a temporary suspension of the works. More weight has been added on the side opposite the inclination, but the works that should guarantee the definite stability and the re-opening of the Tower have not yet begun (the Tower was closed to the public in January 1990; the re-opening will be for small groups at a time).

It is a curious fact that still at the beginning of the 18th century, the question of whether the builders had deliberately intended the tower to lean, or whether it was due to accidental causes, was still open to discussion in Pisa. All these vicissitudes in the construction of the Tower did not alter Bonanno's original design, except for the height and the belfry. It is said, that inspiration for the circular form of the tower had come from Ravenna, but it might also have come from the East. The decoration however is related to Rainaldo's façade, as confirmed by the ground floor gallery of blind arches on engaged columns, and the floors above, with small galleries articulated by cornices, even though the lightness of the colonnades does not cancel the value of the wall behind and the two-colour effect reveals a hint of archaism which brings it close to Buscheto. The belfry is smaller in diameter and is crowned by arches resting alternately on corbels and on small columns to frame the openings of the bells. Although the whole work is uniform, it is still possible to identify the different construction teams involved. The oldest sculptural elements are bound to the workshops of Guglielmo and Biduino, followed by features which characterise the more mature Romanesque style, and finally, the highest tiers are already definitely Gothic. The entrance door is bordered on the sides by peculiar *animal reliefs* and crowned by a half-moon in which there is a 15th-century *Madonna with Child,* carried out by Andrea Guardi (now in the Cathedral Museum). Another relief illustrates the *Entrance of the Port of Pisa,* symbolised by a tower and two ancient ships. The entrance room of the Leaning Tower was once without the ceiling. It was then possible to admire the inside of the cylinder, open at the top, and for a curious optical effect, the tower looked straight and not leaning. The ropes used to peal the bells once passed through this hollow cylinder, before electricity was brought in. In 1935, the decision was taken to put some control instruments inside the Tower, so the floor that today obstructs the view inside was built. Two tombstones, at the entrance of the monument commemorate the 1st Congress of Italian Scientists (taken place in Pisa in 1839, on the tombstone is mentioned the experiments carried out by Galileo from the Tower) and the discovery (1820) of sepulchral fragments and an inscription with the name of Bonanno (today immured in the entrance wall) that could prove the theory that maintains he is buried at the bottom of his "creature".

The stairway winds around the inside structure in the shape of a great cylindrical well, and allows the visitor to go out on the external galleries that have no protection. Finally, at the top of the stairway there is the panoramic terrace of the bell-chamber, embellished with arcades and much smaller in comparison with the whole cylindrical structure of the Tower. We want to hereby remember the names of the seven bells, since the 1960s operated by electricity: *Assunta* (16th century), *Crocifisso* (fused again during the 19th century), *Dal Pozzo* (17th century), *Pasquareccia* (13th century), *San Ranieri* (18th century), *Terza, Vespruccio.* From the top of the monument Galileo carried out his famous experiments on the velocity of falling bodies, allowing weights to fall (1589).

A narrow stairway allows you to go on top of the bell-chamber, from which it is possible to admire the Square and the whole city sweeping from the mountains to the sea. Out of curiosity, it is worthwhile remem-

Pisa, the fine shapes of the Baptistery.

bering that through recent excavations near the Tower, archaeologists have discovered the traces of an ancient Etruscan sanctuary of the 6th century BC and important finds of settlements, datable between the 5th and 4th century BC.

BAPTISTERY – An inscription on the pier to the left of the entrance to the Baptistery of Pisa – the right pier bears the date – says that it was Diotisalvi who began the building in 1152, when the earlier octagonal baptistery (whose foundations came to light in the excavation of the Cemetery) was still being used. The beginning of work on the Baptistery is also confirmed by the *Annales* of the chronicler Maragone. They inform us that in 1164, the columns were set up in only fifteen days, and that some of them had been brought from Elba and Sardinia a few years earlier. The sculptural characteristics of the capitals lead one to believe that in 1221, when the archbishop and the Pisan chapter met to deliberate the investiture of the Work, the interior must have been finished. In 1260, under the direction of Nicola Pisano, the gallery of small columns was added, and the design for the Gothic facing is also his. Work went on at great speed in the last quarter of the 13th century: in 1278, the windows were closed, and in 1299, the Gothic vaulting of the inner gallery was finished. In the meanwhile, in 1284, Giovanni Pisano was also at work on the external decorations. It must be noted that around the middle of the century the main furnishings for the Baptistery were also set: the baptismal font by Guido Bigarelli da Como in 1246, and Nicola Pisano's *pulpit* in 1260. After the middle of the 14th century, the construction of the Baptistery was almost finished, with the decision to cover the building with a dome. The covering of the precedent women's gallery had first to be rebuilt, making it taller, and finally, in 1394, the copper statue was set in place, on the top. On the **exterior** of the Baptistery, the decorative features of the Cathedral and the Tower are used only in the first tier, which is articulated by a row of large blind arches. The four portals open on two orthogonal axes, with the main door opposite the Cathedral. The second tier consists of a loggia with semicircular arches on slender columns, topped alternately with gables and spires, almost hiding the powerful cornice from which the drum of the dome springs, slightly smaller in diameter. Mullioned windows with two lights are set in the drum under a light cornice which is broken over the windows to form high gables decorated with rampant leaves. This same feature appears along the slender ribs which articulate the sections of the vault of the dome. Although the Baptistery, like the other monuments in Pisa, is based on a two-colour scheme, here the most important decorative feature is its sculpture. Examples are the decoration of the portals, especially the main portal with a *Madonna* by Giovanni Pisano in the lunette, and the rich decoration of the galleries where the *human heads* (now replaced by copies) at the imposts of the arches are mostly by Nicola and Giovanni Pisano. The imposing ground plan of the Baptistery of Pisa is circular, and the **interior** consists of a ring-shaped nave covered with vaulting which rests on columns and piers. Over the nave there is a women's gallery, which opens towards the inside with other arches supported by pilasters. The central area is covered by a tall slender pyramid which was originally visible from the outside, as in the Pisan church of Santo Sepolcro and the smaller one of St. Agata. The altar has six plutei by an artist close to Guglielmo, which may originally have been for a transenna in the Cathedral. An inscription reads that the baptismal font, dating from 1246, was by Guido Bigarelli of Como. This large octagonal basin was used for baptism by immersion, the four smaller fonts for the baptism of children. The eight panels with the heads of men have rose-windows which recall those of Guglielmo. The furniture of the Baptistery is completed by Nicola Pisano's *Pulpit* dating from 1260, on which his son Giovanni and Arnolfo di Cambio also seem to have collaborated, although very little. The pulpit, definitely Gothic in style, was carried out without adhering to the old scheme but it is a balanced synthesis between architecture and sculptural decoration. Hexagonal in form, it is supported by seven columns, which alternately rest on lions, plus one in the centre resting on a tall plinth. The columns support trilobate arches, with figures of *Prophets* and *Evangelists* in the spandrels, while *allegorical figures* and *saints* are set over the capitals. The fine panels of the parapet, framed by small columns, contain *Events from the Life of Christ*.

THE MONUMENTAL CEMETERY – The Cemetery of Pisa, definitely Gothic, represents the final touch in the layout of the Piazza del Duomo, on the side facing the walls of Cocco Griffi. Although it was the last addition, it harmonises beautifully with the rest. An inscription reads that the Cemetery was begun in 1278, on a design by Giovanni di Simone who, in 1263, had also built the Hospital on the other side of the square. The Cemetery was built on an area precedently occupied by other religious buildings, such as the early medieval octagonal baptistery, and on the site (according to documents) of the bishop's vegetable garden. It seems likely, that the decision to build the Cemetery was taken when the new baptistery was consecrated, and the old one could be eliminated. Apparently, the idea of building a cemetery for famous citizens, dates back to the early 13th century. Moreover, according to tradition, the bishop, Ubaldo de' Lanfranchi, had a large amount of earth brought from Golgotha by the Pisan ships. Entirely faced with marble in two delicate tonalities, the Cemetery is articulated on a rectangular gallery – the long south side marks the edge of the square – around the field of the old cemetery. **Outside**, the gallery is closed by blind arcading springing from pilaster strips, with sculptured heads at the imposts of the arches. **Inside**, the gallery faces onto the field through an arcaded portico on piers and with slender mullioned windows with four lights. The pavement of the eastern arm is raised higher than the others, since this area

Pisa, the "Final Judgement" can be found in the Hall of the frescoes inside the Monumental Cemetery.

was reserved for worship. Chapels were later added to the external wall of this and of the northern arm. The ceiling, a simple timber roof, was destroyed in a fire during World War II when many frescoes were also damaged, and many sculptures and sarcophagi were lost. The walls around the Cemetery were frescoed, especially in the 14th century, and other tombs were added to those of the famous Pisans. At the beginning of the 18th century, antique sarcophagi, many of which had been used as tombs around the Cathedral, were also transferred here. In the 18th century, ancient and medieval material found in the city was also brought here, so today the Cemetery is one of the most important museums in Pisa, thanks also to the important fresco cycles it contains.

In the **Southern gallery** you should see the frescoes by the Florentine Taddeo Gaddi, illustrating the *Stories of Job* (14th century). The *funerary monument of Algarotti* (18th century) is also interesting. The first thing you see upon entering the **Western gallery** is a Roman sarcophagus: it is made of marble and oval-shaped (3rd century AD). A little further, from the top, hang the chains that used to close the entrance of the Port of Pisa and that were stolen by the Genoese in 1362. Among the many *tombs* there is the one of *Bartolomeo Medici,* generally attributed to Tribolo (16th century). A recent reorganisation has returned to their original places the frescoes by Lomi, Ghirlandaio and Guidotti (16th-17th centuries), and the monuments to *Francesco Vegio* (16th century) and to *Anastasia Schouvaloff* (19th century). As you enter the **Northern gallery** there are Umbrian 14th-century frescoes, illustrating *Episodes from the Genesis*. On the floor it is possible to see the tombstones of famous contemporary Pisans, who distinguished themselves by their scientific studies. At this point you will enter the *Ammannati Chapel*, in which the *funerary monument of Ligo Ammannati* has been put back; from here you can continue on to a hall, built in the early 1950s displaying interesting frescoes taken from the southern gallery. These strong 14th-century interpretations of uncertain artists (Traini, Orcagna, Buffalmacco or an unknown artist of the river Po area) illustrate the *Crucifixion,* the *Triumph of Death,* the *Last Judgement,* and *Hell.* Another fresco of the same period describes the *Stories of the Anchorites.* A second hall (photographic reproductions of the frescoes) houses a Greek marble pot (2nd century AD) embellished with *Dionysian figurations.* Again in the northern gallery, you can admire a fine sarcophagus of the Roman age with a representation of the *Phaedra Myth* (2nd century AD). The 14th century *Aulla Chapel* preserves a valuable polychrome terra-cotta figure attributed to Giovanni della Robbia (16th century). The walls just outside the chapel were once adorned with beautiful frescoes by Benozzo Gozzoli (*Biblical stories*). They were heavily damaged by atmospheric agents and by the war, and therefore, the remaining parts, have been

165

taken down. Now you can admire the *Muses sarcophagus*, embellished with lying figures and niches with fine bas-reliefs: it dates from the 3rd century AD Imperial age. In the **Eastern gallery** there are other funerary monuments, among which those by Lorenzo Bartolini, Giovanni Duprè and Stagio Stagi. The pompous *funerary monument of Boncompagni* (16th century) was made by Ammannati, who also made the figures representing *Justice, Peace* and the *Redeemer*. Passing the *Dal Pozzo Chapel* you will come to the Southern gallery, in which there are Roman age *tomb-stones* (1st century AD). Some of the frescoes of the northern gallery are being restored. As well as the remains of Gozzoli's frescoes the following are also being restored: the *Stories of the Saints Efisio and Potito,* by Spinello Aretino, and the *Stories of St. Ranieri,* by Veneziano and Buonaiuti.

SINOPITE MUSEUM – You will find it in the beautiful edifice built between 1257 and 1286 by Giovanni di Simone (the same architect of the Monumental Cemetery), and enlarged various times during the 14th century. The museum is divided in a number of rooms: on the first floor you can admire the sinopites of some masterpieces frescoed by Buonamico di Buffalmacco, such as *Stories of the Saint Fathers, Last Judgement, Triumph of Death*. A bit further, there is a beautiful *Crucifixion* by the famous Pisan master Francesco Traini, and, next, the powerful *Assumption,* again by Buffalmacco. On the second floor are preserved a few fragments of frescoes with their sinopites. From here you will descend to the ground floor, where you can admire the sinopites of the *Coronation of the Virgin* and *Stories from the Genesis,* by Piero di Puccio; *Stories from the Old and New Testament* by Benozzo Gozzoli.

MUSEO DELL'OPERA DEL DUOMO (CATHEDRAL MUSEUM) – It is among the most rich and famous museums in Tuscany. The edifice is made of two perpendicular buildings on a 13th-century keep, closing on a scenic **cloister**. On the ground floor, there are many sculptural works, ranging from the 11th to the 12th century, among which the fine *Crucifix,* wooden polychrome sculpture by Burgundian artist, and some masterpieces by Tino di Camaino, Giovanni and Nicola Pisano. Also, extremely interesting are the *archiepiscopal tombs,* carried out by Nino Pisano's workshop and dating from the 14th century; and other works by Renaissance sculptors Andrea Guardi, Matteo Civitali, the Stagi and Tribolo. In a big room, at the centre of the museum, is the famous **Treasure of the Cathedral**, which also includes the beautiful ivory *Madonna* by Giovanni Pisano, the Limoges reliquaries (12th century), and many sacred gold-

Pisa, view of the Lungarno.

Pisa, the Sinopite Museum.

work. The first floor houses many paintings ranging from the 16th to the 17th century, by artists such as Battista Franco, Orazio Riminaldi, Aurelio Lomi, Giuseppe and Francesco Melani and Giovan Battista Ferretti. The museum also exhibits a rich collection of wooden tarsias and illuminated codexes dating from the 12th to the 13th century.

CHURCH OF SANTO STEFANO DEI CAVALIERI – The church was built on a design by Giorgio Vasari (1565), and received its marble **façade** from Giovanni de' Medici, in the 17th century. The building is flanked by two wings, added by Pier Francesco Silvani, which were used as dressing rooms by the knights, and then later transformed into aisles. The **Bell tower**, at the end of the right side, is by Vasari and was built after 1570. The **interior** of the church, with a single nave and flanked by the two wings mentioned above to which four doors lead, exhibits works of the artists of the Grand Duke. The ceiling in carved wood has inserts of paintings representing *Memorable events of the Knights* by Cigoli, Allori, Ligozzi and Empoli, while the holy water stoups were made from Vasari's designs, as were other works. The urn on the marble high altar is by Pier Francesco Silvani and Giovan Battista Foggini. The 18th-century organ is by Azzolino della Ciaia; the 17th-century *pulpit* is by Chiarissimo Fancelli, and there are also works by Bronzino, Buti, Lomi as well as a *reliquary bust*, copy of the original by Donatello (in the National Museum of St. Matteo). The fact that in the church there are many banners stolen from the Turks, and other historical relics, makes it a real museum of the Order of St. Stephen.

167

Pisa, Piazza dei Cavalieri is embellished by Palazzo della Carovana and by the Church of Santo Stefano dei Cavalieri.

PALAZZO DEI CAVALIERI – To the left of the church is the Palazzo dei Cavalieri, known also as *della Carovana*, from the name of the course the knights who frequent it had to attend. The palace is the result of a re-modelling by Vasari of the older *Palazzo degli Anziani*, of which a high arch can still be seen on the right side, and part of the brick façade, on the left. The broad uneven line of the façade follows the conformation of the piazza. The strongly projecting roof and the two flights of **Stairs**, which date from the 19th century, give a sense of grandeur. The **façade**, which is decorated by sgraffiti, has a large Medici-Stefanian coat of arms over the first floor windows, as well as six niches with *busts of the Grand Dukes*, from Cosimo I to Cosimo III. The palace has been enlarged at the back and is now the seat of the **Scuola Normale Superiore** of Pisa, a university branch for the specialisation in letters, philosophy, mathe-matics, and science, instituted by Napoleon in 1810, and then reorga-nized by Leopoldo II. The *statue of Cosimo I* with the *Fountain of the Hunchback* by Francavilla, dating from the end of the 16th century, stands in front of the Palazzo dei Cavalieri.

PALACE OF THE CLOCK – The Palace of the Clock is on the north-west side of the *Piazza dei Cavalieri*. It was also built for the Knights of St. Stephen in 1607, on designs by Giorgio Vasari. The palace is also a fine example of town planning, for it resolved the problem of reuniting two precedent constructions without interrupting the use of the road. The Palace of the Clock incorporates the remains of the **Tower of Justice**, the old town prison, and the **Tower of the Gualandi**, known as *Torre della Muda* and then *Torre della Fame* (Tower of Hunger) as a result of the fa-mous episode of Count Ugolino narrated by Dante.

CHURCH OF ST. FREDIANO – The church of St. Frediano, formerly dedi-cated to *Saints Martin and Frediano*, to which a guest house for pilgrims was once annexed, is fully documented from the 11th century – in 1077 it was occupied by a Camaldolite community – and the façade was fin-ished within the first half of the 12th century. Obviously inspired by the Cathedral and well preserved, the **façade** consists of a row of arches, in the lower part, which depart from corner pilaster strips and are sup-ported by corbels and two columns set in corrispondence of the internal division of the church and has three portals and recessed rhombs. The second order springs from a cornice which runs across the entire façade and in the centre, between the sloping sides of the gable, includes three blind arches with a wide mullioned window with two lights under the central arch and the recessed rhombs under the side arches. There are oculi in the lateral connections and at the top, articulated in the shape of a simple raised tympanum.

The **interior** of the church was altered in the 16th and 17th centuries and especially after the fire of 1675. It has a basilican plan, with antique columns dividing the nave from the two aisles. The capitals are in part Romanesque and in part reused, while the original semicircular apse no longer exists. The sides, partially covered by later constructions, are decorated by small arches on corbels and pilaster strips. Among the works preserved here, mention should be made of the 13th-century *Crucifix*, in the first chapel of the left aisle; the *Madonna and Child with St. Francis* by Ventura Salimbeni, in the second chapel; and the *Annunciation* and the *Nativity*, also by Salimbeni, in the third chapel. The chapels at the end of the aisles contain, on the left, poorly preserved frescoes by Passignano and *Events from the Life of St. Brigida* by Tiarini; on the right, the dome is decorated with frescoes by Manetti.

PALAZZO DELLA SAPIENZA – The **University**, which was initially set up by Count Fazio della Gherardesca in 1329, had its seat in this building. Piero de' Medici, Lorenzo's brother, restructured this institution and it was definitively organised by Cosimo I; the Grand Dukes that followed held the University in great esteem, until Leopold II suppressed the faculties for being hotbeds for excessively liberal ideas. Since the middle of the 16th century the Pisan University included scientific institutions such as the **Botanical Garden**, but the organisation of the **Museums of Palaeontology**, **Mineralogy** and **Zoology and Comparative Anatomy** also go back to an early date. They are among the most prestigious institutions of their kind in Italy. From 1981, these museums all became part of the **Museum of Natural History**, which can be visited at the Charterhouse of Pisa (Calci).

CHURCH OF ST. FRANCESCO – The church of St. Francesco was founded in the second decade of the 13th century; work continued in the second half of the century by Giovanni da Simone, and was finished in the 14th century, although the **façade** was not completed until the beginning of the 17th. The building has the normal plan of a single rectangular hall, a transept with chapels and a wooden ceiling (except for the chapels). Light comes from large tall pointed-arch windows, and it contains various works of art. In 1922, the mortal remains of Count Ugolino, his children and grandchildren were recomposed there. The **Chapter room** faces out into the **Cloister**, and it was in the former, that according to tradition, in 1263, Saint Bonaventura, presiding over the Chapter of the Order, instituted the custom of the "*Angelus*". The ancient Franciscan complex also includes a pair of 15th-century **Cloisters**. The tribune has vaulting frescoed by Taddeo Gaddi, and various chapels: in the first chapel on the left is a *St. Francis* of the 13th-century Pisan school, in the second, a *Madonna* by Memmo di Filippuccio; in the third, a 14th-century cycle of frescoes. The *tomb of Count Ugolino and his children* is in the second chapel on the right. The fine Chapter Room is off the cloister, and contains a fresco cycle with events from the *Life of Christ* by Niccolò di Pietro Gerini (1392).

Pisa, Palazzo della Sapienza: the Botanical Garden.

Pisa, National Museum of St. Matteo, the inside courtyard.

CHURCH OF ST. CATERINA – The **façade** of the church of St. Caterina, built by the Dominicans in the second half of the 13th century, is in the great tradition of Pisan Romanesque architecture. The lower part is articulated by three round-headed blind arches which frame the portal in the centre, while the upper part, 14th-century, has two rows of trilobate loggias (like those in St. Michele in Borgo), with a rose-window in the upper one. The **interior** with a single nave, as one can guess from the shape of the façade, and with a trussed timber roof and a transept with four chapels, follows the design of the churches of the mendicant orders, based on simplicity. Giovanni di Simone has been suggested as the architect of the **Bell tower**, in brick with mullioned windows with two and three lights, and with majolica bowls set into the wall. There are many works of art in the church, some of remarkable value. Nearby is the **Archiepiscopal Seminary** and the seat of the **Library Cateriniana**, with more than 30,000 volumes, including manuscripts and incunabuli.

ABBEY OF ST. ZENO – The origins of the abbey of St. Zeno go far back in time. It was founded by the Benedictines before the 11th century, on the remains of Roman buildings. Altered and enlarged at various times throughout the centuries, it has recently been radically restored, thus revealing the various stratifications from the 5th century on. The **interior** on a basilica plan, has a nave and two aisles, separated by piers alternated with columns with reused capitals. Some of the pointed arches are of Arab inspiration. The **façade**, in tufaceous stone, is peculiar, with a deep porch on the front with two-light openings, while the upper part is decorated with pairs of small arches articulated by pilaster strips, between which are set oculi, recessed rhombs and three elegant mullioned windows with two lights.

NATIONAL MUSEUM OF ST. MATTEO – The museum, which should be reorganised through the acquisition of new space belonging to the University, as well as the constitution of a detached section at the ex **Palazzo Reale** (16th century), began its life during the 18th century and found a definitive seat only after the 2nd World War. The art collections are in what once was a Benedectine Convent: a building, with a cloister with arcades and elegant mullioned windows with two lights, transformed and enlarged many times up to the last century.

Among the art-works, the collection of medieval ceramics is particularly prominent, here represented by many *bowls* from the Mediterranean area and mostly from Islamic countries. You should take a look especially at the Egyptian bowls (11th century), as well as the ornamental ce-

170

ramics used to adorn sacred buildings (13th century) and the many objects accidentally found during excavations around the city. 12th and 13th-century Pisan painting is represented here by very valuable pieces: such as the so-called *Calci Bible* (12th century), a fine example of illuminated codexes; the painted *Crosses* that were in the churches of St. Paolo all'Orto, of St. Sepolcro and in the St. Matteo Convent; and the pieces of frescoes taken down from the churches of St. Pietro in Vinculis and St. Michele degli Scalzi.

Among the most esteemed artists of 13th-century Pisan painting are Giunta di Capitino (*Cross of S. Matteo*) and Berlinghiero (*Cross of Fucecchio*); the latter was head of an art school known in Lucca, Emilia and Umbria. The works by Enrico di Tedice and Maestro di St. Martino, who illustrated *Episodes of the life of S. Anna,* have Byzantine influences. Among the 14th-century paintings most famous is the remarkable *Polyptich* created by Simone Martini for the Church of St. Caterina; others are Deodato Orlandi of Lucca, Giovanni di Nicola, Francesco di Traino, Lippo Memmi, Turino Vanni, Jacopo di Michele, Neruccio Federighi, Cecco di Pietro and Francesco Neri of Volterra. Noteworthy are also the *Madonnas* by Barnaba da Modena, the *polyptich* that Spinello Aretino created for the Cathedral, the works by Martino di Bartolomeo and Taddeo di Bartolo and the *Crucifixion* by Luca di Tommè. Among the sculptures the best are those of Nicola and Giovanni Pisano, Tino di Camaino, and of Andrea and Nino Pisano – the last two are the sculptors of the remarkable *Madonna del Latte,* once in the Church of St. Maria della Spina. Andrea Pisano (*Angel*), Agostino di Giovanni (*Annunciation*) and Francesco di Valdambrino (*Angels, Annunciation*) here represent the wooden polychrome and gilt sculpture. The 15th-century art of painting was influenced by the works of Florentine artists or others working in the city. This is the case of Masaccio, of whom you can admire a remarkable *St. Paul* on golden background, Beato Angelico (*Madonna with Child*), Gentile da Fabriano (*Madonna dell'Umiltà*) and Domenico Ghirlandaio (*Madonna with Child and Saints*), while Benozzo Gozzoli mostly dedicated himself to the frescoes of the Monumental Cemetery. Among the 15th-century sculptures there is the excellent *Bust of S. Lussorio,* in fused bronze, embossed and gilded, a beautiful piece by Donatello once in the Church of St. Stefano dei Cavalieri. Finally, there are some glazed Robbian terra-cotta figures by Michelozzo and artists of the school of Jacopo Rustici.

CHURCH OF ST. MARIA DELLA SPINA – This is the only religious building of importance begun in Pisa during the 14th century. It is situated on the *Lungarno Gambacorti*, with one of the side walls lined up with the parapet. The more ancient oratory of St. Maria di Pontenovo was enlarged in its present form in 1323, and takes its name from the fact that it houses a thorn from Christ's crown of thorns, now in the church of St. Chiara. The small edifice has a small rectangular nave with three transverse arches which separate the presbytery. On the **outside**, the marble facing has depressed arches which enclose the portals and the large mullioned windows with three and four lights. Above is a forest of spires, cusps, small and richly decorated aediculae sculptured by artists from the circle of Nino Pisano and Andrea Pisano. The latter also made a *Madonna and Child*, the original of which is now in the National Museum. One of Nicola Pisano's best works, the *Madonna del Latte*, was **inside** but this too, is now in the National Museum, while statues by Andrea and Nino Pisano are still on the altar.

CHURCH OF ST. PAOLO A RIPA D'ARNO – After the Cathedral, the church of St. Paolo a Ripa d'Arno represents one of the major works of the city, and of all the buildings in Pisa it most closely resembles it. Mention goes back as far as the 9th century, and reconstruction may have begun in the 11th century – continued up to the 13th century – while the church was consecrated in 1148, by Eugene III, after having passed to the Vallombrosan friars in 1115. Heavily damaged by bombs in 1943, it has been restored. The church is basilican in plan, with a nave, two aisles and a transept. The arches – supported by columns in granite from Elba – are slightly pointed and set on high piers which reveal ties with the Arab-inspired churches of Sicily. The **dome** is also of southern style, flattened and set on pendentives, and with the form repeated in the covering. On the **exterior**, the right side, to which the cloister was to

Pisa, the Church of Santa Maria della Spina, gothic jewel of the city.

be attached, is decorated only by brick arcading in the transept, while the side and arm of the transept on the left, echo the architecture of the Cathedral. The **façade**, begun in the 12th century, but with some decorative elements which are already Gothic, has the common order of five blind arcades at ground floor level, set over the three portals, the oculi and recessed rhombs. Above, are three tiers of galleries with an exceptional upward thrust. Of note **inside** are the *tomb of Burgundio Pisano* who lived in the 12th century and was a famous jurist and Greek scholar; the frescoes by Buffalmacco on the pier in the left aisle with *Two Saints*; and the 14th-century stained-glass window in the apse with the *Redeemer and Apostles*.

ENVIRONS

The area of **San Giuliano Terme** was already famous in antiquity for the fine marble quarried, and for its abundant springs of curative water. San Giuliano first developed in the Roman period and then, after centuries of inactivity, flourished again in the 18th century. The marble quarries were exploited in antiquity, but later the **spas** became more important, and still today are the town's major attraction. With famous people such as Carlo Alberto of Savoy, Lord Byron, Louis Bonaparte coming here to be treated, the town felt it had to live up to this honour, and the establishments became increasingly elegant and comfortable, including the **Café-Haus**. Not much remains of this past glory, but the establishment is still functional and inviting.

To be noted near San Giuliano, for those who love medieval towns, is the village of **Ripafratta**, overlooked by the ruins of a **Castle** and with a charming central piazza. The imposing **Medicean aqueduct**, which brought water from Monte Pisano to Pisa, can still be seen below **Asciano**.

San Piero a Grado, a majestic basilica in Romanesque style, was built in the 11th century, on the foundations of a precedent early Christian building (excavations have revealed that this was built on a Roman structure, perhaps a warehouse for the port). It was originally on the

172

shore of the banks of one of the numerous inlets which formed the delta of the Arno. According to the legend it was here that Saint Peter, perhaps driven by a storm, landed on his way from the Holy Land to Rome where, divinely inspired, he was to found the Christian Church. It may have been Peter himself, with the help of some of his disciples who built the first church, which was then consecrated by his successor Clement I. During archaeological exploration, a tiny oratory was discovered inside the large basilica, unanimously dated from early christian period (4th-5th century). It is also true that materials, such as the columns, capitals and marbles which were used for construction came from early Roman buildings. Much of the material used in the construction of the basilica, dating from different periods, was also of Roman origin. For instance, the 26 columns, which divide the nave and two aisles, are Roman, and the differing heights have been skilfully adjusted by the use of plinths of various sizes. The frescoes, which line the walls of the nave, are attributed to the Luccan painter Deodato Orlandi, who worked in the basilica at the beginning of the 14th century. The cycle is divided into three tiers: the area above the divisory arches contains the *busts of the popes* up to John XIII, the middle band contains *Episodes from the Life of St. Peter*, and in the clerestory, are the *Walls of the Celestial City* with *Angels* looking out. The spacious building, said to be one of the first examples of Pisan Romanesque architecture, was probably finished in the course of the 11th century, perhaps in two phases, and was longer than it is now, with the façade to the west. Towards the end of the 12th century, when the façade collapsed, the church was supplied with two opposing apses, the only example in Italy. The damage may have been caused by the terrible flood of 1180, of the Arno. The building was then shortened by four bays, and the façade was replaced by a wall and western apse.

The final stage in the building was the **Bell tower**, which went up between the end of the 12th and the beginning of the 13th century. It was of Lombard derivation but with decorative elements in Pisan style, such as the blind arcading and the corbel tables with pilaster strips. During World War II, the bell tower was blown up by the retreating German soldiers. In 1950, it was partially rebuilt.

Environs of Pisa, San Piero a Grado, view of the tripartite apse of the ancient Romanesque Basilica.

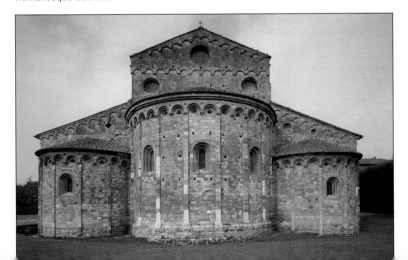

PISTOIA

HISTORICAL SURVEY – *Pistoia is situated on the northernmost extremity of the fertile plain of the Ombrone river, surrounded by the Arno, Mount Albano and the Appenine slopes. The city's charming small historical centre contains extremely fine examples of architecture. In the course of the centuries the city often found itself shadowed by Florence, but despite this managed to achieve an original and personal style in its monuments. The first inhabitants of the area were probably Etruscans with infiltrations of Ligurians. Not until Roman times did Pistoia (then called* Pistorium *or* Pistoriae*) begin to take on the characteristics of a real town, and even became a Roman* municipium. *In antiquity, its importance must have been only relative, to judge from literary and epigraphic evidence, aided by new archaeological finds. Pistoia's ascent began in the 2nd-3rd century AD, when the diocese, referred to in 496, was constituted. It first passed under the dominion of the Goths, and then, for a short time, of the Byzantines. With the subsequent Lombard dominion, its prestige grew and it received the rank of* royal *city. It was already a free Commune in the 11th century, and in 1177 emanated its own constitution, one of the oldest in Italy. In the 12th and 13th centuries, the city flourished economically, culturally and artistically. The presence of a great artist such as Giovanni Pisano testifies to the good cultural exchanges with nearby Pisa. Most of its marvelous monuments were built in these two centuries. Pistoia was by then one of the most powerful and populous cities in Tuscany, but the continuous clashes with Florence, Lucca and Bologna began to weaken its power. After being twice heavily defeated by Florence in 1228 and in 1254, and after variuos vicissitudes it fell under the Florentine sphere of influence. From then on, despite various periods of splendour, it was unable to free itself from the powerful grip of Florence, and in 1556, with the political and administrative reform promoted by Cosimo I de' Medici, it was once and for all integrated into the Tuscan state, dependent on the Medici city.*

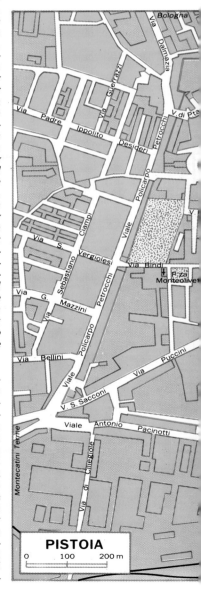

CATHEDRAL – The oldest information there is on this church dates back to the 10th century. It was modified more than once in the Pisan Romanesque style, between the 12th and 13th century. The **façade** with three rows of galleries and a porch is decorated with an important glazed terra-cotta bas-relief by Andrea della Robbia. There are two marble statues in the upper part of the façade: the *Apostle St. James* by Jacopo di Mazzeo, and *Saint Zeno Bishop* by Andrea Vaccà. To the left of the façade is the solid **Bell tower** (67 metres). The lower part was a Lombard watch-tower, modified at the end of the 13th century, and with the addition of three tiers of arches in Pisan style. The tripartite **interior** has a nave covered by timber trusses wider than the aisles from which it is divided by columns and two piers. Immediately to the right of the entrance, is the tabernacle containing what is left of the *Shrine of St. Matthew*, composed of three low reliefs attributed to Agostino di Giovanni (1337); at the centre is *Blessing St. Atto between Two Angels*, and at the sides *Pilgrims at Santiago de Compostela receiving the Relics of St. James and taking them to St. Atto*. To the right of the right portal, is a fine Gothic window, included in the chapel of St. James, in the splay of which is a charming pictorial decoration by Alessio d'Andrea and Bonaccorso di Cino (1347) representing *The Four Virtues*. In the right aisle are, one after the other, a Gothic aedicule, with a tabernacle with the *Madonna and Child between Saints James and Zeno*; a fine *Crucifixion*, a panel painting by Coppo di Marcovaldo (1275); and the **Chapel of St. James**, with the lovely silver altar dedicated to the memory of the saint, one of the most prestigious Italian goldworks with pieces by Andrea di Jacopo d'Ognibene (*Fifteen Stories from the New Testament*, 1316), Leonardo di Giovanni (*Nine Stories of the Old Testament*, 1361-64), Nofri di Buto and

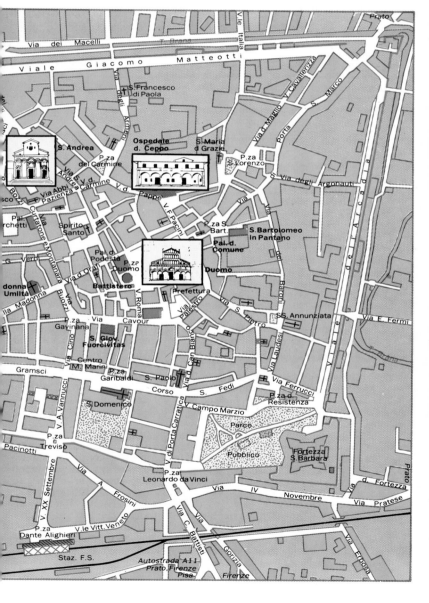

175

Pistoia, majestic buildings that dominate the city centre.

Atto di Piero Braccini (*statue of the Redeemer*). Close by is an altar with a copy by Passignano of the *Annunciation of the Servants*. A few steps further, a brief flight of stairs leads to the upper level, with a large Gothic niche lined with frescoes by unknown painters. In the chapel to the right of the high altar, there is also a very large canvas, *Saints Bernard and Desiderio*, an outstanding work by Mattia Preti. Then in the presbytery there is a rare bronze candelabrum by Maso di Bartolo on the left and, in the vault, frescoes by Passignano. In the chapel to the left of the high altar are other noteworthy works, such as the *Madonna and Child Enthroned between Saints*, by Lorenzo di Credi (1485), probably on a design by Verrocchio. From here you can enter the Romanesque **crypt**: it has marble inlaid panels which belonged to the old choir enclosure, a capital from the Barbarian period, and various other object. In the left aisle particular note should be given to the second altar, with a *Madonna* from the late 14th century, a fresco of Sienese school; the *Monument of Cardinal Niccolò Fonteguerri* (1419-1473), by Verrocchio, Lorenzo di Credi and Lorenzetto. The inside of the façade has a *Madonna and Child with Two Angels* by an unknown painter, while note should be taken of the fine baptismal font by Andrea Ferrucci da Fiesole on a design by Benedetto da Maiano.

BAPTISTERY – This small octagonal building in green and white marble, was designed by Andrea Pisano in the first half of the 14th century. A fine example of Gothic style, the portals are finely decorated and a loggia of blind polylobed arches runs along the top of the wall just below the dome. The main entrance has the architrave sculptured with low relief scenes from the *Life of St. John the Baptist*, and the lunette above contains a *Madonna and Child* flanked by the figures of *St. John the Baptist* and *St. Peter* carried out by the school of Andrea Pisano.

TOWN HALL – Built in the 13th century, the severe **façade** has a Gothic-arch portico, above which are two tiers of mullioned windows with two and three lights as well as a few simple mullioned windows now shut. The **Civic Museum** is installed **inside**. The spacious rooms contain im-

176

portant works from the 13th to the 16th century. Special mention should be made of a *St. Francis* of Pisan school (13th cent.), one of the oldest examples of painting in Pistoia; a *Crucifixion*, a panel painting by Salerno di Coppo (1275); and fragments of various 13th-century frescoes. The Museum also houses the **Puccini Collection**.

BISHOPS' PALACE – The Palace dates from the 11th century, and has recently been restored. The façade is in late 14th-century Gothic style and has eight pointed-arch openings on the first floor, while elegant mullioned windows with two lights face out on the second floor. The palace houses the **Cathedral Museum** in variuos rooms on two floors. The collection contains interesting examples of religious art, including chalices, reliquaries, furnishings, monstrances, and liturgic vestments (chasubles, copes, cassocks, albs, chalice veils, busts, conopeii); the *Chalice* and the *Cross of St. Atto*, both datable to the second half of the 13th century, two very refined objects; the *Reliquary of Saint James* made in the workshop of Lorenzo Ghiberti around 1407; the so-called *Reliquary of the Virgin*, another extraordinary example of late medieval goldwork; a large holy water pail, dating 1642; and an 18th-century monstrance by the great Giovanni Validier, with a lively composition of female figures and angels at the base. In addition the museum also contains archaeological material found in the city territory: as well as a *cippus*, probably Etruscan, there are numerous clay vases from the Roman period, both in simple terra-cotta and in terra-cotta sigillata, coins and various oil lamps. The medieval and Renaissance collections, including majolicas, glass, fibulas, are even richer.

CHURCH OF ST. FRANCESCO – This imposing structure in Franciscan Gothic style, was built in the 13th-14th centuries. In the centre of the **façade** is a finely decorated portal. The **interior** on a Latin-cross plan has a single large nave, terminating in a spacious transept with five pretty chapels covered with ribbed cross vaults. On the walls are fragments of frescoes by Pietro Lorenzetti, Puccio Capanna, Lippo Memmi and other painters of the school of Giotto and from Siena.

Pistoia, a detail of the famous Della Robbia frieze that embellishes the Spedale del Ceppo.

CHURCH OF ST. ANDREA – This 13th-century church, on an ancient pre-existing foundation (8th century), is a true jewel of Pistoian architecture. The lovely **façade** in Pisan style, in green and white marble, has a fine portal with a *Statue of St. Andrew*, in the style of Giovanni Pisano, in the lunette, and a sculptured architrave by Gruamonte, representing the *Adoration of the Magi* and the *Magi before Herod*. The narrow tripartite **interior** is longitudinal in perspective. The church contains the famous *Pulpit* by Giovanni Pisano (1301), and an intense wooden *Crucifix* by the same sculptor, in the right aisle.

HOSPITAL OF THE CEPPO (SPEDALE DEL CEPPO) – This 13th-14th century building in the P*iazza San Giovanni*, has on the **façade** above the porch, the famous glazed terra-cotta frieze (16th cent.) depicting the *Acts of Mercy*, separated by the figures of the *Theological Virtues* and two *Spihnxes*. The first six panels are by Giovanni della Robbia and Michele Viviani. The other one is by Paladini. The five tondos and half tondos with garlands of fruit and flowers representing the most important *Marine episodes* are by Giovanni della Robbia. Antique surgical instruments, once used in the hospital, constitute the patrimony of the singular **Museum of Surgical Instruments**.

PITIGLIANO (Grosseto)

This pretty little village, not far from the Lazio border line, is one of the pearls of the so-called "tufa" centres. Once an Etruscan possession of Vulci, then of the Romans, during the Middle Ages it belonged to the Aldobrandeschi and Orsini. When it passed under the Medicean administration, it became the heart of a Jewish community. The **Cathedral**, named after the *Saints Peter and Paul* and dating back to the Middle ages, is the result of a 16th-18th-century reconstruction. It has a beautiful **Bell tower**, and in the inside hall, you can admire paintings by Francesco Zuccarelli, who was born here, and also by Aldi and Cozzarelli. Between the **Citadel** (16th century) and the great **Palazzo Orsini** you will find the 16th-century arched **Aqueduct**. Palazzo Orsini was built be-

Pitigliano, view of the striking town clinging to the tufaceous cliff.

Poppi, a beautiful panorama of the delightful medieval village.

tween the 14th and 16th century: it is thought that Giuliano da Sangallo and Peruzzi collaborated at its construction.

ENVIRONS – The Etruscan **necropolis** of the **Marsiliana** is one of the most interesting of the **Manciano** district. In the village, where remains of the original **walls** and of the **Fortress** can be seen, there is the **Archaeological Museum** that houses finds excavated in the river Fiora Valley.
Sorano is of Etruscan origin, and so is the entire surrounding. But the Sorano we see now is that of the Middle Ages, when it belonged to the Aldobrandeschi and then to the Orsini, before becoming part of the Medici Grand Duchy. The main square contains the **Parish church**, remodelled in the 18th century. The **Fortress of the Orsini**, built in the 14th century and later enlarged, is also imposing. The coats of arms of the Aldobrandeschi and the Orsini recall past times. From here you can admire a beautiful panorama.

POPPI (Arezzo)

One of the most famous monuments of the feudal period in Tuscany is to be found in Poppi. The **Castle of the Guidi counts** dates from the 13th century and is similar to Palazzo Vecchio in Florence. However, the hypothesis that it was designed by the great architect Arnolfo di Cambio, has not yet been convalidated. Entrance into the courtyard is across the moat, which encircles the castle. The walls of the court are decorated with fine coats of arms of the magistrates and vicars of Florence, who took up residence here after the fall of the Guidi when Poppi was annexed to the Florentine republic. A staircase leads to the first floor, used as a **Museum**, in which special note should be paid to a Della Robbian terra-cotta figure, and a *Madonna and Child* of the school of Botticelli.

The imposing **Library** is also of great interest. It contains more than 15,000 volumes, and many manuscripts and incunabuli. A visit to the chapel on the second floor should be made. It is frescoed with *Scenes from the Lives of Christ and John the Baptist*, attributed to Taddeo Gaddi. Nor should one miss the splendid panorama from the castle tower, which dominates all of Bibbiena and the valley below. The medieval town lies at the foot of the castle. Noteworthy in the town centre is the **Church of the Madonna del Morbo**, begun in 1657 and finished about fifty years later. The central plan church has a dome and a portico on three sides. At the end of the *Via Cavour*, flanked by porticoes, is the **Church of St. Fedele**, a very old structure dating to 1185-95, with a bell tower that was originally a tower in the city walls. The Latin-cross interior has only a nave, covered by a trussed timber roof. Various paintings, from the 14th to the 16th century, are preserved in the numerous chapels.

POPULONIA (Livorno)

The ancient *Popluna* was the only Etruscan city right on the coast; and it was for this particular geographical position that its economy flourished.

The port, situated on the **gulf of Baratti**, under the promontory of the city, was in fact already a centre for trade in Villanovia age (9th-8th century BC), especially for the minerals, such as copper, tin, and lead quarried on the Metalliferous Hills and in the territory of Campiglia. In a following period, with the exploitation of the iron mines on the Island of Elba, and the consequent working of the iron, the city's economy reached its heights; in fact, at this point, trade was also with many cities of the Tyrrhenian coast and of Greece, which exchanged their best products with the precious mineral. Evidence of this rich trade, is from the numerous objects found in archaic tombs, and coming from Sardinia, Corsica, and from the eastern coasts of the Mediterranean Sea. The most ancient necropolises of Populonia are situated on the opposite extremities of the gulf, at **Poggio delle Granate**, at San Cerbone, and might indicate the pre-existence of two different villages, that later joined to become the original Etruscan city. The tombs of this period (9th-8th century BC) are in the typical *well* shape, and contain the urn and some personal objects (terra-cotta vases and simple bronze ornaments). The tombs of the following period are different, both in the architectural structure and in the richness and abundance of the treasures: these contained fine embossed bronze objects and vases with the first geometrical designs, either local or imported. During the 7th century BC, there is a great change in the building of the tombs, which start to follow monumental models.

Examples of this new architecture are the chamber tombs of the **Costone della Fredda** and of the **Porcareccia**, but especially the great tumuli of **San Cerbone**, brought to light at the beginning of the 20th century, removing the great quantity of iron scoriae covering them. Among the many sepulchral monuments, the most interesting is the **Chariots Tomb**, the most imposing in the necropolis of San Cerbone; from this tomb, delimited by a wide cylindrical drum in blocks, with stone slabs for the flow down of the rain-water and surmounted by a great tumulus of earth, come the remains of two war chariots, with coverings in bronze and iron, gold-work, ivory objects, bronze and iron weapons, all of which date the tomb to around the middle of the 7th century BC. Also in the necropolis of San Cerbone you will find the **Tomb of the Cylindrical Ciboria**, the **Tomb of the Balsamer**, and the **Tomb of the Pyriform Aryballos**, which contained fragments of Greek-oriental ceramics and gold and silver ornamental jewels, dating from the middle of the 7th and beginning of the 6th century BC. Not far from here, the **Tomb of the Offerer Small Bronze**, an *aedicula* tomb, with a double weathered roof, was surrounded by a number of open sarcophagi, unfortunately sacked in ancient times, as were most of the other tombs, and which dates from the 5th century BC.

On the **Poggio della Porcareccia**, between the city and San Cerbone, there are two other important sepulchral monuments, dating from the 7th century BC, evidence again, of the well-being reached during this period: the **Tomb of Gold-work**, with gold and silver personal objects, and the **Tomb of the Flabelli**, discovered intact, with jewels, three beautiful embossed bronze fans, weapons, helmets, many bronze vases and Greek and local ceramics. Near these tombs, archaeologists have found an edifice of a number of rooms, which is thought might have been the factory for the working of the minerals, used from the end of the 6th century to the late Etruscan period. Tombs from the Hellenistic period can be found at **Le Grotte**, **Buche delle Fate**, and **Poggio Malassarto**. Unfortunately, there is no certain evidence of the exact extension and site of *Popluna* in antiquity, but it is supposed that the built-up part must have been where the village and the castle of the city are today.

The **city walls** were about 2,500 metres long, and today it is still possible to see some parts of it, big square blocks dating from the archaic phase (6th-5th century BC), when Popluna was a powerful and leading city, evidenced by its coins. Popluna's coins, gold, silver (famous is the series with the Gorgone) and bronze, are the most ancient and large in number of Etruria, and start from the 6th century BC. Today Populonia, typically medieval, looks down on the Piombino Canal and the gulf of Baratti. There also is the Medieval **Fortress**; an **Etruscan Museum** (private) that houses a collection of objects, sarcophaguses, funeral treasures, epigraphs and other finds discovered in ancient necropolises.

Populonia, the Etruscan necropolis dominates the bright setting of the gulf of Baratti.

PRATO

HISTORICAL SURVEY – *The city is situated at the centre of the plain lying between Pistoia and Florence, to the right of the Bisenzio river, at the foot of the Calvana Mountains. It is the most important industrial centre in the Florence hinterland, and is famous throughout the world for its textiles and wool. An Etruscan-Roman settlement probably existed on the site now occupied by the town. Written information begins in the 9th century AD, and it is known that Prato became a free Commune in the 12th century. This was when the town began its economic and artistic development, despite the fact that it was overshadowed by nearby Florence and by Pistoia. In 1351, it fell under Florentine domination from which Prato attempted to escape. After much tribulation and continuous struggles against the Medici power, in 1653, Prato acquired the title of city and diocese. Today Prato is one of the most densely populated cities in Tuscany. It is an industrial city which has developed enormously, with modern streets and buildings, but which still retains the memories of its antique life as a Commune, in its small but charming historical centre. In April 1993, Prato became the 10th Province of Tuscany: a recognition long desired. It is the third city, after Florence and Livorno in terms of population.*

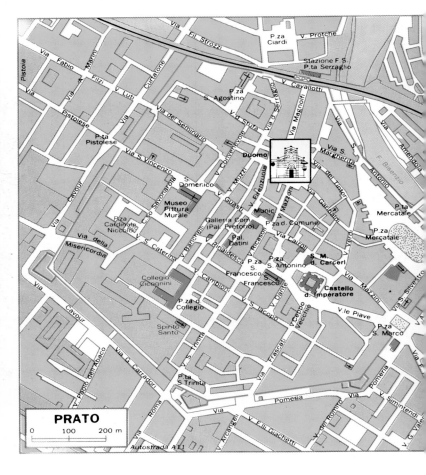

Prato, the Emperor's Castle.

Prato, a modern sculpture in front of the
Contemporary Art Museum.

183

Prato, a beautiful view of the Cathedral with the Pulpit of the Sacro Cingolo.

CATHEDRAL OF ST. STEFANO – The church was founded in the 10th century as a Parish church. In 1211, the architect Guidetto da Como began an extensive remodelling and enlargement. In the first half of the 14th century, the church was further enlarged with the construction of a large crossing with five ogival chapels.

The present **façade** is in polychrome marble and dates from 1385-1456. The *Pulpit of the Sacro Cingolo* (Holy Girdle) projects from the right corner. It was made by Donatello on a bronze capital by Michelozzo. The pulpit consists of a canopy, supported by a column surrounded by a parapet on corbels. The lovely *Dancing putti* on the parapet are by Donatello (copies). The right flank of the façade is characterised by a frieze of small arches and is articulated by arcading on pilaster strips, with two imposing portals decorated with marble inlays and flanked by columns.

The **interior**, divided into a nave and two aisles, is basically Romanesque, with Gothic additions. The solid columns in green marble have charming capitals. The nave is distinguished by the fine *Pulpit* by Mino da Fiesole and Rossellino (1473).

Nearby, under the transept is the underground **Vault** with the fresco portrait of *Convenevole da Prato* (Petrarca's master), buried here, and another fine fresco of a *Pietà* (14th cent.). Nearby, is the **Chapel of St. Stefano**, completely frescoed by local painters at the end of the 14th century. A beautiful bronze *Crucifix* by Ferdinando Tacca (1653) stands on the high altar. In the choir, behind the altar, is a tall stained-glass window done by Lorenzo da Pelago on designs by Filippo Lippi (1459), who also painted the cycle of frescoes in the choir, considered among the most important works of the entire Renaissance. The vault contains the *Evangelists*, the right wall *Events from the Life of St. Stephen*. The first chapel to the right of the high altar, contains other frescoes attributed to Paolo Uccello or the Prato Master, which represent the *Nativity of the Virgin*, *Presentation in the Temple* and the *Dispute of St. Stephen*. The frescoes below were finished by the painter Andrea del Giusto, with the *Lapidation*, the *Burial of St. Stephen* and the *Marriage of the Virgin*. Note should also be taken of Filippo Lippi's *Death of St. Girolamo* (1452) at the back of the transept near the door. There are various early 15th-century frescoes in the first chapel to the left of the high altar. On the right wall are *Events from the Life of St. James the Greater* and on the left, *Events from the Life of St. Margaret of Antioch*. In the second chapel to the left (of the high altar), is the *tomb of Filippo Inghirami* (1480) attributed to Simone di Niccolò de' Bardi.

At the head of the left transept is the **Chapel of the Holy Girdle**, by Agnolo Gaddi (1385-95), with the cycle of frescoes depicting the *Legend of the Holy Girdle*, on the wall. Not to be missed here is the statue of the *Madonna and Child*, a masterpiece by Giovanni Pisano (1317). Below, to the right of the portal, is the small Baptistery, and near the beginning of the right aisle is a fine *Cross* in wood by Giovanni Pisano. Lastly, 14th-century decorations and works by minor artists are preserved in the **Sacristy**

EMPEROR'S CASTLE – The Emperor's Castle, or *St. Barbara's Fortress*, is an extremely original monument which in its structure follows the architectural concepts of the Swabian castles of Puglia and Sicily. It is therefore not only unusual, but unique in Tuscany. It was built in *alberese* from the quarries in the Calvana mountain, between 1237 and 1247, for Frederick II, on the remains of the manor-house of the Counts of Prato. Square in plan, it has square towers at the corners and other towers which serve as abutments. There is a tympanum above the main portal. Performances are often organised in the simple courtyard inside.

CHURCH OF ST. MARIA DELLE CARCERI – This Greek-cross building was built by Giuliano da Sangallo (1484-95). The **façade** in green and white marble was never finished, except for one side terminated in the 19th century. The **interior** is considered one of the masterpieces of Renaissance architecture in the measured placement and perfect balance of its forms. Noteworthy in the dome are terra-cotta medallions of the *Evangelists* by Andrea della Robbia (1490). The high altar in the shape of a tabernacle, was executed in 1515, on a model by Sangallo himself. The side altars, by Alfonso Parigi, contain some interesting works, in particular an *Adoration* by Leonardo Mascagni. The late 15th-century stained-glass windows, with the *Assumption*, the *Visitation*, the *Nativity* and the *Annunciation* are also of high quality.

MUNICIPAL GALLERY – Established in 1850 in the **Palazzo Pretorio** rooms (13th-14th century), it contains important collections especially of 14th and 15th-century Florentine painting. There are several floors to visit. Among the outstanding works mention should be made of the *Tabernacle of St. Margaret* by Filippino Lippi (1498), the predella with *Seven scenes from the Legend of the Holy Girdle*, attributed to Bernardo Daddi; a lovely polyptych of the *Madonna and Child with Saints* by Bernardo Daddi (1328), a lively *Madonna Enthroned with the Child and Saints* by Giovanni da Milano (1354), the famous *Madonna del Ceppo* by Filippo Lippi, the *Portrait of Baldo Magini* attributed to Ridolfo del Ghirlandaio, as well as works by Pier Lorenzo Pratese, Zanobi Strozzi, Giovanni della Robbia, Raffaellino del Garbo, Francesco Botticini, Luca Signorelli, Gian Domenico Ferretti and many others.

CATHEDRAL MUSEUM – Installed in the Bishop's palace, adjacent to the Cathedral, the museum houses works of outstanding level, such as the *Madonna and Child with Angels*, a detached 13th-century fresco; two panel paintings with *Saints* by Giovanni Toscani (14th cent.); *Jacopone da Todi*, a detached fresco attributed to Paolo Uccello; the *Christ Child*, a statuette by Baccio da Montelupo; the mystical *Communion of Saint Theresa* by Livio Mehus (1683) and many others.

CONTEMPORARY ART MUSEUM – You will find it in the **Centre for Contemporary Art Luigi Pecci** and it displays exhibits of both Italian and foreign contemporary artists. Furthermore, in this centre there often are interesting live cultural performances.

TEXTILE MUSEUM – You may visit this museum in the **Palazzo Banci-Buonamici** (17th century): it is an interesting example of the textile production of the 15th-19th centuries. There are many valuable materials from the Loriano Bertini donation.

RADDA IN CHIANTI (Siena)

The communal territory of Radda is situated at the centre of the Chianti; it occupies the high valley of the river Pesa, and to the south, part of the Arbia Valley. Radda was one of the "terzo" of the ancient Chianti League, and today's boundaries are very similar to what they were then. Both archaeology and place names tell us that the entire area around Radda saw many Etruscan-Roman settlements. Traces of inhabited centres have been found at Paterno, Lo Smorto, La Pietraia, and in the immediate environs of Radda. But it is, above all, on the **Poggio di Cetamura**, near the Croce di Porcignano, that the remains of what was probably the most important Etruscan-Roman settlement in Chianti were found. It seems to have been at the centre of a network of roads, from Volterra, Chiusi and the Etruscan centres in the valley of the Arno. With the Middle Ages, the types of settlements changed and the territory was gradually dotted with castles, which in the 12th century belonged to the feuds of the Guidi counts or local lords (the Trebbiesi, the "da Monte Rinaldi"). Soon after however, the area fell under the control of the city of Florence, which, with the peace of Fonterutoli in 1201, had its dominion over the entire region of Chianti recognised.

The administrative organisation of the Florentine state in the early 14th century reunited the "peoples" of Chianti into a "League" divided into "Terzi" (thirds) centred around the principal towns, Radda, Castellina, and Gaiole. The representative of Florence had his residence in Radda, chosen as the chief centre of the league because of the strategically important position. Evidence of its past administrative and jurisdictional importance is the 15th-century **Palazzo Pretorio**, decorated with the coats of arms of the Podestà.

The principal inhabited centres of the Communal territory have retained the typical urban structure of fortified medieval settlement: in addition to Radda, there are **Volpaia**, **Monterinaldi**, **Castelvecchi**, **Albola** and **Montemuro**.

These were all hilltop settlements with defensive constructions dating from the 13th-14th centuries, and which consisted in a circular or elliptical circuit of walls (rarely completely preserved) enclosing the houses. In the bigger centres (Radda, Volpaia), defense towers were set along the walls at regular intervals. Gates opened at the main entrances, often at the ends of the principal road which divided the urban fabric in two parts. A keep completed the fortifications: it consisted of a taller and stronger tower, set into the circuit of walls (as at Volpaia), or at the centre of the settlement, rising up high (as at Albola). In only some cases, a few traces remain of the defensive structures (such as Monterinaldi, Montemuro and Castelvecchi), however the urban fabric of the towns retains memory of their feudal structure.

The **Parish Church of St. Maria Novella** gives an interesting evidence of the great renewal that characterised religious building throughout the west, from the beginning of the 11th century. Despite the fact that the church was remodeled in the 19th century, it still preserves its original basilican ground plan, with the nave divided from the two aisles by a series of arches springing from rectangular piers, alternated with columns

Roselle, the archaeologic area.

and cruciform piers. The presence of elements in sculpture (the capitals) makes the church similar to some of the Romanesque buildings of the upper Valdarno area, rich of Lombard influences. In the past, St. Maria Novella was perhaps the richest and most important parish church in Chianti, as proved by the numerous works of art from various periods inside. These include an *astylar Cross* in gilded bronze, dating from the 12th-13th century; an altarpiece, a late work by the Della Robbia school; a hexagonal baptismal font, also by the Della Robbia, as well as many religious vestments, furnishing and church ornaments.

ROSELLE (Grosseto)

A few kilometres from Grosseto, you can admire the excavations of the Etruscan and Roman city of Roselle, began in the middle of the 20th century and still undergoing.
The town, situated on two low hills divided by a small valley, is surrounded by the **city walls**, long more than three kilometres and still incredibly well preserved from the 6th century BC. This made it possible to study the construction technique of this grand defensive work, which in some points reaches five metres in height. Various gates open the circuit, and from the **Eastern Gate** is the entrance to the excavations. At the end of the street, is the heart of the Roman city, with the **forum**, and

wide streets on which are situated the most important public edifices. One is the **Basilica**, with a rectangular plan and arcade, and once the administration of justice. On the opposite side of the street, there are the remains of the paving, with slabs of the forum of Imperial age. Towards the south, is the **Augustales seat**, with niches on the walls, in which were set the marble statues of the Emperor Claudius, of Livia and others of the dynasty, evidencing the cult for the Imperial family. Under special shelters, you can see the ruins of a few **Etruscan houses** of archaic age (one with two rooms, another with circular enclosure, and other types), found under the Roman level: the ruins consist of parts of walls and paving in pressed clay, dating from the 7th-6th century BC. On the slopes of the northern hill, not far from the access street to the excavations, there is a **Roman thermal plant**, with a mosaic pavement and the base of a medieval **Tower**; while towards the top of the hill, you will find other **Etruscan edifices** of archaic age, and the **Roman Amphitheatre**, dating from the 1st century AD, with four entrances set on the cardinal points. On the southern hill, the excavations have brought to light a vast **inhabited complex**, with streets, houses and artisan workshops, dating from the 6th century BC; one type of this is a successive Hellenistic settlement. The **necropolises** of Roselle have not been as deeply investigated as the town, although the burial-grounds, known since the last century, contained precious treasures, confirming the 6th and 5th centuries BC as the period of greatest prosperity. The oldest tombs, dating from the 8th century BC, are very few and are situated not far from the southeastern gate. Instead, the examples of *chamber* sepulchres, dating from the end of the 7th and beginning of the 6th century, are more numerous; they are covered with slabs, and can be seen along the route that leads to the excavations. The Archaeological Museum of Grosseto can give the visitor a correct and clear interpretation of the city, the necropolises, the artistic production and economy of Roselle.

ENVIRONS – What attracts the attention of the village of **Roccastrada** is the medieval centre, called "il Cassero". You can still see the remains of the 14th-century Sienese fortifications. **Church of St. Nicolò** (13th century).

SAN CASCIANO in Val di Pesa (Florence)

The presence of four **Parish Churches** in the municipal territory of San Casciano bears witness to how densely populated the area was in the Middle Ages. All four date from the 11th-12th century: the churches of **St. Cecilia a Decimo, St. Pancrazio, St. Giovanni in Sugana** and **St. Stefano a Càmpoli**. The most interesting is the church of St. Giovanni, which contains a *Pietà* by Della Robbia. The town of San Casciano developed around the crossing of the routes between the Valley of the Pesa and the Valley of the Greve. From the beginning, the urban layout was rational and spread out around the cross-intersection of two roads. It formerly belonged to the Florentine bishops, and in the 13th century, passed under the jurisdiction of the Florentine republic, which created fortifications also serving to defend Florence, very close to San Casciano. Inside the **walls**, next to the only surviving **gate**, is the **Church of the Misericordia** or of *Santa Maria al Prato*, 14th-century, but with the interior remodelled in the 16th century. The fine works of art it contains include a fine *Pulpit* decorated with bas-reliefs by Giovanni di Balduccio . For the many and fine art works it contains, it is also a **Museum**, although it still serves as a church. Although the other churches in San Casciano are less interesting architecturally, they contain rather important works of art. The **Collegiata** has an *Annunciation* attributed to Ridolfo del Ghirlandaio; **St. Maria del Gesù** has a 14th-century panel painting of Florentine school; and **St. Francesco** has a 16th-century fresco of the *Last Supper*. In the **Church of the Suffragio**, also known as *St. Maria del Gesù*, there is the **Museum of Sacred Art**. Inside you will find many works from the town and country churches of the area: precious liturgical objects and furnishings, vestments, *crosses* and 15th-century *Madonnas*. Among the most famous artists here represented there are Francesco Fiorentino, Neri di Bicci, Cenni di Francesco and Jacopo del Casentino.

ENVIRONS – At **Sant'Andrea in Percussina** there is **Villa Bossi-Pucci**, better known as l'*Albergaccio,* where Niccolò Machiavelli lived.

SAN GIMIGNANO (Siena)

HISTORICAL SURVEY – *Situated at the centre of an area that was already occupied in Etruscan and Roman times, San Gimignano was a free Commune as early as 1130. During the 13th century, it underwent a phase of economic expansion which permitted the principal families of the city to erect the towers which still are an unmistakeable feature of San Gimignano. Florentine influence gradually increased until the city became subject to Florence in 1353.*

THE WALLS – When the Florentines took over San Gimignano, one of the first things they had to do was see to the restoration of the city walls (the first circle dates from the 11th century and the second from the second half of the 13th century). In the middle of the 15th century, and in 1470, the round towers were built as reinforcement of the walls, and in 1553, Duke Cosimo further strengthened the fortifications of San Gimignano, which led to the destruction of the churches and convents of St. Francesco and St. Chiara and the Hospital of the Innocents and resulted in the creation of a counter-gate. However two years later, Cosimo himself had the fortress torn down, and after the end of the war with Siena, the fortified structures of San Gimignano were dismantled and abandoned. Three gates still remain of the oldest set of city walls (the line can still in part be reconstructed) which enclosed the first town, set between the mounds of the Tower and Montestaffoli. To the north is the arch so-called **Arch of Goro**, to the east the imposing **Arch of Becci**, with its overhang still in place, and to the west the two stone arches known as **Arches of St. Matteo** or *Arches of the Cancelleria*. The second circle is on the contrary almost complete. It stretched out eastwards and westwards to include the *borghi* which had risen outside the preceding gates, along the *Via Francigena*, and on the north to enclose the addition to the city towards the hospital of St. Jacopo, including the two fortified hilltops in its circuit. All the gates of this circle of walls, on the whole restored but not excessively, are still extant: the **Gate of St. Giovanni**, with its overhang; (nearby, **Museum of Arts and Crafts**) the **Gate of the Springs** also with an overhang; the **Gate of St. Matteo**, which is better preserved, while the small **Gate of Quercecchio** (in the street that bears the same name, **Ornithological Museum**) near the panoramical **Fortress of Montestaffoli** and the gate near the church of St. Jacopo are simpler.

San Gimignano, the turreted profile of the medieval town dominates the typical Tuscan countryside.

TOWERS AND PALACES – Needless to say that San Gimignano still has the forms it received between the 13th and 14th centuries. The many outstanding examples of architecture, both civil and religious, are exceptionally well preserved. The towers and tower-houses, that have made San Gimignano famous, are concentrated around the two squares, *Piazza del Duomo* and *Piazza della Cisterna*, which constitute the city centre. Mention should be made of the **Great Tower of Palazzo del Popolo**, the **Rognosa**, the **Tower of the Cugnanesi**, the **Twin Towers of the Ardinghelli and the Salvucci**, the **Tower of the Cortesi** (or *of the Devil*) with its crowning in stone corbels. If we were to mention all the medieval tower-houses and small and large palaces which line the squares and streets of San Gimignano the list would be too long. But special attention must be given, in the Piazza della Cisterna, to the 14th-century **Palazzo Tortoli** (now *Treccani*), with two rows of mullioned windows with two lights, the **Razzi** and **Salvestrini Houses** (the latter formerly Hospital of the Innocents or foundling home, and now a hotel), the **Palazzo dei Cortesi**, next to the tower of the same family. In the *Via di San Matteo* in addition to the 13th- 14th-century **Palazzo della Cancelleria** (which belonged to Marsili), and the **Tower-house of the Pesciolini**, outstanding examples are **Palazzo Vichi**, formerly *Bonaccorsi,* with frescoes of the school of Poccetti, the **Baccinelli House**, with the façade decorated with recessed majolica bowls, the 14th-century **Palaces Mori** and **Lorini**, and finally the **Palazzo Tinacci**, which consists of two buildings, one of which has a portal with a depressed arch and Florentine style windows on the first floor, and with a large mullioned window with three lights, similar to those of the palaces in Lucca, on the second floor, while the other reveals Sienese influence in the ogival mullioned windows with two lights in the second floor. The **Houses of the Ceccarelli-Franzesi** are in the *Via del Castello*, as is the **Palazzo Moronti**, with a small courtyard and well and an external staircase. Near the **Arch of the Becci** is the **Palazzo** which belonged to the same family, and in the adjacent *Piazzetta Cugnanesi*, the **Palazzo Cugnanesi**, with the tower next to it. Lastly, in the *Via di San Giovanni*, particularly striking are the **Palazzo Campatelli**, with its tower, and the 14th-century **Palazzo Pratellesi**, with elegant two-light mullioned windows in brick, now seat of the **City Library**, founded in 1449 (it contains codexes, parchements, autographs), and the **City Historical Archive**, with the old statues of the first half of the 13th century. There are also other tower-houses and dwellings in the same street, adapted from the 14th-century **Convent of St. Caterina**.

PALAZZO DEL PODESTÀ AND PALAZZO DEL POPOLO – The architecture of the public buildings around the *Piazza del Duomo* is particularly noteworthy. The old **Palazzo del Podestà**, rebuilt in 1239 and enlarged a hundred years later, is flanked by the tower known as **Tower Rognosa**, and has a large vestibule on the ground floor, with barrel vaulting and stone benches along the walls, as well as a fresco by Sodoma. Around the middle of the 16th century, a **Theatre** was built inside, remodelled at the end of the 18th century and now out of use. Across from it, is the **Palazzo del Popolo** (or *Palazzo Nuovo del Podestà*, now the townhall), built in the second half of the 13th century and enlarged in the early part of the 14th, but the battlements date from 1882. On the right, is the highest **Tower** in San Gimignano, preceded by two flights of stairs which lead to a speaker's platform (*arengo*), while on the left is a large loggia with three arches. An inscription in the palace commemorates the fact that Dante Alighieri stayed here when he came to plead the cause of the Guelph league. An external staircase in the picturesque courtyard, leads to the rooms which were once the seat of the civic magistrature, and now house the **City Museums** and the **City Gallery**. For the former, mention here will be made only of the *Maestà*, which Lippo Memmi (1317) frescoed, obviously inspired by the one Simone Martini had painted two years earlier in the Palazzo Pubblico of Siena. The Gallery contains a fine collection of paintings of Sienese and Florentine schools from the 13th to the 15th century, including the two tondos with the *Annunciation* by Filippino Lippi.

THE SPRINGS – Evidence of civil architecture in medieval San Gimignano also includes the imposing **Springs**, not far from the **Gate of the Springs**, built on the model of the Sienese springs and consisting of ten arcades with different types of arches and supports, built between the 12th and

14th century (although they were restored in the middle of the 19th century), and which were also used for the washing of wool.

COLLEGIATE CHURCH – The most famous monument of religious architecture in San Gimignano, worthy of a large city, is the Collegiate church (improperly also called *Duomo*), which is the old parish church of San Gimignano consecrated in 1148 by Eugene III. In 1239, the orientation of the church was reversed (remains of the semi-circular apse have been brought to light near the 13th-century façade), and in 1460, it was enlarged by Giuliano da Maiano with the addition of the tribune. The Romanesque structures of the aisles, which belonged to the parish church, with the colonnades of Pisan type and the sculpture of the capitals, are closely related to the neighbouring parish church of Cellole, and may be the work of the same workshop. Of the same period as the parish church is the **portico** with two superposed tiers, brought to light on the left side, on *Piazzetta Pecori*. In the 14th century, the **interior** of the church was already being enriched with frescoes – by Taddeo di Bartolo, Barna da Siena, Lippo Memmi, Bartolo di Fredi – but even more after it was enlarged in the 15th century, and the **New Sacristies** and the

San Gimignano, the tower and the arch of the Becci are among the most salient architectural elements of the medieval centre.

Chapels of the Conception and **of St. Fina** were added. The Chapel of St. Fina also received the magnificent altarpiece by Benedetto da Maiano. Artists such as Benozzo Gozzoli, Domenico Ghirlandaio, Pier Francesco Fiorentino, Sebastiano Mainardi worked on the great 15th-century fresco cycles. But the church was also enriched with other works of art, such as Jacopo della Quercia's wooden sculptures, the inlaid benches by Antonio da Colle, and other works and religious objects of value, today preserved – with Etruscan and Roman finds and objects from the churches of the environs – in the **Museum of Sacred Art**, installed, together with the **Archive of the Works and of the Chapter** in the Piazzetta Pecori.

CONVENT AND CHURCH OF ST. AGOSTINO – The ancient Dominican convent, where Savonarola once stayed, is now a penitentiary. A sign of the presence of the mendicant orders in San Gimignano (and further proof of how populous the city was in the 13th and 14th centuries) is the Church and the **Convent of St. Agostino**, secluded in the western part of the city in a piazza that is a true masterpiece of town planning.
Consecrated in 1298, the **Church**, in brick on the outside, has the simple ground plan of the poorer religious orders, with a single large luminous nave and a presbytery slightly wider and terminating in three vaulted chapels. From the 15th century on, altars (one by Benedetto da Maiano) and fresco cycles were added, among which best-known are those in the choir, by Benozzo Gozzoli depicting the *Life of Saint Augustine*. The **Cloister**, which also contains Etruscan urns from Cellole, is also 15th-century.

OTHER CITY CHURCHES – San Gimignano has an incredible number of minor Romanesque buildings which testify to the intense religious life, and confirm the early prosperity of this town in the Valdelsa.
The *Piazza Sant'Agostino* also contains the **Church of St. Pietro**, with a single aisle and no apse, built in two successive periods. The older portal is on the left side, and the principal decorative elements are the arched lintels in molded brick on the archivolts of the doors and windows.
The two tiers of blind arcading which decorate the brick façade of the **Church of St. Bartolo** are more clearly inspired by Pisan architecture. The building, near the gate of St. Bartolo in the first circuit of city walls, has an extremely simple ground plan. It dates from 1173, but the façade,

"St. Gimignano supporting the townspeople" by Taddeo di Bartolo (detail).

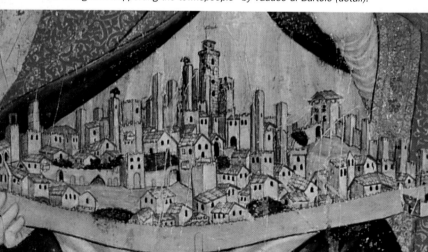

192

in clear contrast with the rest, seems to date from the early 13th century. What is left of the façade of the former **Church of St. Giovanni**, later dedicated to *St. Francesco*, is of the same date as the façade of St. Bartolo. It also has a tier of blind arcades in Pisan style. The church belonged to the Hospitallers and may originally have been a hospice.

The **Church of St. Jacopo** also belonged to the same order of Hospitallers. The church is near the gate of St. Jacopo and, according to tradition, was founded by the people of San Gimignano in 1096 on their return from the First Crusade. The ground plan is simple with a single aisle and no apse, and the church is small but displays unusual features in the vaulting sustained by transverse arches which spring from enganged piers with engaged columns set against the walls and with rich capitals. The northern elements obviously seem to have come from beyond the Alps, through the *Via Francigena*. Romanesque also is the **Church of St. Lorenzo in Ponte** (the draw-bridge of the old castle was nearby) with a nave only, but after the heavy restoration of 1929 the church is better known for the frescoes by Cenni di Francesco di ser Cenni.

Other religious buildings in San Gimignano include the **Church of Guercecchio**, the **Conservatory of St. Chiara** with works by Matteo Rosselli and Vincenzo Tamagni in the small church, the **Hospital of St. Fina**, and the **Oratory of St. Girolamo** with works by Sebastiano Mainardi and Vincenzo Tamagni.

ENVIRONS

None of the castles or other settlements scattered throughout the territory were able to compete with San Gimignano, the fortunes of which rose so rapidly. **Castelvecchio di San Gimignano** became relatively important as a settlement because it belonged to the bishops of Volterra, but around the middle of the 13th century it once and for all passed under the control of San Gimignano, and became relatively prosperous thanks to the discovery of silver in the vicinity. It seems to have been abandoned as early as the second half of the 15th century. The ruins of the settlement have a romantic air: the remains of the walls and towers are among the rich vegetation. **Castelnuovo di San Gimignano** (at present **Castel San Gimignano** on the road that runs from Colle to Volterra) was more fortunate. It also belonged first to the bishop of Volterra, and subsequently from the 14th century on, was under the firm control of San Gimignano. At present it is rapidly developing thanks to its site along a state motorway, but it preserves traces of its medieval fortifications. Little remains of the **Castle of Casaglia** which was dominated by Count Ugo, passing to the Carolingians and finally to the bishops of Volterra. It was the object of bitter struggles between San Gimignano and Volterra as early as the 12th century; and war even broke out between San Gimignano and the inhabitants of Colle. In 1230, it was destroyed during another war between San Gimignano and the bishop of Volterra. **Collemucioli** also belonged to the Carolingians, although it was contested by the bishops, to whom it was confirmed by papal privileges. A fine stone tower, now used as a house, still remains. A brick tower also remains of the important **Castle of Fosci** (now **Castellaccio**), situated at the border with the territory of Colle, in an area full of ancient settlements. In the territory of San Gimignano, you will also find the **Parish Church of Cellole**; it was situated along the old *Via Francigena* which joined Rome to France. The **interior** has the usual tripartite form, with a semi-circular apse, but the subdivision with columns is particularly striking: the capitals are slightly different with a low abacus decorated with the star-shaped flowers that are typical of the Romanesque in the Valdelsa. This decoration is particularly rich in the blind arcading, in the supporting corbels, and in the lunettes that are both on the inside and on the outside of the apse. A typical feature of the church of Cellole is the fact that the nave is not much taller than the aisles, so the **façade**, heavily restored, almost has the shape of a hut. To be noted, is also the absence of the bell tower, originally set on the first bay of the right aisle and, when transformed, was torn down in 1860. The building shows various phases of construction: while the columns, in Pisan style, can be dated from the end of the 12th century, the apse with its decorations might date from the beginning of the same century, and the façade, except for the outer walls, would seem to date from the first part of the 13th century, as deduced from an inscription with the date 1238.

SAN GIOVANNI VALDARNO (Arezzo)

Well known town of the lower Valdarno, was used by Florence to control Arezzo.

The most interesting monument here is probably **Palazzo Pretorio**, embellished by a portico and coats of arms on the façade. Although it is originally 14th-century it has been restored many times up to the Renaissance. The **Church of St. Maria delle Grazie**, 15th century, in spite of its 19th-century façade, has a terra-cotta figure by the Della Robbia brothers, works by Jacopo del Sellaio and Maestro del Cassone Adimari. In the sacristy there is a wooden bust of *St. Lorenzo*, attributed to Ghiberti. In *Piazza Masaccio* note the **Oratory of St. Lorenzo** (14th century) and the **Palazzo Ricorboli** (15th century).

SAN MINIATO (Pisa)

Initially a possession of Federico Barbarossa (Frederick II), San Miniato, also known as *San Miniato al Tedesco*, was a free Commune in the 14th century, and at the end of the 14th century became subject to Florence and followed its fate. It developed mainly along the ridge of three hills and stretched out along a single street. The great number of fine works of art it contains makes it more important than many larger and better known cities. The majestic **Tower of Frederick** rises up over the entire town. The **Cathedral** too, dominates the town, but from a slightly lower position. It is situated in front of what was probably the site of the *palatium*, the seat of the imperial vicar. Orginally built in the 13th century, its present aspect is the result of a subsequent radical remodelling and enlargement that brought the back all the way to the so-called **Tower of Matilde** once part of the defenses of the city and only later, bell tower of the Cathedral. The interior was modified (in the 18th century and later) and nothing remains of the original Romanesque structure except for the façade: it is in brick and has three large rose windows set over the entrance portals. Various majolica bowls are set into the upper part of the façade as decorative elements. The **Diocesan Museum**, next to the church, houses a number of works from other churches in the diocese.

The **Church of St. Francesco**, which was built as an enlargement of an older small church dedicated to *St. Miniato*, was finished, according to an inscription, in 1276. The **Convent** was added later, and between 1343 and 1480, the whole complex was radically remodelled. But of all the religious buildings the **Church of St. Domenico** dedicated to *Saints James and Lucy* best preserves its original features. It was built in 1330, and like St. Francesco, it rises from the steep hillside and is supported by imposing piers and great sustaining walls. The original nave and two aisles have now been reduced to the nave alone, and the façade was never finished. The five chapels contain many extremely important works: the Samminiati Chapel houses the *sepulcher of Giovanni Chellini* by Bernardo Rossellino on design by Donatello (although this is now contested); the Armaleoni Chapel contains a fresco by Masolino and a panel painting by the San Miniato Master. Striking too, is a terra-cotta roundel of an *Annunciation* by the Della Robbia brothers.

The **Town Hall**, built in the 15th century as the residence for the city magistrates, still has a number of frescoes by Cenni di Francesco di Ser Cenni, in the Council Hall. There are also various coats of arms of the 'podestà', including that of Franco Sacchetti who guided the city's fate in 1392. Of interest too is the **Bishop's Palace** on the same square of the Cathedral, and was once the residence of the Captain of the Militia and since 1622 has been the bishop's headquarters. The **Church of the Loretino** was built at the end of the 14th century, as a chapel for the Signori del Popolo and it communicates with the Town Hall. It contained a miraculous *Cross*, dating from the 10th century, which is now in the **Church of the Crucifix** it was built between 1706 and 1712 on a design by the architect Anton Maria Ferri. Other interesting examples of architecture are the **Palace of the Seminary**, with a number of 14th-century shops ('botteghe') on the low and wide façade; the **Oratory della Misericordia**, 16th-century; the 14th-century **Church of the Hospital of St. Caterina**; the **Oratory of Saints Sebastiano and Rocco**; the **Church of St. Paolo**; the **Church of the Conservatory of St. Chiara**; the 14th-century **Or-**

San Miniato, one of the ridges on which the ancient town develops.

atory of **St. Maria a Fortino**; the **Church of the SS. Annunziata**; and the **Grifoni, Ruffoli, Formichi** and **Buonaparte Palaces**.

Mention must be made of at least one of the persons who played an important role in the history of San Miniato. Francesco Sforza (1401-1466) was born here. His father Muzio Attendolo was a commander. A papal bull nominated Sforza marquis of Ancona and gonfalonier of the Church in Umbria. He later became duke of Milan. Another important man of San Miniato was the painter Ludovico Ciardi, better known as "Cigoli" from the hamlet where he was born in 1559. He studied first with Buontalenti and the with Alessandro Allori, and worked prevalently for the Medici court. He later moved to Rome where he died in 1613.

SAN QUIRICO D'ORCIA (Siena)

This ancient town, already subject to Siena in the 13th century, is of great interest. Upon entering the town one is immediately struck by the lovely Romanesque **Collegiate Church** dedicated to *Saints Quirico and Giuditta*, built in the 12th century on a pre-existing building. The central portal, and the one in the right side are magnificent with their low relief decorations. The one on the side can probably be attributed to the school of Giovanni Pisano. A third portal, dated 1298, opens off the end of the right arm of the transept and is Gothic in style. Inside, remarkable are a fine triptych by Sano di Pietro, and the wooden choir stalls, carved by Antonio Barili in the 15th century. Near the Collegiate Church is the **Palazzo Chigi**, built by Carlo Fontana around 1679, heavily damaged in the last war. Also noteworthy is the Renaissance **Palazzo Pretorio** and the **Church of St. Maria di Vitaleta**, in front of which is the **New Gate**. On one side is the entrance to the **Horti Leonini**, a large public park built by Diomede Leoni in 1540. The Romanesque **Church of St. Maria** should also be visited. Dating from the 11th-12th century, the portal was built with material from the Abbey of Sant'Antimo. It is worthwhile visiting **Vignoni**, a small town in the vicinity of San Quirico, with its tower, church and castle of the Ameringhi, lords of the area, and **Bagno Vignoni**, a fascinating spa where the water springs up in an antique pool in the center of the town.

San Quirico d'Orcia, view of the Collegiate Church and the Horti Leonini.

SANSEPOLCRO (Arezzo)

HISTORICAL SURVEY – *This ancient town is one of the most important in the area. A legend says that the town grew up around an oratory dedicated to St. Leonard, in which various relics of the Holy Sepulcher were kept. Sansepolcro became a free Commune in the 13th century, but soon fell under the dominion of various noble families, including the Della Faggiuola and the Tarlati. In the 15th century, it became the property of the Church, but in 1441 it was sold to Florence. Today it is a commercial and industrial town, known above all for its historical center, developed on a 15th-16th-century urban fabric. Its palaces, churches and streets which cross each other creating fascinating corners and beautiful views, have a severe beauty and undeniable charm.*

CATHEDRAL – This powerful building in Romanesque-Gothic style dates back to the first half of the 11th century. It was frequently transformed as the centuries passed. The linear **façade** has a fine splayed portal of Lombard school, above which is a large rose window. The tripartite **interior** with columns is Romanesque, and has a fine trussed timber roof. Among the most important works mention should be made of the *Madonna and Child*, a large 14th-century fresco of the school of Romagna, in the right aisle near the entrance. Nearby is another fresco, the *Crucifixion*, by Bartolomeo della Gatta. On the altar, to the left of the presbytery, is a large polychrome wooden *Crucifix* from the end of the 11th century. Also noteworthy, on the left wall, is an *Ascension* by Gerino da Pistoia, and on the right, a polyptych, *Saints Peter and Paul*, by Matteo di Giovanni. On the second altar of the left aisle is a lovely *Assunta* by Palma the Younger, and the *tomb of Abbot Simone Graziani* of the school of Rossellino.

MUNICIPAL PICTURE GALLERY – It is situated in the fine **Palazzo Aggiunti**, and has works of great artistic interest, including the famous fresco of the *Resurrection*, masterpiece by Piero della Francesca; *St. Sebastian*, a fresco of the school of Piero della Francesca; *Resurrected Christ and Four Saints*, a late 14th-century work by the Sienese school; *Saints Egidio and Anthony Abbot*, another masterpiece by Luca Signorelli; the *Pietà* and a *San Nicola da Tolentino*, both by Santi di Tito, as well as works by Raffaellino del Colle, Agostino Ciampelli, the Della Robbia brothers, Cigoli, and Passignano.

CHURCH OF ST. FRANCESCO – The church dates from the end of the 13th century, and the original structure can still be seen in part of the striking **façade** with the Gothic portal and large rose window. The 18th-century **interior** contains a fine painting on canvas of the *Dispute in the Temple* by Passignano. Next to the church is a sober **Cloister**.

CHURCH OF ST. MARIA DELLE GRAZIE – This Renaissance building has a fine portal decorated with bas-reliefs symbolising death. The single nave **interior** has a finely worked wooden ceiling. Raffaellino del Colle's famous *Madonna delle Grazie* is on the high altar.

CHURCH OF ST. ROCCO – The church, in Renaissance forms, preserves a fine *Resurrection* by Raffaellino del Colle and, on the high altar, a late 13th-century wooden *Christ* in a tabernacle. Englobed in the church is the **Oratory of the Company of the Crucifix**, completely frescoed in 1588 with *Stories of the Passion*. Adjacent to the Oratory, is the **Chapel of the Holy Sepulchre**, a small delightful shrine in sandstone built at the end of the 16th century.

CHURCH OF ST. MARIA DEI SERVI – The church, frequently remodeled in the course of the centuries, presents traces of an antique Gothic building to be dated around the end of the 13th century. The presbytery, in the small intimate **interior**, houses the *Madonna in Glory*, a striking altar-piece by Matteo di Giovanni (1487).

CHURCH OF ST. LORENZO – Built in 1556, the fine **façade** is preceded by a porch. The **interior** contains an authentic masterpiece – the *Deposition* by Rosso Fiorentino, one of the most famous works of the Mannerist period.

CHURCH OF ST. AGOSTINO – The date of the original church is not known, but the present church dates from 1771. **Inside**, on the second altar to the right is a rustic wooden *Crucifix* of the late 14th century.

MEDICI FORTRESS – Probably built by Giuliano da Sangallo (16th cent.), it is a good example of military architecture in a fine landscape setting.

HOUSE OF PIERO DELLA FRANCESCA – This fine small 15th-century palace has Michelozzo modules in the portal and the windows.

THE PALACES OF SANSEPOLCRO – This small town has many great buildings which constitute the urban fabric. Some of the most interesting include **Palazzo delle Laudi**, now the Town Hall, built by Alberto Alberti and Antonio Cantagalli at the end of the 16th century; **Palazzo Graziani Mercati**, a fine structure with Gothic portals; **Palazzo Pretorio**, which has the façade covered with Della Robbia coats of arms; the delightful **Palazzo Graziani**, realised in the 16th century under the influence of Ammannati; **Palazzo Cherici-Rigi**, finely decorated with sgraffiti and frescoes, now in poor condition; **Palazzo Ducci**, clearly Mannerist in inspiration; the Romanesque **Palazzo Benci**; the Mannerist **Palazzo Galardi**; and **Palazzo Turini**, **Palazzo Bofolci** and **Palazzo Pichi**.

ENVIRONS – It is worthwhile taking the deviation to **Monterchi**. In the Cemetery of this Medieval village - inside a Chapel – there is the famous *Madonna del Parto*, a remarkable work by Piero della Francesca.

Sansepolcro, a detail of the Palio della Balestra that takes place in September.

SANTA FIORA (Grosseto)

The peculiarity of the historical centre of Santa Fiora is in its division in two distinct parts: the upper part, characterised by the feudal palaces, and the lower part, enclosed in walls. In **Castello** the remains of the **Fortress** are still extant. Adjacent to the **Palazzo Sforza-Cesarini** is the Romanesque **Parish Church**, remodelled in the 16th century and with various Della Robbia terra-cotta figures inside. A gate with a window above leads to the town below, with the **Oratory of the Madonna delle Nevi**, frescoed inside by the 17th-century painter Francesco Nasini. Of interest too, is the so-called **Peschiera**, built in the 18th century to collect the waters of the Flora river and now also the point of departure for an aqueduct which supplies a large area of the Maremma.

SAN VINCENZO (Livorno)

Here, between the sea and the pine woods, stretches the so-called Etruscan Riviera, which also includes the interesting **Natural Park of Rimigliano**. Already in 1304, Pisa had built here a **Tower** to watch out for the Saracens. About two centuries later, the Florentines won on Bartolomeo d'Alvano, who wanted to free Pisa from the siege. Today the town is well organised for summer tourism.

SARTEANO (Siena)

The houses of Sarteano are arranged in a semicircle at the foot of the castle. The double **circuit of walls** is still visible. Inside is the **Church of St. Martino**, already mentioned in documents in the 13th century, and remodelled in Neo-classic style around the middle of the 19th century. The church contains the *Annunciation*, an important work by Beccafumi. Also interesting is the **Collegiate Church of St. Lorenzo**, 16th century, inside which are various interesting paintings. Opposite is the fine **Palazzo Cennini**, built in brick in the 15th century, but transformed in the 18th century. After passing through **Monalda Gate**, the *Via della Rocca* leads to the **Castle**, with its perfectly preserved medieval structures. Building began in the 10th century, but it was remodeled various times. What we see now is the result of work done in 1464-70 by the Republic of Siena, which had conquered the town in 1379. You should see the **Thermal pools** of the "Bagno Santo", at the Park-Camping delle Piscine. The beneficial properties of these waters were also known by the Romans; Orazio called them *Fontes Clusini*. In the environs of Sarteano, see the **Abbey of Spineto**, fortified and today transformed in villa, founded in 1085.

Sarteano, view of the town dominated by the Castle.

Saturnia, detail of the Roman road and gate.

SATURNIA (Grosseto)

This small village is all inside the circuit of walls, built by the Sienese in 1461 on the ruins of the pre-existing walls, probably Etruscan. The **Roman Gate** runs on an ancient Roman street. In **Villa Ciacci**, where there are the ruins of the Sienese donjon, there is a collection of Roman-Etruscan antiquities. The **Church**, despite all the reconstructions, is Romanesque. The village is especially known for the **spa** of sulphurous water (37,5°C), beneficial for affections of the respiratory tract and rheumatology problems. The visit to the **Etruscan necropolises** is also very interesting: it preserves various tombs in travertine slabs, and is only a few kilometres away from Saturnia.

SCARPERIA (Florence)

The area of the municipality of Scarperia developed along the main route that joined Florence to Bologna, crossing the Appenines through the Giogo pass. Evidence of the importance of this road are the numerous **Parish Churches** along the route. They were places of worship but also of refuge for the wayfarers. The most important are those of **St. Agata** and **St. Maria a Fagna**. The former seems to have been built in the 12th century on older foundations. The tripartire interior has a lovely baptistery with an ambo that dates from 1175. The Parish Church of Fagna, originally dating from the 11th century, was rebuilt in the 18th century but the carrying structures are still Romanesque. Inside there are an ambo and a baptismal font, also in inlaid marble, both datable to the 12th century. The **Palace of the Vicar** in the main square in Scarperia, dates from the 14th century, when the city was founded. In 1306, the Florentines built Scarperia to control the Ubaldini, lords of this side of the Apennines. The coats of arms of the vicars of Florence who came to live here, can still be seen on the façade. On the other side of the square is the **Provostship**, an Augustinian convent until 1812. It is a typical church of the mendicant orders with only a nave. Of the many works inside, mention should be made of the marble tondo with the *Madonna and Child* by Benedetto da Maiano, a tabernacle, by Mino da Fiesole, a wooden *Crucifix,* which some critics attribute to Sansovino. Next to the Provostship is the 14th-century **Oratory of the Madonna di Piazza**, decorated inside with frescoes by Jacopo del Casentino, who also painted a *Madonna and Child* in the same church. The Commune of Scarperia is well known for the motor-racing track "del Mugello".

SIENA

HISTORICAL SURVEY – *On the soft hills of the countryside, between the valleys of the Arbia, the Elsa and the Merse rivers, lies Siena. This city, with its alleys, small streets, narrow suburbs, and squares, reveals all its sober medieval beauty. It is truly one of the finest examples of medieval city. The few finds testify that the area now occupied by the city, was already inhabited in the bronze age. An Etruscan settlement also seems to have been present on the site of the current town. But the first*

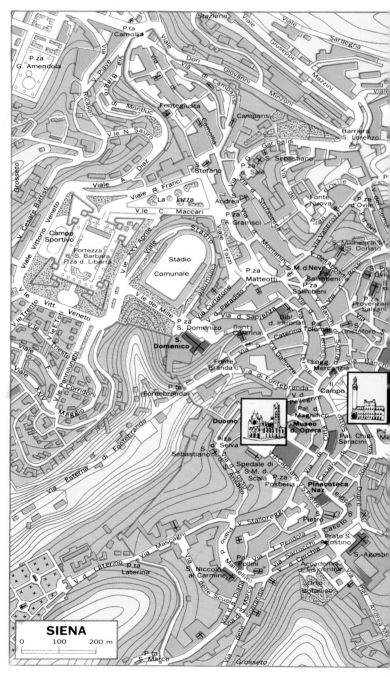

detailed information dates from Roman times. We, know, for instance, that Siena, then Sena Julia, must have been a Roman civitas, founded as a military colony by Caesar (a legend says that the city was founded by Aschio and Senuo, Remo's two sons). In the Lombard period, Siena was already quite famous. After the Carolingian conquest, it was subject to the pre-eminence of the Bishops, until the 11th century, when it became a free Commune. This was when the city experienced its first great period of territorial and urban expansion, thanks to the flourishing commerce and trade on the route Via Francigena which put the city in communication with the area north of the Alps. During the 12th and 13th centuries the city, by then rich and powerful (Sienese bankers used to lend considerable sums to sovereigns, popes and princes), often clashed with the neighbouring city of Florence on which it inflicted a heavy defeat in 1260, in the famous battle of Montaperti. These were also the years in which some of the most important trends in medieval painting took form in Siena. Outstanding personalities, such as Duccio di Buoninsegna, Simone Martini, and Ambrogio Lorenzetti, were born and left inimitable masterpieces, influencing, with their works, all of 14th-century art. In 1269, the Sienese were drastically defeated at Colle di Val d'Elsa, by the Florentine troops. It meant the beginning of a decline which, with its ups and downs, intensified in the course of the following centuries. In fact in 1487, Siena became a dominion of the aegis of Pandolfo Petrucci. In the 16th century Siena became an ally of the French and in 1559 surrendered to the troops of Giangiacomo de' Medici passing under the dominion of Cosimo I. In the following centuries, it fell under the Lorraine, becoming part of the Grand Duchy of Tuscany. In 1859, it was the first Tuscan city annexed to the Kingdom of Italy.

CATHEDRAL – The Cathedral marks the passage from Romanesque to Gothic forms, and developed as the city grew: it summerises the most vivid artistic experiences. Dedicated to the *Virgin of the Assumption*, it was certainly built on the site of a precedent church. Construction began towards the end of the 12th century, and in the third decade of the 13th century there is unmistakable mention of the 'Opera di Santa Maria', a group of citizens commissioned with the construction. Work on the Cathedral continued throughout the 13th century. Shorty after the middle of the century, the dome and the first apse of the building were finished, but they were torn down in the second decade of the 14th century, when Camaino di Crescentino, father of Tino, began the extension of the apse towards Vallepiatta. In the meanwhile, around 1290, Giovanni Pisano had built the lower part of the façade. But before the middle of the 14th century, work on the Cathedral came to a halt, because the economic and demographic growth of the city, together perhaps with the desire to emulate the great cathedral of its rival Florence, induced the Sienese to plan a church of such a size, that the existing building would have served as transept. Lando di Pietro began the construction in 1339, then it was continued by Giovanni di Agostino and by Domenico di Agostino. But either due to statics errors, or to the change in the economic and political situation,

Siena, the majestic Cathedral represents a jewel of gothic architecture.

as well as the plague of the middle of the century, the ambitious project was abandoned in 1355. This decision once more focussed attention on the old Cathedral, and the apse was finished in 1382, while the vaulting of the nave was raised higher. Giovanni di Cecco, clearly inspired by the Cathedral of Orvieto, completed the upper part of the main façade, setting it, not without difficulty, on the lower part already completed. These endless vicissitudes are the reason why the Cathedral of Siena is still a sort of mysterious object for architecture critics, even though as a whole, the church is one of the principal churches in Italian Gothic style. Derivations from Romanesque culture can still be seen in the oldest parts of the Cathedral, which has a basilica plan, with a nave and two aisles and a projecting two-aisled transept. This Romanesque influence can be seen in the piers with engaged columns in Lombard style, and in the erection of the dome that changes from hexagonal to dodecagonal through the pendentives at the corners; but the dome, instead of being contained by a lantern, shows its shapes also on the outside. Here the loggia surrounding it, clearly demonstrates ties with the Cloister of the Abbey of Torri, and it is worthwhile remembering that Bruno, bishop of Siena between 1182 and 1215, had in precedence been abbot of that monastery. Other elements with echoes of Romanesque culture include some of the capitals of the piers in the nave, where next to the foliage already typically Gothic, there are elements still echoing the pre-Romanesque features so diffused in the Romanesque art of the Valdelsa and the Sienese countryside.

The **Bell tower** is also Romanesque in structure, although lightened by the two-colour marble facing. It seems to have been built on a precedent tower of the Bisdomini, and is pierced by a succession of mullioned windows with one to six lights, and topped by an octagonal base pyramid. The Cathedral of Siena not only offers a great variety of architectural solutions and an intense note of colour in its rich marble facing, but also contains an incredible number of works of art, which together with those preserved in the adjacent Cathedral Museum provide a complete survey of the artistic culture at its height. Obviously only the most important are here mentioned: in the **façade** there are Giovanni Pisano's statues, carried out around 1290, and now replaced by copies (the originals are in the museum).

Inside, the first thing to admire is the marble pavement decorated in sgraffiti or intarsia, subdivided into about fifty panels, carried out between the middle of the 14th and the middle of the 16th century. A group of about ten artists, mostly Sienese, including Domenico di Niccolò and Domenico Beccafumi, collaborated in the work. The high altar in the presbytery is by Baldassarre Peruzzi, with the large ciborium by Vecchietta; two of the *angels* are by Francesco di Giorgio Martini and others are by Beccafumi. The round stained-glass window in the apse, with events from the *Life of the Virgin, Evangelists and Patron Saints of Siena* was made at the end of the 13th century, on cartoons by Duccio di Buoninsegna, and seems to be the oldest example extant of an Italian-made stained-glass window. The apse also contains fine 14th-century wooden choir stalls, completed in the 16th century. In the left transept, near the area covered by the dome, is the famous octagonal *Pulpit* by Nicola Pisano with *Events from the Life of Christ* in the parapet, separated by *Prophets* and *angels*: executed with the help of Nicola's son Giovanni, Arnolfo di Cambio, Donato and Lapo di Ricevuto, it must be considered as one of the basic stages in Gothic sculpture. In the centuries that followed, the Sienese continued to focus their attention on the Cathedral, as shown by the addition of numerous chapels.

Mention must be made of the **Chapel of St. Ansano** with the *monument of Cardinal Petroni* by Tino di Camaino, and the *tomb slab of Bishop Giovanni Pecci*, and a bronze work by Donatello. The **Chapel of St. John the Baptist** is a Renaissance structure by Giovanni di Stefano, with a bronze *Baptist* by Donatello and frescoes by Pinturicchio. The **Chapel of the Sacrament** is also rich in works of art, while the **Chapel of the Madonna del Voto** (or *Chigi Chapel*) was commissioned by Alexander VII, shortly after the middle of the 17th century, from a design by Bernini: it is a rotunda with a gilded drum and dome, rich in marbles and bronze decorations. It also contains a panel painting (the *Madonna del Voto*) of the school of Guido da Siena.

To the right of the Cathedral stands what remains of the **New Cathedral**, among which the **façade**, the portal on the right side leading to the

Siena, a beautiful view of the monumental interior of the Cathedral.

Sabatelli stairs, while in the right aisle, the rooms for the **Museum of the Metropolitan Works** were obtained by closing off the first three arches. From the end of the left aisle you can enter the **Piccolomini Library** founded towards the end of the 15th century by Cardinal Francesco Todeschini Piccolomini (future Pius III), to house the rich library of his uncle Pius II. Preceded by a monumental front, it consists of a large rectangular hall, completely lined with frescoes by Pinturicchio, with *Scenes from the Life of Pius II*. At the centre, on a Renaissance support, is the group of the *Three Graces*, a Roman copy of a Hellenistic Greek original.

THE BAPTISTERY OF ST. GIOVANNI – The Baptistery is built as if it were the crypt of the Cathedral, set underneath the end of it and making use of the drop in the land. It was begun in 1316. The **façade**, realised towards the end of the century and never finished, is traditionally attributed to Giacomo di Mino del Pellicciaio, but no proof exists. Three portals lead into the **interior**, which consists of a rectangular hall, divided into three aisles by two piers. It is the work of Camaino da Crescentino and his son Tino. At the centre is the baptismal font by Jacopo della Quercia, begun in 1417, typically transitional in style. The sculptural decoration is not by Jacopo alone, but also includes works by Ghiberti and Donatello, as well as other Renaissance masters.

MUSEUM OF THE METROPOLITAN WORKS – The museum was established in the second half of the 19th century, and contains mostly works of art that were removed from the Cathedral. This is why it contains some of the most important works of Sienese and Tuscan art from the 13th to the 15th century. Represented with their masterpieces are artists such as Giovanni Pisano, Duccio di Buoninsegna, Simone Martini, Pietro Lorenzetti, and Jacopo della Quercia. The ten statues Giovanni Pisano made for the façade of the Cathedral, and which were in place until the late 1950s, are now here, as well as his small wooden *Crucifix*. The relief sculpture by Jacopo della Quercia which was on Cardinal Casini's altar in the Cathedral, has been recomposed in the museum. This late work represents the *Madonna and Child, St. John and Cardinal Casini*, and is one of Jacopo's finest. The most precious work in the Museum is Duccio di Buoninsegna's *Maestà*, which was on the high altar until 1505. Painted at the end of the first decade of the 14th century, the Maestà is Duccio's most famous painting, and the key work in the development of the great period of Sienese painting – a work in which the Gothic experiences arriving in Siena through miniatures from north of the Alps, and the sculpture of the Pisano, fuse with the Byzantine tradition and at the same time, frees itself from it. The large panel which was carried to the Cathedral with great festivity after it was finished, was painted on both front and back. In 1771, these were split apart. What was the front contains the *Madonna Enthroned Surrounded by Angels and Saints*, while the other side is covered with 26 *Scenes from the Passion*. Other panels with *Events from the Life of Christ and of the Virgin* were part of the crowning and the predella, but some of these are now in various museums in USA and in London. The *Madonna and Child* from the church of St. Cecilia a Crevole, is an early work by Duccio. A masterpiece of Ambrogio Lorenzetti's maturity is the triptych with the *Birth of the Virgin,* which the Master signed and dated in 1342. Various figures of *Saints* from a dismembered polyptych are also by Ambrogio. Simone Martini is here represented by *The blessed Agostino Novello*, a splendid art work carried out around the year 1130. The Museum also contains numerous other works of art: in addition to the paintings, there are the illuminated codexes from the Cathedral, and the fine pieces from the Cathedral Treasure (including works by Valdambrino, Sano di Pietro, Beccafumi, Riccio, and unknown 13th- and 14th-century masters).

CHURCH OF ST. DOMENICO – Of the large churches of the mendicant orders in Siena, the one which has most retained its original character is the church of St. Domenico. It was begun in the first half of the 13th century, but was soon enlarged, and building continued throughout the 14th century. Finally finished after the middle of the 15th century, it was damaged by fire a few decades later. The **Bell tower** set against the left side is also 14th-century, although lowered during the 18th century. The church has a single large nave and is simple but imposing, with an openwork timber roof and a projecting transept with seven chapels, the central one of which projects from the end wall. Like the rest of the church, the tribune is in brick with an occasional row of stone ashlars. Especially from the exterior with its buttresses, and from the way in which the openings are distributed, the tribune seems to have been influenced by Cistercian architecture. A large **crypt** lies under the ending part of the church, a result of the steep slope on which it was built. The crypt, divided into three aisles by robust piers supporting the cross vaulting, was restored shortly before World War II after having been abandoned for centuries. The **Cloister** to the right of the church is 15th-century, but it was in part remodelled in the restorations of the late 1940s. Mention **inside** should be made of the frescoes by Sodoma in the **Chapel of Saint Catherine** (which preserves a venerated relic of the saint, the head with a funeral mask); the ciborium and the *angels* on the high altar, by Benedetto da Maiano; a detached fresco by Pietro Lorenzetti; and then works by Matteo di Giovanni, Vanni, Francesco di Giorgio Martini, Sodoma, Casolani, Sano di Pietro, and Manetti, while some of the stained-glass windows are by modern or contemporary artists.

CHURCH OF ST. AGOSTINO – Built shortly after the middle of the 13th century, this church was transformed at the end of the 15th century, and finally completely remodelled by Luigi Vanvitelli in the middle of the 18th century. It is known, in fact, that in 1258, the land on which the convent was to be built was bought, and in 1262, the Republic of Siena, assigned 50,000 bricks for the building – *pro hedificatione ecclesiae Sancti Augustini*. The church was originally built on the usual monastic plan, but with Vanvitelli's transfiguration became one of the most successful Sienese examples of Baroque. As usual the many examples of works of

Siena, the Church of St. Domenico rises over the arches of Fontebranda.

art confirm the wealth achieved by these orders, despite their original devotion to poverty. These include the *Slaughter of the Innocents* by Matteo di Giovanni, works by Sodoma, Perugino, Petrazzi, Ventura Salimbeni, Vanni, Maratta, Rutilio Manetti, and Flaminio del Turco. The *altarpiece of the Blessed Agostino Novello* by Simone Martini, now in the Museum, originally came from this church.

CHURCH OF ST. NICCOLÒ AL CARMINE – The church rose as part of the Carmelite monastery in the Plain of Mantellini. Although it is said that hermits were already living here at the beginning of the Middle Ages, the Carmelites settled here around the middle of the 13th century, and the church as it is now dates from the successive century. The edifice was erected following the common standards of simplicity: a single rectangular nave covered with an openwork timber roof terminating in a presbytery with vaulted chapels. The simple gabled **façade** is half hidden by the old entrance to the monastery, now occupied by university institutes. Inside is a frescoed **Cloister**. The fine **Bell tower** in four tiers rises up on the left side of the church, remodelled internally at the beginning of the 16th century, perhaps by Baldassarre Peruzzi - who built his masterpiece right across from the church, Palazzo Pollini. The **Sacristy** also dates from this period, and was built by Vannoccio Biringucci, apparently from designs by Francesco di Giorgio. The works of art inside date from various centuries: the artists include Beccafumi, Gualtieri di Giovanni, Riccio, Girolamo del Pacchia, Casolani and remains of a fresco attributed to Ambrogio Lorenzetti.

CHURCH OF ST. PIETRO ALLA MAGIONE – Not far from the **Gate of Camollia**, on the old *Via Francigena*, this Romanesque church was indicated as a Templar hospital in 1240, after which it passed to the Knights of Malta. The church, with the remains of the original rooms that were annexed to its foundation, is one of the most significant medieval complexes in the urban fabric of Siena, enriched by the most important remains of tower houses in the city lying along the *Via di Camollia*. Structurally, St. Pietro is very simple, with a single nave and a semi-circular apse, and with an openwork bell tower set onto an arch that springs from the terminal wall to a building near the church. It is interesting to note that the **façade** of St. Pietro, rebuilt with its present portal perhaps in the early 14th century, retains on either side the remains of two flanking portals. It is a rather unusual feature in Tuscany, and is present in only a few religious buildings, significantly set along the medieval Via Francigena, including, for example, the Abbey of Isola, near Monteriggioni.

HOSPITAL OF ST. MARIA DELLA SCALA (SPEDALE DI SANTA MARIA DELLA SCALA) – The name of the Hospital of St. Maria della Scala derives from its location right across from the steps of the Cathedral. According to a tradition, it was founded by a Sienese shoemaker, Beato Sorore, in the first half of the 9th century. Whatever the case, in view of the part played by Siena as one of the stopovers on the *Via Francigena,* this hospital was one of the most important medieval institutions of its kind and was often taken as a model. The extant building went up under the auspices of the Canons of the Cathedral, and its style is that of Sienese architecture of the late 13th and early 14th centuries, with a broad **façade** in stone and brick, pierced by numerous mullioned windows with two lights and other large windows. Of the many particular additions made throughout the centuries, mention should be made of the monumental medieval structures, such as the **Church of St. Maria della Scala** (or *of the SS. Annunziata*), built around the middle of the 13th century but restructured after the middle of the 15th century by Guidoccio d'Andrea; it has a broad nave with a raised presbytery with an apse containing the large fresco by Sebastiano Conca representing the pool in Jerusalem used to wash the animals for sacrifice. The whole church, though, is richly decorated, starting with the polychrome coffered ceiling to the wooden choir stalls that date from the end of the 16th century. They were made by Ventura Turapelli who also carved the organ. Also noteworthy is the *Resurrected Christ*, a bronze statue by Vecchietta on the high altar. The **Sacristy** preserves the **Treasure**, with a rich collection of goldwork from the 10th to the 16th century, and pharmaceutical ceramics from the 14th to the 16th century. The architecture of the Pilgrim House is also extraordinary, with the vast covered hall, and large arches and frescoes by various 15th-century artists. The **Infirmary of St. Pius** is also frescoed with *Beato Sorore in Ectasy*, by Domenico di Bartolo, as well as the **Hall of St. Pietro**, later used as the library, frescoed by Vecchietta shortly before the middle of the 15th century. The Hospital is in part seat of the **National Archaeological Museum**. It contains a rich collection of archaeological material found in the territory of Siena: finds from the prehistoric to the Roman period are on exhibition. The museum is divided into three sections: prehistory, topography and numismatics. The **Prehistoric section** includes flint weapons, vases, bone and bronze instruments and various archaeological material; the **Topographical section**, in nine rooms, includes material arranged according to the area of provenance and comprises stone objects, bronze fibulae and weapons (7th-6th cent. BC), and in particular a *crouching lion in stone* (5th cent. BC), a magnificent female torso in travertine (6th cent. BC), Etruscan and Roman urns, and various precious vases from the 6th and 5th centuries BC. As well as coins, the **Numismatic section** contains various interesting objects from the areas of Chiusi, Chianciano and Montepulciano, such as '*buccheri*', Attic vases, and ornaments.

Siena, a spectacular aerial view of Piazza del Campo and the historical centre.

CHURCH OF ST. FRANCESCO – The large church of St.Francesco was only later enclosed in the circle of the city walls, and is no longer the one built for the first Franciscan convent on the land Bishop Buonfoglio donated to the Franciscans, not far from the church of the Ovile, shortly after the death of the saint. The present building was not begun until 1326, and was meant to enlarge the precedent church. It was finished in the second half of the 15th century, with the possible collaboration of Francesco di Giorgio Martini. Baroque elements were added after the fire of 1655, and it was restored at the end of the 19th century by Partini, at which time the Gothic style **façade** was rebuilt. The **Bell tower** rose right after the middle of the 18th century, and is by Paolo Posi. The **interior** is typical of Franciscan churches: a vast nave with a wooden ceiling, illuminated by large windows – outstanding is the mullioned window with four lights in the apse – and terminating in chapels. Frescoes by Pietro and Ambrogio Lorenzetti, now detached, decorated the building. A large **crypt** stretches out under the transept, with a vault supported by robust piers, and which served various purposes in the past. In the adjacent **Convent**, now occupied by the Faculty of Economic and Banking Sciences, there is a noteworthy square **Cloister** in Renaissance style.

Siena, the Tower del Mangia and Palazzo Pubblico in Piazza del Campo.

CHURCH OF ST. MARIA DEI SERVI – The original structure of the church of St. Maria dei Servi, dating from the 13th century, has been remodeled but the original façade can still be seen in the present unfinished **façade**. The **Bell tower**, thoroughly restored in the 1920s, is also 13th-century. The **interior** of the church of the Servi was rebuilt between the 15th and 16th century, in a tripartite Latin-cross plan, with marble columns, attributed to Baldassare Peruzzi or Porrina. Of the many works of art mention should be made at least of the *Madonna and Child with Two Angels,* signed and dated 1261, by Coppo di Marcovaldo; the *Slaughter of the Innocents* by Pietro Lorenzetti; and the *Madonna of the People* by Lippo Memmi. Other works are by Manetti, Vanni, Segna di Bonaventura, Pacchia, Cozzarelli, Mino del Pellicciaio, and Fungai.

PIAZZA DEL CAMPO – The *Piazza del Campo,* stage of the most important events in the history of Siena, and where still today the *Palio* is held, probably was built around the middle of the 12th century, when the public administration began to acquire the land on which then it was built. The decision to set the square on a spot where the three main thoroughfares came together at the *Croce del Travaglio* (the *Via di Città,* the *Banchi di Sopra* and the *Banchi di Sotto*) had the double scope of eliminating most of the city traffic from the square, while leaving it as a principal point of reference for the entire city. Very much has been said, and much more could be written, about the famous shell shape of this square. The placement of the square at the beginning of a valley, on a slope, contributed to the shape . Work terminated, with the laying of the brick pavement in nine triangular sections, apparently referring to the nine magistrates, in 1346. But the pre-existant natural elements do not in the least diminish the merits of that medieval culture, which gave such importance to the form and the urban decorum, as to require that the windows of the houses overlooking the piazza harmonise with those of the Palazzo Pubblico (this is just one example). Suitable complement to the piazza is the monumental **Fonte Gaia**, decorated with sculptures by Jacopo della Quercia, the originals of which are now in the Palazzo Pubblico.

PALAZZO PUBBLICO AND THE TORRE DEL MANGIA – In Siena the first meeting place for the city magistrates had been the church of St. Cristoforo, and the need was soon felt to find more appropriate headquarters for the representatives of a city which was fast growing.

In 1282, when these headquarters for the civic authorities were urgently required, the **Palazzo Pubblico** of Siena, a whole with *Piazza del Campo*, was built as an enlargement of an existing building. The central part went up first and, at the beginning of the 14th century, it was enlarged in depth in the direction of the *Piazza del Mercato*, crowning this part with a loggia. Shortly thereafter (1307), the left wing was begun as residence of the 'Podestà', while the right wing was the residence of the 'Nove' (the nine magistrates). In the 1320s, the 'Podestà's' residence was further enlarged with an external staircase of its own and a loggia for the reading of the sentences, which was eliminated shortly after the middle of the 15th century. It should also be recalled that the figures of the rebels used to be painted on this part of the façade.

In the meanwhile work was begun on the **Torre del Mangia**, by Minuccio and Francesco di Rinaldo. The model for the crowning part was commissioned to Lippo Memmi, but the iron scaffolding was not erected until

Siena, Piazza del Campo.

Images of the Palio of Siena and of the folklore events that surround it.

Siena, a dynamical picture of the famous Palio.

1665. It is interesting to remember, that around the middle of the 15th century it was proposed to build another tower like the one already there, in a symmetrical position. In 1327, the addition on the right between the *Via di Salicotto* and the Market was in construction designed to be a prison, later it became a theater, and before the middle of the century the Hall of the Great Council had also been built.

The Palazzo, of which we can see the original version in a panel painting by Sano di Pietro, has a central higher body and is decorated with the common arcading and crenellations flanked by wings, set at an angle so as to follow the curve of the piazza. At the end of the 17th century, a floor in perfect keeping with the original forms was added. The ground floor, in stone, has doors and windows in typical Sienese style with barred lancet arches.

The two upper floors have elegant mullioned windows with three lights, while the topmost floor of the central body has smaller mullioned windows with two lights, the central one of which was replaced in 1425 by the *coat of arms of San Bernardino*. At the foot of the Torre del Mangia – the name derives from that of a bellringer, Giovanni di Duccio, known as 'Mangiaguadagni' (eat your earnings) – the so-called **Chapel of the Square** was built as the result of a vow made during the plague of 1348. It was begun in 1352 by Domenico di Agostino, and finished by Giovanni di Cecco. The Renaissance arcades and crowning were not added until after the middle of the 15th century by Antonio Federighi. The **interior** of the Palazzo was richly decorated by the most important Sienese artists, as in the Hall of the Map of the world and the Hall of the Peace as well of course as the Chapels. These rooms today form part of the Civic Museum.

In the **Hall of the Map of the World,** which took its name from the large rotating map painted by Ambrogio Lorenzetti, then lost, (an interesting fresco has been discovered on the corresponding wall, now being studied), contains outstanding works of art, such as the *Maestà,* dating 1315, by Simone Martini (that went through accurate restoration in 1994) and his *Guidoriccio da Fogliano at the Siege of Montemassi,* which took place in 1328. The knight, in the foreground, is set against a hilly and dull landscape, with the castle of Montemassi, incredibly faithful in its

214

details to what is still left of the actual castle on his right. On the knight's other side is a 'battifolle' (fortress of timber in the shape of a tower) built by the Sienese for the 'trabucco', the launching machine for the siege, as well as the encampment. This was one of the frescoes whose scope was to celebrate the stages of Siena's territorial expansion, promoted by the government of the 'Nove'. We know for example, that Simone himself, in addition to having frescoed Sassoforte, was sent to Arcidosso and Castel del Piano, evidently to make on-the-spot sketches. Moreover, the fresco fragments found where the map was, also reproduce a castle. These earliest examples of celebrative frescoes were doubtless destroyed, to make room for other pictorial cycles, also of a celebrative nature, such as Lippo Vanni's *Victory of the Sienese at Sinalunga* (1363) and *Victory of the Sienese at Poggio Imperiale* painted by Giovanni di Cristofano and Francesco d'Andrea, in 1480. Other paintings in the room are by Sodoma, Sano di Pietro and Vecchietta, as well as a *Madonna Enthroned*, dated 1221, but almost certainly repainted later. The **Hall of the Peace**, where the lords met, is famous for the frescoes by Ambrogio Lorenzetti, the largest pictorial cycle of profane nature, carried out in the Middle Ages. The image Lorenzetti offers of the *Effects of Good Government* is not only allegorical. In this sense see *Good Government*, *Magnanimity*, *Temperance*, *Justice*, *Prudence*, *Fortitude*, *Peace* and other figures. Lorenzetti's vision is also that of the city and its surroundings, one of the most significant examples of what medieval life in the countryside and within the city walls was like, although it must be kept in mind that this was basically propaganda painting. Opposite, is the other fresco with *Bad Government and its Effects*, unfortunately in poor condition, where the allegorical figures can barely be deciphered. Mention should also be made of the **Pilasters Hall** containing the bell from the church of St. Cristoforo which called the Sienese together the day of the Battle of Montaperti; the **Antichapel**, with frescoes by Taddeo di Bartolo, and the **Chapel** with a fine 15th-century wrought-iron gate, carved and inlaid wooden choir stalls by Domenico di Niccolò, and with paintings by Taddeo di Bartolo and Sodoma, as well as a precious 16th-century organ. Then there is the **Hall of the Cardinals**, with various works of art, the **Hall of the Concistory**, entrance to which is through a marble portal by Bernardo Rossellino, with frescoes by Beccafumi, Florentine and Gobelin tapestries, and a *Judgement of Solomon* by Luca Giordano; the **Hall of Power** or *of the Priors*, divided into two parts by a frescoed arch; and finally the **Hall of the Risorgimento**, decorated with mediocre conventional frescoes by late 19th-century Tuscan painters illustrating *Episodes from the life of Victor Emmanuel II*. The **Civic Museum**, in other rooms, contains minor art objects, coins, seals and paintings. Inside the wing of the palace, near the Torre del Mangia, is the fine **Courtyard of the Podestà**, built in the 1320s, but restored shortly before 1930, with a ground-floor portico and an upper story with large Gothic mullioned windows with three lights. In the courtyard is the entrance to the **Communal Theatre of the Rinnovati** , which was originally the hall for the Great Council of the Republic, until 1560. After two fires the hall was remodelled by Antonio Bibbiena in 1753.

PALAZZO TOLOMEI – Palazzo Tolomei is one of the finest 13th-century Gothic civil structures in Siena. Powerfully built in stone, the elegant façade with its two tiers of mullioned windows with two lights above a tall ground floor with a large central portal, faces onto the *Piazza Tolomei*. The decorative elements of the architecture however, would seem to indicate that the palazzo was not built before the end of the 13th century.

PALAZZO CHIGI-SARACINI – The Palazzo, which belonged to the Marescotti, was begun in the 12th century but finished early in the 14th century, remodelled in the second half of the 18th century and thoroughly restored by Arturo Viligiardi around 1920 in line with the canons of Sienese architecture, as can be seen in the two orders of mullioned windows with three lights in the façade. The palace houses a **Gallery** with important works of art (Sassetta, the Maestro dell'Osservanza, Sano di Pietro, Matteo di Giovanni, Riccio, Beccafumi, Mariotto di Nardo, Botticelli, Biagio d'Antonio, Salvator Rosa, Francesco di Giorgio and others) and is the seat of the **Musical Academy Chigiana**, a music school founded in 1932, and now internationally famous.

Siena, the embattled Palazzo Sansedoni is one of the architectural jewels of Piazza del Campo.

PALAZZO SANSEDONI – This palace, in late Gothic style, bears signs of later remodelling. The original Gothic **façade** looks on the *Banchi di Sotto* and has been profoundly altered; the palace also overlooks the *Piazza del Campo*, with a majestic curved brick **façade** over which rises the tower with its rhomboid ground plan. The tower – once much higher – has three orders of mullioned windows with three lights, and is an early 18th-century adaptation in Gothic style.

LOGGIA DELLA MERCANZIA – The 15th-century Loggia della Mercanzia (*of San Paolo* or *dei Mercanti*) was designed by Sano di Matteo in 1417, and then continued by Pietro di Minella.

CHURCH OF SANTO SPIRITO – The church of Santo Spirito was built almost at the end of the 15th century (1498). The large brick building with a single nave and a transept has a simple gabled **façade**, with a stone portal said to be by Baldassare Peruzzi. The heavy dome at the crossing is, like the portal, 16th-century, and has also been attributed to Giacomo Cozzarelli. The church, near which is the *Fountain of the Pispini* dating from 1534, contains numerous 16th-century works of art.

ACADEMY OF THE ROZZI AND ACADEMY OF THE INTRONATI – The origins of the Academy of the Rozzi and the Academy of the Intronati go back all the way to the late Middle Ages, while the Academy of the Fisiocritici was instituted at the Sapienza at the end of the 17th century. They achieved their greatest success however, in the age of Enlightenmnent, when the Academy Tegea was also created by the great Sienese economist, Sallustio Bandini. The **Academy of the Rozzi** was purely social, as proved by the imposing **Theatre of the Rozzi**, and the **Academy of the Intronati** had distinctly cultural aims, as for example in the publication of the *Bullettino Senese di Storia Patria* (a journal dealing with history), and its name has been connected with the **Communal Library of the Intronati** which vaunts a collection of more than 300,000 volumes and manuscripts. These include Francesco di Giorgio's sketchbook and Giuliano da Sangallo's notebook, and various drawings by Sienese artists, including Peruzzi, a Byzantine gospel of the 10th century, and various illuminated codexes, including works by Giovanni di Paolo, Sano di Pietro, and Filippo de' Corbizzi.

PALACE OF THE CAPTAIN OF THE PEOPLE – Originally the property of the Grottanelli, and then of the Piccolomini family, the Palace was built between the 13th and 14th century, and was thoroughly restructured shortly after the middle of the 19th century. Its peculiarity is the **front** on two levels: below a series of arcades with oculi over the bar, enclosing an alternating series of portals and barred windows. The upper floor has an equal number of mullioned windows, with an oculus inserted under the external arch; while the building is crowned by an austere embattlement as well as the usual corbel tables. The courtyard, with its external staircase, is also outstanding. The palace is now the seat of the Faculty of Economic and Banking Sciences.

PALAZZO SALIMBENI – Built in the 14th century, the palace was frequently restored in the past. It overlooks the *Piazza Salimbeni* and was considerably restored and enlarged by Partini around the end of the 19th century. It is today the seat of the Monte dei Paschi di Siena, which was instituted in 1624 as a loan bank but since it incorporated the Monte Pio of 1471 it can boast being the oldest bank in Italy. The main **façade** of the palace, with its three stories, has to all accounts been redone, and the **back face** is certainly more interesting. This is in brick, overlooking the *Piazza dell'Abbadia*, and is flanked by two powerful towers. Recent restoration has brought to light the **keep** of the old Salimbeni fortress, as well as the warehouses and other rooms of the original house of this renowned Sienese family. Noteworthy is the bank's rich historical archives, with extremely interesting items, as well as the collection of works of art.

PALAZZO BUONSIGNORI – The most recent, but also the best preserved of the large private palaces of Gothic Siena is the Palazzo Buonsignori, formerly *Tegliacci*, finished in the first half of the 15th century. The **façade** is all in brick, with a stone base in the form of a bench. The central portal on the ground floor is of a typically Sienese Gothic style, flanked symmetrically by two false doors and intercalated with small lancet windows. Cornices set on arcading mark the two upper orders which are each articulated by seven elegant mullioned windows with three lights, perfectly aligned with the real or false openings on the ground floor.

NATIONAL PICTURE-GALLERY – Installed in Palazzo Buonsignori, it is the most important museum in Siena, giving a full understanding of Sienese painting, from its origins up to the middle of the 17th century. The collection began with the first group of paintings collected towards the end of the 18th century by Abbot Giuseppe Ciaccheri. It was subsequently enriched with works of art from country churches, suppressed convents, acquisitions, bequests and deposits. It was not installed in its present site till 1930, when the collection became the property of the State. Sculpture and architectural elements are on display in the colonnaded courtyard, including the marble portal from the monastery of the Olivetani, which once stood outside the Tufi Gate. A room on the ground floor contains several large cartoons with *Biblical scenes* carried out by Beccafumi for the pavement of the Cathedral. The ideal itinerary to follow in a visit to the Gallery begins on the second floor, and chronologically follows the stages of Sienese painting, here represented by all its principal masters, sometimes with outstanding masterpieces. Brief mention of some of the names and some of the titles will be enough to provide an idea of the enormous artistic patrimony enclosed within these walls. Among the earliest pieces mention should be made of the late 12th-century *Painted Cross* from the small Romanesque church of St. Pietro in Villore in San Giovanni d'Asso, while an altarpiece dated 1215 may be the oldest example of Sienese painting known. The early period of Sienese painting is of course represented by works by Guido da Siena, including an altarpiece, unusual as it is painted on canvas. The greatest period of Sienese painting, from Duccio di Buoninsegna to the death of the Lorenzetti brothers in the plague of 1348, is represented by its most important exponents. Duccio, who renewed Sienese painting, here has

Siena, detail of the Sanctuary of St. Caterina.

the fine *Madonna of the Franciscans* a small painted panel, but this is not the only painting by this great master, in the Gallery. He also had many followers, most of whom are represented in the Gallery, such as for example the "Master of the City of Castello", Ugolino di Nerio, and Segna di Bonaventura, perhaps the closest of all to Duccio. The Gallery owns one of the finest works by Simone Martini, who so exquisitely interpreted Gothic refinement, his *Madonna and Child* from the parish church of Lucignano d'Arbia. Another *Madonna and Child* is by Lippo Memmi who was Simone's collaborator as well as his brother-in-law. The Lorenzetti, who interpreted Giotto's lesson in their own original way, are present with some of their major works. There is a *Madonna and Child with Saints, Doctors of the Church, and Angels* by Ambrogio and an *Annunciation,* which he signed and dated 1344. But the two famous panels with the *City on the Sea* and *Castle on the Shore of a Lake* have also been attributed to Ambrogio Lorenzetti, one of the most complex artistic personalities of his time. These two small paintings, considered autonomous compositions, have been indicated as the only extant examples of European landscape painting before the end of the 15th century, but which are more probably fragments of a larger composition, perhaps a predella. Pietro Lorenzetti was a more dramatic painter than his brother, and outstanding examples of his work are the *Madonna and Child with Saints* and the *Stories of the Carmelite Order*, both parts of a large dismembered altarpiece the master painted in 1328-29 for the church of the Carmine in Siena. One of the major exponents of Sienese art of the middle of the 14th century is Barna, who was influenced both by Duccio and by Simone, although he made no great innovations. Nor should one forget Lippo Vanni, inspired by the Lorenzetti, as was Luca di Tommè, Bartolo di Fredi, Niccolò di ser Sozzo Tegliacci who, it must be remembered, was also the most important 14th-century Sienese illuminator, Naddo Ceccarelli, Niccolò di Buonaccorso, Paolo di Giovanni Fedi, Giacomo di Mino del Pellicciaio, and Andrea Vanni. Towards the end of the 14th century and the beginning of the 15th, the Sienese school seemed to have made a comeback with Taddeo di Bartolo, but Andrea di Bartolo and others, such as Martino di Bartolomeo and Gregorio di Cecco continued weak re-elaborations of the more fortunate past.

The only one, in the early decade of the 15th century, to introduce the elegant style of International Gothic, with attempts at perspective, was Stefano di Giovanni, known as 'Sassetta.' Domenico di Bartolo though, was the painter who most felt the influence of the Masaccio lesson, or in any case of the Florentine school. Sassetta is represented in the Gallery by a *Last Supper* and a *Saint Anthony being beaten by Devils*, and seems to have been the inspiration for Sano di Pietro, a pleasant prolific painter (as can be seen by the great number of works in the Gallery, including a *Madonna recommending Siena to Calixtus III* and the polyptych, dating from 1444), Pietro di Giovanni d'Ambrogio, Giovanni di Paolo who elaborated definitely Gothic features throughout the 15th century and for whom we will mention the *Madonna of Humility*. Lorenzo di Pietro, better known as 'Vecchietta', became a point of reference for Sienese art of this period. He was a painter and sculptor, influenced by Sassetta as well as by Florentine art – note should be taken of some of his works from the Hospital of the Scala. Matteo di Giovanni, here represented by his *Madonna and Child with Angels*, was Sienese by adoption (he was born in Sansepolcro), and adapted to the local tradition although he was also influenced by other currents. Guidoccio Cozzarelli, who seems also to have been successful as an architect, may have been his pupil. Neroccio di Bartolomeo, initially bound to Sassetta, was a partner in the workshop of Francesco di Giorgio Martini who was destined to become one of the greatest military architects of the Renaissance. Neroccio is here represented by the *Madonna and Child with Saints Jerome and Bernardino*, and Francesco di Giorgio by the *Annunciation*, to mention only the most famous of the various works the two masters have in the Gallery. Bound to Vecchietta, and perhaps a pupil, was Benvenuto di Giovanni, influenced both by Matteo di Giovanni and by Francesco di Giorgio, as was also the case with his son Girolamo di Benvenuto, all painters represented in the collections of the Gallery. At this point, it is worth remembering that the school of Sienese painting was at an end: at the beginning of the 16th century it was still reflecting the art produced two centuries earlier. The chief merit for renewal goes without doubt to Sodoma, and a certain merit can also be attributed to Perugino and Pinturicchio. Bernardino Fungai seems to have been particularly influenced by the latter while Giacomo Pacchiarotti seems to owe something to Signorelli, even though he was basically a traditionalist. On the other hand, Girolamo del Pacchia seems to have lost his ties with the Sienese environment and have entered the Florentine sphere. A wider range and a greater cultural opening appears in Domenico di Jacopo di Pace, known as 'Beccafumi', to be considered perhaps as the greatest Sienese painter of the 16th century. Works by Beccafumi in the Gallery include *St. Catherine Receives the Stigmata*, with an outstanding predella, the *Birth of the Virgin* and the *Descent of Christ into Limbo*, to mention only the most famous in the Sienese collection. Beccafumi also influenced Bartolomeo Neroni, known as 'Riccio', who distinguished himself as a sculptor and architect as well. Among the painters mention must lastly also be made of Baldassarre Peruzzi, who distinguished himself especially as one of the greatest high Renaissance architects. In the second half of the 16th century a numerous group of painters flourished in Siena, some of good standard, such as Alessandro Casolani, who also worked in northern Italy, Francesco Vanni, influenced by Barocci, Ventura Salimbeni, and Sorri. In the 17th century Caravaggism was not foreign to Siena, and in this sense was represented above all by Rutilio Manetti, and then by Bernardino Mei, Tornioli, Rustichino, to end with Astolfo Patrazzi. The Nasini family, born in Castel del Piano, worked in Siena between the 17th and 18th centuries. The most famous of them was Giuseppe Nicola.

THE CITY SPRINGS – In the early decades of the 13th century there was a growing desire in Siena to organise the urban spaces. This led to the installation of the springs: **Follonica**, **Pescaia**, **Ovile**, **Fontebranda**, and later **Fonte Nuova**. These were not only oustanding examples of Gothic architecture, interpreted in an original way – the large strongly pointed arches are definitely Sienese – but also are the visible part of a complex underground network of acqueducts (the 'bottini') which brought water to the city from springs distant many kilometres (towards the Chianti), a masterpiece of medieval hydraulic engineering of which very little is known.

THE WALLS – The great growth of the city, between the 13th and 14th centuries, brought to the enlargement of the existing city walls. In Siena, unlike other cities, this was not done through concentric rings, but by a series of additions. The orography of the ground played an important role, and Siena was forced to develop the inhabited areas along rigidly determined lines. In the course of the 14th century, it was particularly the southern part of Siena which outgrew its previous limits. Some of the gates in the city walls, especially the older ones, open, or opened (like the **Campanasi Gate**, now walled up) with the vault in the curtain wall, such as the **Camollia Gate**, the northernmost gate on the road to Florence, restructured at the beginning of the 17th century by Alessandro Casolani and with the famous inscription *Cor magis tibi Sena pandit* addressed to the traveler in arrival, and meaning that Siena willingly opened the heart of the gate to the traveller. In the Middle Ages, the city's defenses on this side were also guaranteed by a "countergate" with the passageway in a robust tower, now standing by itself. Other gates that open directly in the wall include the **Laterina Gate**, the **San Marco Gate**, the **Tufi Gate**. Other 14th-century gates had a more complex structure with the passageway in a tower preceded by a fortified courtyard serving as countergate. The **Gate of Ovile** and **Pispini Gate** were like this, but above all the **Roman Gate**, the most imposing. Built in 1327, and attributed to Agnolo di Ventura, this gate is comprised of a tower with two floors, the upper one of which open, as customary, towards the city. There is a fresco by Taddeo di Bartolo dating from the second decade of the 15th century on the external arch. This model was also used on other arches, as in the Pispini Gate. The side of the gate facing the countryside is protected by a counter wall (or counter gate) with loop-holes at the bottom and crowned, like the tower, by corbel tables and crenellations. The arcading, which was very flat, did not have the function of a supporting projection, but was purely decorative and was an element often used in public and private palaces during the Gothic period in Siena.

PALAZZO PICCOLOMINI – When Enea Silvio, who was also a brilliant humanist, became pope (Pius II, 1458-64), the Piccolomini family achieved the heights of their prestige. Pius II himself promoted the construction of the **Loggias**, called **of the Pope**, by Antonio Federighi in 1462. Not far from here, a few years later, the imposing Palazzo Piccolomini was begun. It was one of the Sienese buildings most clearly influenced by the characteristics of the Florentine Renaissance, re-evocating the forms of Alberti's Palazzo Ruccellai. It was begun by Pietro Paolo Porrina, perhaps on a project by Bernardo Rossellino, and repeats the features he adopted for the Palazzo Piccolomini in Pienza.

The stone **façade** has two floors in addition to the ground floor, articulated by large cornice moldings and crowned by a fine cornice. Various state offices are now installed in the Palazzo, which is also the seat of the **State Archives of Siena**. The archives contain the principal documents of Sienese history, going as far as 736, and some of them are on exhibition: for example the famous collection of *Small panels of the Biccherna*, the painted panels that were used as covers for the account books of the Biccherna and the Gabella. Famous painters, including the Lorenzetti, Vecchietta, Francesco di Giorgio Martini, and Beccafumi decorated these covers. The palace known as **Palace of the Popesses**, now the seat of the Banca d'Italia, also belonged to the Piccolomini family: it was inspired by Florentine models, although greatly restored, and Rossellino has been mentioned as the architect.

SANCTUARY OF ST. CATERINA – The complex had developed around the saint's house which was transformed into a sanctuary in 1464. The **façade** of the house has a fine Renaissance portal and a small loggia in brick on stone columns. The interior consists of several rooms, the first of which is the **Upper Oratory** with a fine coffered ceiling with gilded rosettes. At the altar is a lovely *St. Catherine with Stigmata* by Bernardino Fungai, and all around various paintings by Riccio. There are seventeen paintings on the walls including, from the left of the altar, *Jesus Shows Catherine the Cross She had given to a Poor Man*, by Riccio; a touching *Communion of the Saint* by Pomarancio; the *Saint Illuminated by the Holy Spirit*, by Rutilio Manetti; the *Canonisation of the Saint*, by Francesco Vanni, and other paintings by minor artists. A small loggia attributed to Baldassarre Peruzzi leads to the **Oratory of the Crucifix**, entirey lined with frescoes, most of which are by Giuseppe Nasini. On the right-hand altar, *St. Catherine meeting Gregory XI*, by Sebastiano Conca; on the left-hand altar, *Apotheosis of Saint Catherine*, by Rutilio Manetti; and lastly, on the high altar, a fine *Crucifix* on panel of the school of Pisa, dating from the early 13th century. Turning right at the entrance to the sanctuary, the path leads to the so-called **Oratory of the Bedroom** with *Seven events from the Life of the Saint*, by Alessandro Franchi (1886) on the walls, and *Catherine Receives the Stigmata*, by Girolamo di Benvenuto, on the altar. Next to the Oratory is a small **cell**, where the Saint spent most of her time and where objects which belonged to her are still kept.

A small door on the lower floor leads into the **Church of St. Caterina in Fontebranda**, known also as *Oratory of the Contrada*. It is a small single-aisled church with cross vaulting: on the right wall are frescoes by Girolamo del Pacchia, and on the left, two 17th-century paintings on canvas by Vincenzo Tamagni and Ventura Salimbeni. At the altar, is a polychrome wooden statue of the *Saint*, an outstanding work by Neroccio (late 15th-century); *Five angels* by Sodoma crown the altar and, further up, is another *Saint Catherine with the Stigmata* by Girolamo del Pacchia.

ORATORY OF ST. BERNARDINO – This delightful and unique edifice was built in the 15th century on the spot where the saint used to address the crowds. The structure consists of two superposed oratories: the **Upper Oratory** in particular is architecturally interesting and has a fine ceiling and walls in stuccoed wood, by Ventura Turapilli (1496). In addition, the areas between the divisory pilasters are occupied by small frescoes by Sodoma, Girolamo del Pacchia and Beccafumi. Beginning on the left of the wall facing the entrance, see the *St. Louis* by Sodoma, the *Nativity of Mary* by Pacchia, the *Presentation of the Virgin in the Temple* by Sodoma, the *Marriage of the Virgin* by Beccafumi, *St. Bernardino* by Pacchia, the *Archangel Gabriel* by Pacchia, the *Madonna in Glory and Saints* by Beccafumi (1537), the *Virgin of the Annunciation* by Pacchia, *St. Anthony of Padua* by Sodoma (1518), *Visitation* by Sodoma, *The death of the Virgin* by Beccafumi (1518), *Assumption of the Virgin* by Sodoma (1532), *St. Francis of Assisi* by Sodoma, and *Coronation of the Madonna* by Sodoma. At the altar is a fine *Madonna and Child* by Sano di Pietro. The vestibule leads to the **Lower Oratory**, completely decorated in the 17th century by important painters, including Ventura Salimbeni and Rutilio Manetti. Noteworthy at the altar, is a charming *Madonna and Child with Saints Bartholomew and Ansano* by Andrea del Brescianino.

ENVIRONS

The **Church of the Osservanza** was built between 1474 and 1490 on the ruins of a 12th century hermitage. The simple **façade** is preceded by a porch.

The **interior** has a single nave with eight chapels with two dome vaults, and a cupola in the presbytery. Noteworthy on the right wall in the first chapel is *St. Anthony of Padua*, a fine 17th-century wooden statue, and a *Crucifixion and Saints*, a fresco by Riccio (1548-50); in the third chapel, on the altar, the eye falls on a *Madonna and Child between Saints Jerome and Bernardino*, by Sano di Pietro; in the fourth chapel, a fine triptych, *Madonna with Saints Ambrose and Jerome*, attributed to Sassetta; on the pilasters of the triumphal arch, the *Virgin of the Annunciation* and *Saint Michael Archangel*, outstanding terra-cotta figures by Andrea della Robbia. On the left wall see the *Madonna and Child with Angels* by Sano di Pietro, in the first chapel; the glazed terra-cotta *Coronation of the Virgin* by Andrea della Robbia, in the second; a *Crucifixion and Saints* by Riccio in the third; and a fine polyptych, *Saints John the Baptist, Francis, Peter and John the Evangelist*, by Andrea di Bartolo (1413), in the fourth chapel.

After the chapels is the entrance to the **Sacristy**, where there is an imposing group of the *Pietà* by Giacomo Cozzarelli. Next to the Sacristy is the small **Aurelio Castelli Museum** with a collection of paintings, sculpture, prints, incunabuli and choir books of considerable value. Upon leaving the sacristy, a staircase leads to the **crypt** with 17th-century frescoes. Nearby is the **Loggia of Pandolfo** from which you may admire a magnificent view of Siena.

Sovana, the monumental Ildebranda is among the most famous Etruscan tombs of the area.

SOVANA (Grosseto)

The origins of the pretty village date back to prehistory. The largeness of the cemetery areas, instead, is evidence of the remarkable expansion of the Etruscan civilisation (3rd century BC). Romanised as *Suana*, was known, during the Middle ages, for being the birth town of Pope Gregory VII (Hildebrand from Sovana). From the 15th century it was under the dominion of Siena. Around the picturesque *Piazza del Pretorio* there are some beautiful medieval buildings: **Palazzo Pretorio** (13th century) with the portico **Loggetta del Capitano**; **Palazzo Bourbon del Monte** (16th century); **Palace of the Archive** (12th-13th centuries); **Church of St. Maria**, sublime example of 13th-century Romanesque architecture. Inside there is a pre-Romanesque ciborium (8-9th century) and Sienese frescoes. The **Cathedral**, built before the year 1000, has Lombard Romanesque influences. It has a beautiful side doorway, and inside, divided in a nave and two aisles, there is the 15th century *sarcophagus of St. Mamiliano*.
Outside the village, under the **Aldobrandeschi Fortress**, you will see, among the vegetation, a large **necropolis**. It displays various types of sepulchres: die, temple, as for example the famous **Hildebrand Tomb** (3rd-2nd century BC), shrine, as is the **Sirens Tomb** (3rd-2nd century BC) and the **Typhoon Tomb** (2nd century BC), tympanum, and loculus. The necropolis of **Poggio Stanziale** and of **Sopraripa** date back to the 7th and 6th centuries BC, thus the oldest. In this area there also are many Etruscan roads carved in tufa, called "**cavoni**".

SUVERETO (Livorno)

Dominating the Cornia valley, from a hillock in the Pisan Maremma, there is this small town, a fine example of a well preserved medieval village. Suvereto was a posession of the Aldobrandeschi, of Pisa and of Piombino; and it seems to have taken its name from the many cork-oaks that grow in this area (*Suberetum*). The towered **Town Hall** is of the 13th century; it has a pretty external stairway with loggia. On top of the hill the ruins of an ancient **Fortress** (10th century) are still visible, rebuilt by the Pisans during the 14th century. The town is situated inside **walls** with cylindrical embattled towers. At the 15th-century **Church of the Crucifix** you may visit the **Cloister of St. Francesco**. The portal of the **Church of the Madonna** (18th century) is adorned with good 15th-16th-century sculptures in the lunette. The **Church of St. Giusto**, Romanesque (12th century), is dominated by a bell tower crowned by merlons. The portal is decorated in Byzantine style.

ENVIRONS – In the high Cornia valley, on a marble rock extending from thick forests, there is **Sassetta**. It has medieval features, ruins of a **Castle** and a **Parish Church** which is home to the 15th-century *Virgin and Saints.* The **Sanctuary of the Frassine**, is a popular destination for tourists and pilgrims. In the **Church**, although of ancient origins, now modern, there is a wooden statue representing the *Madonna with Child*. It is thought to be by sculptors of the 14th-century Pisan school.

TORRE DEL LAGO PUCCINI (Lucca)

The town of Torre del Lago is relatively modern, for it was built after the 18th-century reclamation of the area on the site of a defense tower dating at least from the 17th century. The centre remained rather small until after World War II, despite the fact that it became famous in the early 1900s due to the presence of the Luccan composer Giacomo Puccini, who built his residence on the shores of the lake on what was left of the ancient tower. Today the **Villa of Giacomo Puccini**, lies only a few metres from the lake, and contains musical and hunting mementos of the artist in the dusky rooms, furnished in Art Nouveau style, at that time in fashion. The *bust* in the small square overlooking the lake is also dedicated to Puccini. Every summer, in Torre del Lago there is an interesting musical event, the **Puccini festival**, during which there are open-air performances, in the fairy-like setting of the **Theatre of the 4000**, of the great composer's most famous operas.

Suvereto, view of the historical centre towards the Town Hall.

Torre del Lago Puccini, among the many palaces, Villa Orlando faces directly on lake Massaciuccoli.

Vetulonia, traces of the polygonal walls near the ancient acropolis.

VETULONIA (Grosseto)

Only at the end of the 19th century, after centuries of disputes and researches, the millenary sleep of Vetulonia came to an end. It is cited by Greek and Latin historians as being one of the most powerful Etruscan cities; then it disappeared rapidly without a trace. In the medieval part of the town, you can still see the ruins of the great Etruscan **circuit of walls**, built with very big blocks. The excavations of the **urban centre** dating from the Hellenistic-Roman period, are near Vetulonia, at the **Costa Murata**, and along the road leading to the Aurelia. They include paved roads, houses and shops built on a precise plan, drains, pavements, basins and cisterns dating from the Etruscan-Roman period. From the exploration of these structures, many finds have come to light, but the most interesting are the many coins with the Etruscan name of the city, *Vatl*. It is however, the **necropolises** that reveal the richness and power of this town, which started during the 8th century BC with the exploitation of the copper, silver and lead mines of the Metalliferous Hills. The tombs of the archaic phase, situated in the high grounds near the city (**Poggio alla Guardia**, **Colle Baroncio**, **Poggio alle Birbe**, etc.) have brought to light a remarkable quantity of embossed bronze objects and gold and silver jewels produced locally, as well as other precious objects imported from the eastern Mediterranean area, and from Phoenicia, Egypt and Sardinia. The trade and exchange of the Vetulonia manufactured objects with those from other countries was possible thanks to the existence of the lake Prile, or *Prelius*: a large basin situated in the hinterland of Grosseto, delimited by the high grounds of Vetulonia and Roselle, and joined to the sea by a canal used until the Roman conquest; later, with the abandonment of the port structures, the canal silted up, and the lake became a lagoon. The frequent relationships with the Etruscan cities of northern Lazio, allowed the arrival of exotic products, as confirmed by the findings of rich treasures in the so-called *circular tombs.* These sepulchrals were probably built to bury more than one person belonging to the same family, and have pits for the depositions and others for the funerary treasures, which included extremely fine bronze objects and gold-work. The most outstanding, for preciousness and abundance of finds, and dating from the 8th to the middle of the 7th century BC, are the **Circles of the Jewels, of Bes, of the Furs, of the Lebeti, of the Trident**, and the **Tomb of the Duce**. During the second half of the 7th century BC, the aristocratic monumental tumulus tombs make their appearance: these have a quadrangular-plan chamber and are covered by a false dome supported by a central pilaster. Along the **Via dei**

Sepolcri you can admire two remarkable examples: the tombs della Pietrera and del Diavolino. The **Tumulus of the Pietrera** has a diameter of more than 60 m, and a long corridor leading to the central chamber, where a few limestone statues, representing crying women and male figures, were found; moreover, on the slope of the tumulus, other pit tombs have come to light, with precious treasures, datable from the same period of the principal sepulchre (middle of the 7th century BC). Not far from this, is the **Tumulus of the Small Devil**, dating from the same period and taking its name from the animal figure, resembling a small devil, carved on a stone situated near the left door jam. This sepulchre, with a big tumulus delimited by a tambour of stone blocks, also has the covering with a false dome, starting from the corners of the chamber, and supported by a central pilaster, of which only the base remains. There is not much documentation on the successive centuries, but some finds let suppose that life at Vetulonia continued without interruption all through the 6th and 5th centuries BC, resulting in a new period of prosperity during the 3rd century BC, as suggested by the building development discovered in the excavations on the **Acropolis** of the city, and by the bronze coin series with the legend of *Vatl*. In an **Antiquarium** you will see various pieces, which describe the development of the Vetulonia settlements, from prehistoric times, to the Hellenistic age, up to the Roman-Etruscan civilisation.

VIAREGGIO (Lucca)

It was around the end of the 18th century that the fortunes of Viareggio as a holiday resort started. This was when several prosperous families of Lucca chose the small port, which had only recently been freed from the plague of malaria that for centuries had hindered its development, as their vacation spot. Later, Paoline Bonaparte, whose **Villa** in the city centre can still be seen, and Maria Louisa of Bourbon, who opened the *Viale dei Tigli* and endowed the city with an urban plan, established

Viareggio, view of the Burlamacca canal.

Viareggio, aerial view on the parade of the famous Carnival.

their summer residences. But the real tourist boom of the city dates from the early 1900s, in full *Belle Epoque*, when Viareggio was considerably enlarged and the elegant Art Nouveau architecture, still existing, was built. The loveliest buildings of the period still to be seen are the **Bagno Balena** and the **Gran Caffè Margherita** designed by A. Belluomini, with decorations by G. Ghini, while 19th-century Viareggio is represented by the majestic **Palazzo delle Muse**, overlooking *Piazza Mazzini* and now housing the **Civic Archaeological Museum A.C. Blanc**. Very little is left of the old 16th-century town, except for the imposing **Matilde Tower**, built after 1534 as a result of an ordinance by the Luccan senate. The first masonry structures of the small port were built around this defense tower. As time passed the port continued to grow in importance thanks both to commercial fishing and to ship-building activities, still today playing an important role in the local economy, side by side with the flourishing resort activities.

Lastly, speaking of Viareggio mention of its famous **Carnival** is mandatory. The bizarre floats made by real artists of papier maché, need months and months of preparation.

VICCHIO (Florence)

The painter Fra' Angelico was born in Vicchio, while the nearby Vespignano was Giotto's birthplace. Moreover, the area played an important role in the political vicissitudes of medieval Florence, for it was part of the 14th-century fortification system Florence created in its surroundings and which served to protect the city itself, considering the proximity. The ancient **city walls** of Vicchio, in the shape of a hexagon, are in part still extant. Inside, in the *Piazza Giotto*, is the **Palazzo Pretorio** with the annexed **Civic Museum** which houses works of art and archaeological finds from the surrounding territory, including some fine Della Robbias, and Etruscan vases. The **Parish Church** with a Renaissance portal also overlooks the square. The building itself however, was completely redone in the 19th century. Inside is a *Madonna and Child* attributed to Michele di Ridolfo del Ghirlandaio. Also noteworthy is the **Oratory of the Archiconfraternity of the Mercy**, with a fine *Madonna and Child* of the Della Robbia school, and the **House of Benvenuto Cellini**, who lived here from 1559 to 1571.

VICOPISANO (Pisa)

It is a beautiful medieval hamlet, clinging to a hill, on the southeastern slopes of the Monte Pisano. The locality, the ancient *Vico Auserissola*, was one of the many contended by Pisa and Florence, until the latter finally managed to conquer it (end of the 15th century). The hamlet is dominated by the ruins of the **Fortress**, the towers, among which the one **Of Brunelleschi** (in honour of the artist who carried out the work during the 15th century), the one **Of the Clock**, and the so-called **Of the Four Gates**. Among the many antique small palaces, see the fine **Palazzo Pretorio** (14th century), recently restored to its ancient dignity. The **Parish Church**, Pisan-romanesque, was built during the 11th and 12th centuries: the interior is divided in an aisle and two naves, embellished by a byzantine *Cross* in silver and a wooden *Deposition* (13th century).

VINCI (Florence)

This small village (14,000 inhabitants) lies on the slopes of Monte Albano, in the midst of the gentlest of landscapes. It is famous everywhere as the birthplace of Leonardo da Vinci, and the anniversary is celebrated every year on the 15th of April with celebrations and cultural events. Vinci surrounds the castle of the Guidi counts. The **Castle**, still dominating the town, dates from the 13th century and looks like a fortress. Inside there are the remains of frescoes, decorations and coats of arms of various periods. Two big halls on the ground floor contain the **Vinci Museum**, with a collection of drawings, paintings and models of machines designed by Leonardo. The Sala Consiliare, on the same floor, also contains a glazed terra-cotta *Madonna* of the school of the Della Robbia. The antique **Church of Santa Croce** lies in the vicinity of the Castle and contains the baptismal font where Leonardo was baptized. Also interesting is the Leonardo Library (important centre for the study of the great artist and scientist) and, in the nearby Anchiano, the Native house of Leonardo (visitable).

Vinci, the Tuscan countryside seen from the Vinci Museum.

VOLTERRA (Pisa)

HISTORICAL SURVEY – *The earliest information of the city dates from prehistoric times, that is to the iron age (9th-7th cent. BC). As* Velathri, *it was for a long time one of the most powerful lucumonies in Etruria. It was so important that in the 3rd century BC it had around 25,000 inhabitants and was the last lucumony to fall to the Romans after a siege that lasted two years (81-80 BC). It thus became first a Roman municipium, and then a Lombard gastaldato (an official administrated the city on behalf of the king). The city was quite powerful between the 12th and 14th centuries and fighting Pisa, Florence, Siena and San Gimignano for questions of territory. In 1340, it passed under the lords of the Belforti, and finally fell to the Florentines, in 1361. From then on the fate of the city was that of the Tuscan Grand Duchy.*

PALAZZO DEL POPOLO – Not only is the Palazzo del Popolo or *of the Priors* probably the first example of its kind erected in Tuscany, but it served as inspiration for the architects of the Palazzo della Signoria in Florence and for many other civic buildings. The **façade**, where the many mullioned windows with two lights are surrounded by the polychrome coats of arms of the 'podestà', is crowned by the pentagonal **Tower**, the top of which was added after the earthquake of 1846. Open to the public, **inside**, on the first floor, is the **Council Hall**, decorated with a large late 14th century fresco of the *Annunciation and Saints*, and the **Junta Hall** which has a beautiful wooden ceiling.

Guarnacci Museum, the Etruscan collection.

Volterra, panorama towards the embattled Palazzo dei Priori.

Volterra, a view of the Fortress (or "Mastio") from the Archaeological Park Enrico Fiumi.

GATE OF THE ARCH – The so-called 'Gate of the Arch' (Porta dell'Arco) is set into the Etruscan city walls, on the south side of the city of Volterra, towards the sea. The road that leaves the city at this point, with a slight descending curve, was the *cardo maximus*. The barrel-vaults with piers of the gate seem to be reinforced on the outside by various rows of stone square blocks. There is a rectangular chamber with a barrel-vault between the two passageways. Both the front and the back of the gate, have a large arch, over four metres wide, built in dry masonry with blocks of tufa. On the side outside the city, three *heads* in dark stone are set in the arch, so much ruined by time that they are unrecognisable. Many hypotheses have been advanced as to their meaning – they may have been a triad of divinities protecting the city, or perhaps the Dioscuri and Jupiter, or warriors, symbolising the trophy heads of enemies. Various phases of construction can be identified: originally there was a passageway with wooden fixtures in the wall, which can be dated from the first half of the 4th century BC. This was then replaced by the arched gateway still to be seen, dating from the middle of the 3rd to the end of the 2nd century BC. The monument continued to be used in medieval times and later, when a tower, subsequently torn down, was built on top of it.

CHURCH OF ST. FRANCESCO – Next to the gate that bears the same name, there is the 13th-century Church of St. Francesco. The simple Romanesque **façade** has a portal with a lunette decorated by fine sculptures. The **inside** is a big hall that lets into the **Chapel of the Cross of the Day**, embellished by 15th century frescoes, by Cenni di Francesco Cenni (*Legend of the Holy Cross*).

CATHEDRAL – The Cathedral dates from the 12th century, although minor 13th-century changes are also evident. The **façade** is simple, linear and enriched by a finely decorated marble portal and blind arcading in the tympanum. The lovely **interior** consists of a nave and two aisles with columns and an exquisite coffered ceiling of the 16th century. The

Volterra, view of the very ancient Porta dell'Arco.

Volterra, Guarnacci Museum, the famous "Shadow of the Evening".

Cathedral preserves a variety of important works. In the nave there is a magnificent *Pulpit* decorated in part with 12th-century church ornaments, by the school of Guglielmo Pisano. The right arm of the transept has a striking polychrome wooden *Deposition* from the middle of the 13th century. The high altar in the presbytery has an important ciborium in marble by Mino da Fiesole, who probably also made the two *angels* on either side; in the left transept there is a polychrome *Madonna* by F. di Valdambrino. The **Chapel of Our Lady of Sorrow** is situated off the left aisle at the entrance. Two niches in the chapel contain an *Epiphany* and a terra-cotta *Crib*, both 15th-century. A marvelous *Arrival of the Magi* was frescoed on the walls of the chapel and reveals the unmistakably elegant hand of Benozzo Gozzoli. Various interesting objects in wood, furniture, choir stalls, church ornaments dating from the 15th century, are in the **Sacristy**.

BAPTISTERY – The Baptistery is a 13th-century Romanesque building of great architectural interest, standing across from the Cathedral. It is octagonal in plan. The portal, richly decorated with sculptured heads, leads into an **interior** striking for its spirituality. The room is quite bare, adorned only by niches and mullioned windows under the dome, which was restored in the 16th century. Particularly lovely are the holy water stoup (made out of an Etruscan cippus), the lively baptismal font (1502) perhaps by Andrea Sansovino, and the altar by Mino da Fiesole.

DIOCESAN MUSEUM OF SACRED ART – Works of great interest, most from Volterra and its diocese, are on exhibit here. Under the portico, at the entrance to the museum, is a collection of objects from the ancient abbey of the Camaldolites (now practically in ruins). Among the most outstanding works in the museum: a *Madonna and Child with Angels*, a marble sculpture by Giovanni d'Agostino, the *sepulchre of St. Ottaviano* by Tino di Camaino; a glazed terra-cotta *bust of St. Lino* by Giovanni della Robbia; the *Conception*, a splendid panel painting by Taddeo di Bartolo; a 15th-century monstrance-reliquary in gilded copper; a *reliquary-bust of St. Vittore* in silver and enamel, Sienese work of the 14th century; a magnificent *Madonna Enthroned with Saints John the Baptist and John the Evangelist*, a panel by Rosso Fiorentino (1521); a gilt bronze *Crucifix* by Giambologna, and numerous illuminated choir books, pyxides, censers, chasubles, dalmatics, and copes. Not far there is the **Quadrivio dei Buonparenti**, a picturesque medieval architectural composition of buildings, towers and tower-houses.

Volterra, noble palaces and tower-houses embellish Piazza dei Priori.

COMMUNAL PICTURE-GALLERY – This picture-gallery is among one of the minor museums with the greatest number of paintings on canvas and panel. The rich collection is installed in the lovely rooms of **Palazzo Solaini**, a building with a fine Renaissance **façade** and charming **Courtyard**. Works by many renowned artists are on exhibit, including Luca Signorelli with an *Annunciation* (1491) and an ecstatic *Madonna and Child with Saints*. Other works include a triptych by Taddeo di Bartolo, a *St. Sebastian between Sts. Bartholomew and Nicola of Bari*, by Neri di Bicci (1478); the beautiful triptych by Alvaro de Pirez with the *Madonna Enthroned and Saints*; the marvelous *Deposition* by Rosso Fiorentino (1521); *Christ with Sts. Benedict, Romualdo, Attinia, Grecina*, by Ghirlandaio; a splendid *Madonna and Child with Saints* by Volterrano, and works by Leonardo da Pistoia, Maso da St. Friano, Giuliano Bugiardini, Donato Mascagni, Daniele Ricciarelli and Pieter Witte. Some of the most important works in the **Civic Museum** which deserve mention are the two wooden statues of the *Annunciation* by Francesco di Valdambrino, medieval marble sculpture, a medal cabinet and a coin cabinet.

ETRUSCAN MUSEUM GUARNACCI – The Etruscan collection in this museum is one of the most important in Italy. Begun in 1732, by Cardinal Franceschini, with a collection of cinerary urns, it has been gradually enriched with outstanding archaeological material. The museum includes a **Prehistoric section**, which contains material from the bronze age and iron age tombs; an **Etruscan section**, the most important both in quantity and quality (over 600 cinerary urns are included), and lastly the **Roman section**, with sculptures, inscriptions, objects in gold and pottery. One of the most important pieces on exhibition is the tufa *stele*, representing a warrior with a lance, from the second half of the 6th century BC. Figures of *demons*, *gorgons* and *geni*, *furies*, *Scylla* and *tritons*, as well as the *Scenes of journey to the nether world on horseback*, are represented on the many cinerary urns. The most bizarre piece is the famouse *Shade of Evening*, a long slender enigmatic statuette in bronze dating from the 2nd century BC.

THE PALACES OF PIAZZA DEI PRIORI – The *Piazza dei Priori* is a wide, well-balanced square framed by an austere mosaic of palaces: the **Palazzo del Monte Pio**, a solid elegant building that has recently been restored; **Palazzo Pretorio**, a union of several buildings dating from the 13th century; the **Tower of the Podestà**, in the upper part of which a humorous beckoning figure of an animal, baptized by the inhabitants of Volterra the *porcellino* (piglet), stands on a ledge; the **Palazzo Incontri**, seat of the Cassa di Risparmio of Volterra, in great part rebuilt in style, and finally, the **Palazzo Vescovile** with a unique overhanging roof.

FORTRESS AND FIUMI-PARK – The imposing noble mass of the large **Fortress**, whose sad fate was for many centuries that of being a prison, rises up at the end of the historical centre. The structure consists of two parts that were once separate: the **Old Fort** (*Rocca Antica* or *femmina*) which dates 1343, and which rises at one side of the Selci gate, and the **New Fort** (*Rocca Nuova* or *maschio*) which Lorenzo the Magnificent had built later (between 1472 and 1475), right after he had conquered Volterra. This has a square layout and is articulated in five splendid towers that give the complex a fascinating austere air. Near the Fortress is the **Fiumi-Park**, with interesting traces of the Etruscan acropolis with its temples, roads and cisterns, waiting for further study.

Volterra, Roman traces near the roman Theatre.

Volterra, the wild natural setting of the "Balze".

ROMAN THEATRE AND BATHS – What remains of the imposing **Roman Theatre** dating from the 1st century BC lies on the north side of the city. Partially recomposed, very interesting evidences of this large complex were brought to light, and are an indication of the importance and power that Volterra had achieved during Roman times. A good part of the stage, the cavea and the very fine portico are fairly well preserved. The **Baths**, which have mostly disappeared, were near the portico.

BALZE – One of the characteristics of Volterra is also the land it stands on. Throughout the centuries the city has had to struggle against the clayey humid earth. There have been frequent landslides in the area known as *Le Balze* to the west of the plain of the Guerruccia, and these are responsible for its present appearance – an enormous chasm that falls away to the plain below. One by one these continuous landslides have swallowed up the iron-age necropolis, various stretches of the **Etruscan walls** (a magnificent panorama can be seen from what survives), churches, such as St. Clemente and St. Giusto, the monastery of St. Marco, and many old houses. This slow and inexorable corrosion has in part compromised the expansion of the city, which has remained concentrated and compact, on the hill.

THE ETRUSCAN NECROPOLISES – As usual, the necropolises lie outside the city walls. Excavation is still being carried out in some of them. They include the **Necropolis of the Portone**, with chamber tombs of the 6th-5th century BC; the **Guerruccia**, which has disappeared in the landslides of the Balze; the **Guardiola**; the **Marmini** with its two hypogeum tombs; and **San Girolamo**.

ENVIRONS – On the northern side of the Metalliferous Hills, is **Pomarance**, with traces of its ancient medieval centre. The **Country Church** preserves works by Cristoforo Roncalli "il Pomarancio", born here. The 14th-century **Palazzo Pubblico** is enriched by armorial bearings on the façade. The village is also the birthplace of Niccolò Circignani, a 16th-century painter, known as Niccolò Pomarancio.

INDEX

INDEX OF PROVINCES